∂les to
Practice in Education for
Intercultural Citizenship

MIX
Paper from
responsible sources
FSC
www.fsc.org   FSC® C014540

LANGUAGES FOR INTERCULTURAL COMMUNICATION AND EDUCATION

Series Editors: **Michael Byram**, *University of Durham, UK* and **Anthony J. Liddicoat**, *University of Warwick, UK*

The overall aim of this series is to publish books which will ultimately inform learning and teaching, but whose primary focus is on the analysis of intercultural relationships, whether in textual form or in people's experience. There will also be books which deal directly with pedagogy, with the relationships between language learning and cultural learning, between processes inside the classroom and beyond. They will all have in common a concern with the relationship between language and culture, and the development of intercultural communicative competence.

Full details of all the books in this series and of all our other publications can be found on http://www.multilingual-matters.com, or by writing to Multilingual Matters, St Nicholas House, 31–34 High Street, Bristol BS1 2AW, UK.

LANGUAGES FOR INTERCULTURAL COMMUNICATION AND EDUCATION: 30

From Principles to Practice in Education for Intercultural Citizenship

Edited by
Michael Byram, Irina Golubeva, Han Hui and Manuela Wagner

MULTILINGUAL MATTERS
Bristol • Buffalo • Toronto

Library of Congress Cataloging in Publication Data
Names: Byram, Michael, editor. | Golubeva, Irina, editor. | Hui, Han, editor.
| Wagner, Manuela (Educator), editor.
Title: From Principles to Practice in Education for Intercultural Citizenship
/Edited by Michael Byram, Irina Golubeva, Han Hui and Manuela Wagner.
Description: Bristol, UK; Tonawanda, NY: Multilingual Matters, [2016] |
Series: Languages for Intercultural Communication and Education: 30 |
Includes bibliographical references and index.
Identifiers: LCCN 2016022808|ISBN 9781783096558 (hbk : alk. paper) | ISBN
9781783096541 (pbk : alk. paper) | ISBN 9781783096589 (Kindle) | ISBN
9781783096572 (Epub)
Subjects: LCSH: International education. | Multicultural education. |
Intercultural communication. | Languages, Modern—Study and teaching.
Classification: LCC LC1090 .F76 2016 | DDC 370.116—dc23 LC record available at
https://lccn.loc.gov/2016022808

British Library Cataloguing in Publication Data
A catalogue entry for this book is available from the British Library.

ISBN-13: 978-1-78309-655-8 (hbk)
ISBN-13: 978-1-78309-654-1 (pbk)

Multilingual Matters
UK: St Nicholas House, 31-34 High Street, Bristol BS1 2AW, UK.
USA: UTP, 2250 Military Road, Tonawanda, NY 14150, USA.
Canada: UTP, 5201 Dufferin Street, North York, Ontario M3H 5T8, Canada.

Website: www.multilingual-matters.com
Twitter: Multi_Ling_Mat
Facebook: https://www.facebook.com/multilingualmatters
Blog: www.channelviewpublications.wordpress.com

The policy of Multilingual Matters/Channel View Publications is to use papers that are
natural, renewable and recyclable products, made from wood grown in sustainable for-
ests. In the manufacturing process of our books, and to further support our policy, preference is given to printers that have FSC and PEFC Chain of Custody certification. The FSC
and/or PEFC logos will appear on those books where full certification has been granted
to the printer concerned.

Typeset by Nova Techset Private Limited, Bengaluru & Chennai, India.
Printed and bound in the UK by Short Run Press Ltd.
Printed and bound in the US by Edwards Brothers Malloy, Inc.

Contents

Foreword   vii
Acknowledgements   xi
Contributors   xiii
Introduction   xvii

Section 1: The Baseline: Learners' and Teachers'
Perceptions of Intercultural Citizenship   **1**

1 Comparing Students' Perceptions of Global Citizenship in
Hungary and the USA   3
Irina Golubeva, Manuela Wagner and Mary E. Yakimowski

2 Exploring Perceptions of Intercultural Citizenship among
English Learners in Chinese Universities   25
Han Hui, Song Li, Jing Hongtao and Zhao Yuqin

3 Intercultural Encounters in Teacher Education – Collaboration
Towards Intercultural Citizenship   45
Ulla Lundgren and teacher students

Section 2: Teachers Cooperating   **79**

4 Beyond Language Barriers: Approaches to Developing
Citizenship for Lower-level Language Classes   81
Etsuko Yamada and Jessie Hsieh

5 Incorporating Environmental Action into Intercultural
Dialogue: Personal and Environmental Transformation
and the Development of Intercultural Communicative
Competence   104
Stephanie Ann Houghton and Mei Lan Huang

Section 3: Learners Cooperating   **129**

6 Green Kidz: Young Learners Engage in Intercultural
      Environmental Citizenship in an English Language
      Classroom in Argentina and Denmark   131
   *Melina Porto, Petra Daryai-Hansen, María Emilia
      Arcuri and Kira Schifler*

7 Understanding Intercultural Citizenship in Korea and the USA   159
   Catherine Peck and Manuela Wagner

8 Mural Art and Graffiti: Developing Intercultural Citizenship
      in Higher Education Classes in English as a Foreign
      Language in Argentina and Italy   181
   Melina Porto

9 Language and Intercultural Citizenship Education for a Culture
      of Peace: The Malvinas/Falklands Project   199
   Melina Porto and Leticia Yulita

10 Human Rights Education in Language Teaching   225
   Leticia Yulita and Melina Porto

Reflections: Learning from the Challenges and Seeking
      Ways Forward   251
Michael Byram, Irina Golubeva, Han Hui and Manuela Wagner

Index   260

Foreword

This book is about intercultural citizenship, and how intercultural citizenship may be fostered through foreign language education. Intercultural citizenship occurs when people who perceive themselves as having different cultural affiliations from one another interact and communicate, and then analyse and reflect on this experience and act on that reflection by engaging in civic or political activity.

Particular attention is laid in this book on intercultural *democratic* citizenship. This occurs when democratic values and attitudes are mobilized and deployed in the activity that is undertaken as a consequence of the reflection on intercultural experience. By democratic values and attitudes, I mean things like respect for the inherent dignity and rights of all human beings, respect for others as equals irrespective of their specific cultural affiliations, an openness to and a willingness to learn about the perspectives and opinions of others, a commitment to decisions being made by majorities but also a corresponding commitment to protecting minorities and their rights, and a conviction that conflicts must be resolved peacefully. The current book is extremely important because today the world is in desperate need of many more citizens who are interculturally and democratically competent. In case anyone doubts this statement, consider a few facts.

Globalization processes are currently bringing people from different cultural backgrounds into contact on a scale that was unimaginable just a few decades ago. International migration is one major source of such contact. There are now estimated to be about 232 million international migrants in the world, more than at any time before in human history, and this number is expected to rise further in the future, with demographic change, economic disparities, environmental change and violent conflict being the major drivers of migration (United Nations, 2013). In addition, technological innovations mean that we now have the opportunity to communicate and exchange information with other people almost anywhere in the world nearly instantaneously. It is estimated that, by the end of 2015, there will be more than 3 billion internet users and 7 billion mobile phone accounts, in a world which contains 7.3 billion people (United Nations, 2015). Increases in contact across countries are also driven, of course, by international trade, and in the past 10 years, global trade in goods and services has nearly doubled from $13 trillion in 2005 to nearly $24 trillion in 2014 (United Nations, 2015).

However, and very sadly, other statistics reveal that these levels of contact between peoples have not led to greater intercultural understanding. For example, data collected in Europe (one of the three principal destinations for migrants, alongside North America and Oceania) have revealed very high levels of prejudice, intolerance, discrimination and hate crime towards minority ethnic and religious groups. For example, in 2008, 26% of persons of African origin within Europe reported that they had been victims of assault, threat or serious harassment with a perceived racist motive in the previous 12 months (FRA – EU Agency for Fundamental Rights, 2013a). In 2014, 46% of survey respondents in France, Germany, Greece, Italy, Poland, Spain and the UK admitted holding anti-Muslim views (FRA – EU Agency for Fundamental Rights, 2015). In 2011–2012, 26% of European Jews reported that they had experienced verbal insults or harassment owing to their religion and 4% had experienced physical violence or threats of violence (FRA – EU Agency for Fundamental Rights, 2013b). Even more shockingly, in 2014, 66% of Muslims in the UK reported that they had experienced verbal abuse (an increase from 39.8% in 2010) while 17.8% had experienced physical assault (an increase from 13.9% in 2010; Ameli & Merali, 2015). These levels of prejudice, intolerance and hate crime are deeply disturbing.

While governments can create institutions, laws and policies that attempt to reduce levels of hate crime and enable the police and the courts to prosecute the perpetrators of such crime, something far more fundamental is required to tackle these levels of prejudice, racism and intolerance. What is required is a change in people's attitudes to other human beings who do not happen to share their own cultural affiliations and/or 'racial' characteristics. In other words, there is a need for much greater respect for the inherent dignity, needs and rights of all human beings; a willingness to engage with those who are perceived to have other cultural affiliations; a willingness to speak out against expressions of prejudice and intolerance; a willingness to defend those who are disempowered and disadvantaged; and a willingness to take civic or political action for the greater good if this is required. In short, active intercultural democratic citizenship is required.

One of the principal means that is available to societies for instilling socially acceptable attitudes and values in its citizens is education. Indeed, formal educational systems have been used for this purpose since schools were first created (Bekemans, 2013). Indeed, the Education Ministers of the member states of the Council of Europe have recently re-affirmed that education should be concerned not solely with preparing young people for future employment but also with preparing them for life as active citizens in democratic societies (Council of Europe, 2013). The latter entails equipping young people with the values, attitudes, skills, knowledge and critical understanding that are required for living as active citizens in democratic and increasingly diverse societies.

While all areas of the educational curriculum have a role to play in achieving this goal of equipping young people with these resources, foreign language education arguably provides one of the most important and useful educational contexts in which this goal can be addressed. As Byram, Golubeva, Han and Wagner point out in their Introduction to this book, foreign language teaching necessarily directs the attention of learners to the world beyond their own national community, especially to other countries where the language which they are learning is spoken. Link projects and exchange schemes involving learners in those other countries provide an ideal opportunity to foster the development of intercultural understanding, communicative skills and the capacity for critical reflection on social, societal and political issues. Furthermore, if such projects and schemes also require learners to undertake some kind of civic or political action in their communities, the setting is ideal for equipping them with the values, attitudes, skills, knowledge and critical understanding required for intercultural democratic citizenship.

This is the reason why the work that is reported in this book is so extremely useful and important. Together, the chapters report the results of a collective research venture that was conducted through the Cultnet research network, a group of researchers sharing an interest in the cultural dimension of language teaching and learning. Many of the chapters report fascinating investigations of what took place when foreign language learners in different countries cooperated together on projects. The findings reveal how these learners came to form 'bonded' international groups, developed common international identifications, gained new intercultural and international understandings, acquired skills of criticality, and were able to apply the new intercultural and citizenship competences that they had acquired through action in their own communities. The book also contains very informative investigations of young people's understanding of the concepts of global citizen and intercultural citizen, two concepts that have direct relevance to current developments in the field of civic/citizenship education. All of the authors who have contributed chapters to the book are to be congratulated on producing such an impressive and insightful body of work.

I very much hope that the present book will be just the first step along a continuing road, and that many of these studies will continue into future years with future cohorts of learners. Having documented and understood some of the processes that take place in learners during these collaborative projects, the next step will be to develop a more detailed understanding of exactly how these projects are serving to enhance specific components of intercultural and democratic competence in learners and what the best and most effective ways to foster individual components are.

I welcome the significant contribution which is made by the present book. The findings that are reported will be of great interest to all who are concerned about the problems associated with globalization, cultural diversity, intercultural understanding and democratic citizenship. I wish this collective venture well for the future in its ongoing developments.

Professor Martyn Barrett
London, January 2016

References

Ameli, S.R. and Merali, A. (2015) *Environment of Hate: The New Normal for Muslims in the UK*. London: Islamic Human Rights Commission.

Bekemans, L. (2013) Educational challenges and perspectives in multiculturalism vs. interculturalism: Citizenship education for intercultural realities. In M. Barrett (ed.) *Interculturalism and Multiculturalism: Similarities and Differences* (pp. 169–187). Strasbourg: Council of Europe.

Council of Europe (2013) *Final Declaration, Council of Europe Standing Conference of Ministers of Education 'Governance and Quality Education'*, 24th Session, Helsinki, Finland, 26–27 April 2013.

FRA – EU Agency for Fundamental Rights (2013a) *FRA Brief: Crimes Motivated by Hatred and Prejudice in the EU*. Luxembourg: Publications Office of the European Union.

FRA – EU Agency for Fundamental Rights (2013b) *Antisemitism: Summary Overview of the Data Available in the European Union 2003–2013*. Luxembourg: Publications Office of the European Union.

FRA – EU Agency for Fundamental Rights (2015) *Fundamental Rights: Challenges and Achievements in 2014*. Luxembourg: Publications Office of the European Union.

United Nations (2013) *Trends in International Migrant Stock: The 2013 Revision – Migrants by Age and Sex*. New York: United Nations.

United Nations (2015) *Human Development Report 2015: Work for Human Development*. New York: United Nations.

Acknowledgements

We are above all grateful to the necessarily anonymous learners and teachers who have worked with us and made this project possible.

We would also like to thank the equally anonymous reviewer for valuable suggestions which have helped us improve the book. We are grateful to Martyn Barrett for his foreword and for his help with deciding how we should organize the book.

Our authors have been patient and cooperative. We thank them for that and take responsibility for any remaining blemishes, but hope they will be happy with the final product as one of the outcomes of a network of dedicated and imaginative teachers and researchers.

The Editors
(in the UK, Hungary, China and the USA)

Contributors

María Emilia Arcuri is a teacher of English at the Escuela Graduada Joaquín V. González, Universidad Nacional de La Plata.

Michael Byram is Professor Emeritus at Durham University, England, and Guest Professor at Luxembourg University. He has worked in initial teacher training and doctoral supervision, and taught courses on intercultural competence. He has researched bilingual and minority education, residence abroad for language students and intercultural competence in foreign language learning. **m.s.byram@dur.ac.uk**

Petra Daryai-Hansen holds an Associate Professorship position at the Department of English, German and Romance Studies, University of Copenhagen and the Department of Research, Development and Internationalization, University College, Denmark. Her main research areas are internationalization of education, intercultural pedagogy and plurilingual education. **pdh@ruc.dk**

Irina Golubeva is president of AEDE-Hungary. She has been working for more than 20 years in different sectors of education, including Higher Education. Since 2000 she has been lecturing in Intercultural Communication and Translation Studies related subjects. Her main research interests concern FLT and intercultural communication, including conceptualization of intercultural citizenship. **golubeva@almos.uni-pannon.hu**

Jing Hongtao is an Assistant Professor of English education and intercultural communication at Waseda University in Japan. He holds a PhD in English education from Waseda University. His research interests focus on intercultural communicative competence, global awareness, global citizenship, and teacher cognition within language education in East Asia. **tonyhongtaojing@gmail.com**

Stephanie Ann Houghton is an Associate Professor in Intercultural Communication at Saga University, Japan. She has published numerous articles and books on intercultural communication. She is a co-editor of the book series *Intercultural Communication and Language Education* (Springer), and the AILA ReN Coordinator for a research network focusing on native-speakerism. **steph_houghton@hotmail.com**

Jessie Ju-Chen Hsieh is an Assistant Professor at the Center of General Education of National Chi Nan University, Nantou, Taiwan. She holds an EdD in Intercultural Education from Durham University, UK. With her other professional involvement in community practice, Jessie is integrating her courses with intercultural communication and social practices. **jessiehsieh@gmail.com**

Mei-Lan Huang holds an EdD in Language Education and Intercultural Education from Durham University, UK. She is an Assistant Professor of Foreign Language Education Department in Chang-Gung University of Science and Technology, Taiwan. Her research interests include intercultural communicative competence, foreign language education, and identity politics. **mhuang4220@gmail.com**

Han Hui is Professor of Foreign Languages at Zhejiang Yuexiu University, China and received her PhD at Durham University, UK and has published numerous papers. She has been teaching English for over 30 years. Her research areas focus around language education, teacher education and intercultural communicative competence. **hanhellen@163.com**

Song Li is Professor of English at Harbin Institute of Technology, Harbin, China. Her major research interests centre on the intercultural dimension of language education, such as intercultural dialogicality, intercultural communicative approach to ELT, native speakerism, critical language–cultural awareness, teacher cognition of ICC and intercultural citizenship education through ELT. **slhrb@126.com**

Ulla Lundgren is a former Assistant Professor of Education, Jönköping University, Sweden. Her research interest is in the intersection of language education and citizenship education. Her earlier background includes secondary schools, adult education and teacher education where she has *inter alia* developed and taught interdisciplinary international courses on Intercultural Encounters. **ulla.lundgren@hlk.hj.se**

Catherine Peck is an academic developer at RMIT University Vietnam, with a background in teacher education. She has taught and trained teachers in diverse contexts in Ireland, Spain, Korea and Vietnam. She is particularly interested in researching foreign language-mediated intercultural encounters within and beyond formal educational settings. **cbmpeck@gmail.com**

Melina Porto is Professor at Universidad Nacional de La Plata and Researcher at the Instituto de Investigaciones en Humanidades y Ciencias Sociales, Consejo Nacional de Investigaciones Científicas y Técnicas (UNLP-CONICET), Argentina. She holds an MA in ELT from the University of Essex, UK, and a PhD in Sciences of Education from Argentina. **melinaporto@conicet.gov.ar**

Kira Schlifer is an English, Danish and Drama teacher at Randersgades Skole, the International Profile School of Copenhagen. She has been working at Randersgades Skole for 17 years. **schlifer71@gmail.com**

Manuela Wagner is Associate Professor of Foreign Language Education at the University of Connecticut. Her teaching and research interests include intercultural competence, first and second language acquisition, humour, pragmatics, advocacy for language education, and teacher education. She enjoys collaborating with colleagues in order to bridge theory and practice. **manuela.wagner@uconn.edu**

Mary E. Yakimowski is Assistant Dean and in the Departments of Teacher Education and Educational Literacy and Literacy at Sacred Heart University at Fairfield, Connecticut, USA. Her teaching and research interests are in urban education, programme evaluation, school improvement, assessment and programming for students who are at-risk. **yakimowski@aol.com**

Etsuko Yamada is Associate Professor at Hokkaido University, Japan. She teaches intercultural education for Japanese and international students and Japanese as a foreign language. She holds a PhD in Education from Durham University, UK. Her research interests lie in criticality and critical thinking. **yamada_etsuko@hotmail.com**

Leticia Yulita holds a PhD from the University of East Anglia, England and lectures in Spanish and intercultural communication at the same university. Her research interests include language and intercultural citizenship education, Critical Pedagogy, curriculum internationalization and identity in language learning. **l.yulita@uea.ac.uk**

Zhao Yuqin holds a PhD in Applied Linguistics from Auckland University of Technology, and has been Professor, teaching English at the School of Foreign Languages of Harbin Institute of Technology since 1989. Research interests include Second Language Acquisition, Discourse Analysis, Cross-cultural Communication and English language teaching. **1982585933@qq.com**

Introduction

This book is based on a project – originally called 'Citizenship Education in the Language Classroom' – which was a collaboration among some of the members of an informal network of researchers 'Cultnet' (http://cultnet-world.wordpress.com). The network consists of teachers and researchers who are interested in foreign language teaching and its cultural dimension and, in particular, in introducing intercultural communicative competence into foreign language teaching on a systematic basis. This network was formed by Michael Byram and has grown over almost two decades from a small group of PhD students who came together in mutual support to an email list of over 200 people who share information and ideas. The idea for this project was born at the annual Cultnet meeting 2013, attended by about 20 members of the network, and then advertised to the whole group by email, inviting anyone to join. Eventually a much smaller number – the authors of this book – became the settled group, working together in pairs or small groups but aware of each other's work through sharing a pbworks page, a real-time collaborative editing system. The page was provided by Robert O'Dowd, a Cultnet member, who also facilitated the use of and interaction on this social network.

This book is one of the outcomes of the project. Its purpose is to show how teachers and researchers – who are sometimes the same people, i.e. teacher–researchers – can work together to develop new curricula and pedagogy. Put briefly, this involves first the creation of new theory – of 'intercultural citizenship' – and an imagined procedure for implementation. Secondly, there has to be a group willing to implement experimentally, and describe for other teachers the processes and procedures. Thirdly, there is a review of the ups and downs of implementation so that other teachers might attempt replication with full knowledge of the realities and willingness to experiment in their own classrooms.

With this purpose in mind, we have planned a book in which the first group of authors explain their attempts to understand how learners and teachers think about citizenship and interculturality, followed by a section in which teachers in different countries collaborate, followed in turn by a third section describing how groups of learners in two or more countries and continents can collaborate across the internet. These three sections are preceded by this introduction to the theory and followed by reflections on the lessons learnt from implementation and how these can help readers who are encouraged to try out our ideas for themselves. For, as teachers ourselves, we are very much aware that theory and innovation cannot be simply 'applied'; all practice is a further challenge to theory and can and should lead to further innovation.

In the next part of this introduction, our purpose is to explain the immediate theory behind the project and how it was shared among the group. In the following part, we explain the implementation of the project and we then locate the project in a wider theoretical context of scholarship on citizenship education.

Finally there is an overview of the sections and chapters that explains the contents and focus of each chapter. Readers can thus identify the chapters that may be of immediate interest, for example because of the age group of the learners or whether the focus is on surveying how learners and teachers think about intercultural citizenship, or how they can create cooperation across continents in real or virtual time. Readers may also wish to turn immediately to the Reflections for an overview of how the groups of teachers worked together in practice, what their difficulties were and how they tried to overcome them. We have thus tried to allow for a number of ways of using this book according to readers' various interests and preferences.

Theoretical Foundations

The evolution of the theory behind the project took place in several stages and over more than a decade of work but it can be summarized as a move from the concept of 'intercultural speaker' to 'intercultural citizen'.

The phrase *intercultural speaker* was coined by Byram and Zarate in a working paper requested by the Council of Europe to help the group of authors who were writing the *Common European Framework of Reference for Languages* (2001). In that paper, Byram and Zarate (1994, 1997) attempted to refine the concept, which up to that point in Council of Europe papers (e.g. van Ek, 1986) was called *sociocultural competence.* They did this by defining four *savoirs*, four dimensions of knowledge, skills and attitudes. In 1997, Byram published a monograph, *Teaching and Assessing Intercultural Communicative Competence*, which built on but modified substantially the Byram and Zarate Council of Europe paper. During this process, the coining of the phrase 'intercultural speaker' was accompanied in the first paper by the introduction of the phrase 'intercultural competence' into the field of foreign language education and then, in the monograph, the coining of 'intercultural communicative competence'.

The phrase *intercultural speaker* was a deliberate attempt to distance the notion of intercultural competence from the cultural competences of a native speaker. It is important to notice that the use of the term 'intercultural speaker' and the subsequent models of intercultural competence do not have any implications for or against using the native speaker as a model for linguistic competences. That is a different issue.

The phrase 'intercultural' speaker was not taken into the Common European Framework of Reference (CEFR), although there are many references to intercultural skills, awareness and competence and one reference to 'intercultural personality'. The original description of the competences of an intercultural speaker proposed by Byram and Zarate (1994), was much amended in the CEFR, even though the terminology of four *savoirs* was adopted. Furthermore, although Byram (1997) is cited in the references of the CEFR, there is no discernible influence. In particular, there is no reference to *savoir s'engager*, a fifth *savoir*, which is the crucial educational dimension of intercultural competence.

The CEFR thus presents a 'list' model substantially different from Byram and Zarate (1994) and from Byram (1997). Nonetheless, one element of the concept of 'intercultural speaker' – namely, that of 'mediation' – is present in the CEFR and is described as the ability to 'act as an intermediary between interlocutors who are unable to understand each other directly – normally (but not exclusively) speakers of different languages' (Council of Europe, 2001: 87). Cultural intermediary roles would include 'the ability to bring the culture of origin and the foreign culture into relation with each other' and, *inter alia*, 'the capacity ... to deal effectively with intercultural misunderstanding and conflict situations' (Council of Europe, 2001: 104–105). This concept of 'mediation' is an important element of 'intercultural citizenship' and can be found in several of the projects in the chapters of this book, as learners take on the responsibility of explaining viewpoints and beliefs in one country to people in another country.

Intercultural competence and intercultural communicative competence

Among linguists, the term 'competence' is often linked to 'performance' and the distinction made by Chomsky. However, Fleming (2009) traces a more complex and longer use of the term in the field of education. He shows that, in this context, the term 'competence' has had a chequered history but can usefully be adopted to refer to observable behaviours as well as to the implicit understandings within them. The emphasis on behaviours as indicators of understanding and as performance skills allows us to observe and to measure people's interculturality as a state of mind, as well as their ability to act interculturally.

Although so far we have referred to interactions among people of different countries (and by implication, languages), someone with 'intercultural competence' acting as a mediator is often just as important in interactions among people of the same country and 'the same' language, as it is in mediating among people of different countries, with different languages and cultures. In the same vein, mediation is important among people of different countries with 'the same' language, e.g. US Americans and Australians. A fine-grained analysis would show that different groups apparently speaking the same language also have different discourses, and that intercultural mediation is just as relevant here as when languages and cultures are visibly and obviously different. Families, for example, have their own family language – often with specific words or expressions – in which they refer to their shared knowledge and past. The fact that people believe that they speak the same language, where there is indeed much in common, can make the task of the mediator more difficult than when languages are obviously different, because mediation in the same language requires sensitivity to fine-grained differences. Mediators are also important in industrial disputes among people who believe that they speak the same language although the degree of awareness of linguistic distinctions may not be high and other skills are the main focus of training such mediators (Hermann *et al.,* 2001).

Where two groups have languages and cultures that are mutually incomprehensible,[1] the linguistic competences of the mediator are more obvious. The mediator needs to be bilingual to some degree, although this must not be understood as having native speaker linguistic competence in both languages. It is to emphasize this linguistic dimension that the distinction is made between 'intercultural competence' (IC), where 'the same' language is being used, and 'intercultural communicative competence' (ICC), referring to mediation between mutually incomprehensible languages. The latter thus combines the use in recent decades of the concept of 'communicative competence' in another language – with emphasis on the ability to use a language not only with correct application of knowledge of its grammar but also in socially appropriate ways (Savignon, 2013; Warren, 2012) – with 'intercultural competence'. It also recognizes the importance of the relationship between language and culture.

The nature of that relationship is not simple. Risager's (2006) comprehensive and authoritative analysis, starting from Agar's (1994) notion of 'languaculture', has shown that a language spoken by a specific group of people – be they 'native speakers' or not – is not necessarily tied to a specific set of beliefs, values and behaviours, a specific culture. Furthermore, in foreign language use, the relationship between a language and the culture it embodies may be highly complex, as Risager shows in her example:

> If I, with Danish as my first language, travel round the world, I take my Danish idiolect with me, with the personal languaculture I have developed during my life. But I also take my special forms of English,

French and German with me – the languages I have learnt as foreign languages. My foreign language resources are, without a doubt, influenced to a great extent by my Danish languaculture. So I contribute to the spreading of Danish languaculture, but to a lesser extent to the spreading of English, French and German languaculture. (Risager, 2006: 134)

Here Risager refers to being a learner of English, French and German and using them around the world, but in most foreign language teaching, learners focus on one language and usually associate it with one country, although proposals for plurilingual curricula now exist (Council of Europe, 2010) and attention is being paid increasingly to multilingualism in research on language acquisition (May, 2013). Learners thus acquire a systematic way of developing intercultural competences by concentrating on the relationships between their own languaculture and one other.[2] Nonetheless, they simultaneously develop ICC, which is transferable to other languacultures they may learn subsequently.

In the model of ICC presented in Byram (1997), the crucial development from the work of Byram and Zarate and the CEFR was the inclusion of the fifth *savoir*, the concept of 'critical cultural awareness' or *'savoir s'engager'*. This was influenced by theory of 'politische Bildung', which is usually translated as 'political education', but this is a translation that misses some of the connotations of *Bildung* (Løvlie & Standish, 2002). Although it was evident that the phrase, in the English translation, might be misunderstood and confused with schooling as indoctrination, the importance of emphasizing the educational value of ICC outweighed the possible disadvantages of mistranslation. At approximately the same time, theoretical work in Germany on 'politische Bildung' was also beginning to use the term 'Demokratielernen' (Himmelmann, 2006), where the emphasis on learning to be and act in a democracy was more evident in the label.

Comparing foreign language education and citizenship education[3]

A comparison of the competences described in models of ICC – especially where 'critical cultural awareness' is a core concept as in Byram (1997) – with models of the competences needed to be and act as a democratic citizen reveals much overlap but also some differences. This comparison was carried out in detail in Byram (2008) with a strong emphasis on the German tradition of 'politische Bildung' and the work of Himmelmann (2006) in particular. The book presents an integrated 'Framework of Education for Intercultural Citizenship', which combines appropriate parts of Himmelmann's approach to setting objectives for citizenship education/democracy learning with the approach in Byram (1997) to setting objectives for language teaching for ICC.

In brief, and at the risk of simplification, it is suggested that there are limitations to both approaches that can be remedied by a combination of ideas from both. Citizenship education and learning to act democratically include as objectives that learners should become active in their world as a consequence of what they learn in their political education, and that this should take place contemporaneously with their classroom-based learning. It is not a matter of learning 'for later life', as is often assumed about much of education. On the other hand, the world where learners should act is assumed to be their community, whether their local community or their national community. There is no transnational level of action in the world; there is no reference to transnational communities.

In foreign language teaching, in contrast, the attention of learners is directed to the world beyond their national community, especially to countries where the language they are learning is spoken. Yet in the interpretation of 'politische Bildung' on which the concept of critical cultural awareness is founded in Byram's (1997) model of ICC, there is no suggestion that criticality should lead to *action* in the learners' world or community/ies. Combining the two approaches to setting objectives for teaching, which develop the competences of an 'intercultural citizen', is therefore the purpose of the analysis and the heart of the framework that is presented in Byram (2008). It was argued there that 'transnational communities' should be created in foreign language teaching and that these become the basis of political action/action in the world. Five levels of engagement were identified:

Pre-political

(1) Learners engage with others (through documents and artefacts or 'in person', which might be face-to-face or virtual) and reflect critically on their own assumptions, and those of the other; and
(2) learners engage with others, reflect critically and propose/imagine possible alternatives and changes.

Political

(3) Learners engage with others seeking their perspective/advice, reflect critically, propose change and take action to instigate change in their own society;
(4) learners create with others a transnational community, reflect together, propose and instigate change in their respective societies; and
(5) in a transnational community, learners from two or more societies identify an issue which they act upon as a transnational group.

The framework and the five levels of engagement were the basis for the proposal put to the Cultnet network:

Citizenship Education in the Language Classroom

Foreign Language Education (FLE) which includes teaching for ICC necessarily involves:

- criticality/critical cultural awareness;
- a focus on 'others' who live beyond our national boundaries and speak another language;
- comparative analysis of our situation and theirs.

It does NOT include 'service to the community' as Citizenship Education (Cit. Ed.) does.

Cit Ed. includes (not only):

- teaching which leads to activity/'service to the community' in the here and now;
- a focus on 'community' as local, regional, national but NOT international.

It does NOT include criticality/critical cultural awareness towards 'our' community.

My proposal is to develop complementarity taking 'activity in the here and now' from Cit Ed. and 'criticality' and 'internationalism' from FLE.

In terms of *methodology*, I propose that the FL classroom become a Content and language integrated learning (CLIL) classroom i.e. where the FL is used as a medium of instruction and the content is 'intercultural citizenship'.

An example model project would be:

- a group of learners of English as FL in country X engaging in a Cit Ed. project with a group of English as FL learners in country Y. They would decide on a project of significance in their community, share ideas and plans with each other, critically analyse the reasons/assumptions in their plans by comparison with the plans of the other group, carry out and report to each other their projects.

(In doing so they would become a (temporary) community of intercultural citizens with an international identity. Such a project might last only a short time – a few weeks/months.)

There are other possible models/combinations …

Mike Byram

References to relevant theoretical and empirical work were provided. Participants were reminded that 'criticality' was the focus of a book by a network member, Manuela Guilherme (2002), with the telling title *Critical Citizens for an Intercultural World*, and that another member, Stephanie Houghton (2012), had published *Intercultural Dialogue in Practice: Managing Value Judgment through Foreign Language Education*. Furthermore, the principles of intercultural citizenship education were presented as they had been developed in a collection of articles dealing with policy and practice in several countries (Alred *et al.*, 2006):

Education for Intercultural Citizenship

There are two purposes for this statement of 'axioms and characteristics' of education for intercultural citizenship. They act first as an approach to planning of education for intercultural citizenship in whatever form deemed desirable, and second as criteria for evaluating the degree of intercultural citizenship education already present in existing education systems.

The axioms define what being intercultural entails and the characteristics are what might be expected in education in any form which helps people to think about their experience and to determine how they should respond to it.

Axioms

- intercultural experience takes place when people from different social groups with different cultures (values, beliefs and behaviours) meet;
- 'being intercultural' involves analysis and reflection about intercultural experience, and acting on that reflection;
- intercultural citizenship experience takes place when people of different social groups and cultures engage in social and political activity;
- intercultural democratic experience take place when people of different social groups and cultures engage in democratic social and political activity – not avoiding values and judgements;
- intercultural citizenship education involves:
  - causing/facilitating intercultural citizenship experience, and analysis and reflection on it (and on the possibility of further social and/or political activity, where 'political' is taken in broad sense to mean activity which involves working with others to achieve an agreed end);
  - creating learning/change in the individual: cognitive, attitudinal, behavioural change; change in self-perception/spirituality; change in relationships with others i.e. people of different social

groups; change which is based in the particular but is related to the universal.

Characteristics of education for intercultural citizenship

- a comparative (juxtaposition) orientation in activities of teaching and learning e.g. juxtaposition of political processes (in the classroom, school ... country...) and a critical perspective which questions assumptions through the process of juxtaposition;
- emphasis on becoming conscious of working with Others (of a different group and culture) through (a) processes of comparison/juxtaposition and (b) communication in a language (L1 or L2/3/...) which influences perceptions and which emphasizes the importance of learners becoming conscious of multiple identities;
- creating a community of action and communication which is supranational and/or composed of people of different beliefs values and behaviours which are potentially in conflict – without expecting conformity and easy, harmonious solutions;
- having a focus and range of action which is different from that which is available when not working with Others, where 'Others' refers to all those of whatever social group who are initially perceived as different, members of an out-group;
- emphasizing becoming aware of one's existing identities and opening options for social identities additional to the national and regional etc. (e.g. the formation of perhaps temporary supra-national group identities through interaction with Others);
- paying equal attention to cognition/knowledge, affect/attitude, behaviours/skill;
- all of the above with a conscious commitment to values (i.e. rejecting relativism), being aware that values sometimes conflict and are differently interpreted, but being committed, as citizens in a community, to cooperation.

In order to give more theoretical depth to the concept of 'action', as planning took place, a further paper discussing criteria was posted where the crucial new element was a more thorough explanation of 'criticality' and the work of Barnett (1997):

Criteria for intercultural citizenship projects

As you form your groups and plan your projects, it will be important to ensure that projects are not simply international groups where learners get to know each other and learn something about each other. This is important but not enough.

A project will have to meet certain criteria if it is to develop 'intercultural citizenship'.

Here are some ideas about what is needed, what to think about as you plan – and what you could use as a list for evaluation of success afterwards:

Identification and competences

- opportunities for learners to create and cooperate in groups of several nationalities, forming 'bonded' international groups;
- i.e. learners identify with 'our group' during the course of the project; such identification may only be temporary but leads learners to suspend their identification with the national culture/way of thinking and acting to find new 'international' ways of acting;
- teaching and learning which include critical thinking as intended outcome;
- this is the notion of 'critical cultural awareness' or *'savoir s'engager'*;
- teaching and learning which leads to learners becoming aware of the presuppositions they hold and the national basis of many of these;
- this is related to 'critical cultural awareness' and refers to questioning/ challenging/wondering about what learners would have done/thought if the project had not involved people from another country;
- Intercultural competence as a basis for successful cooperation and 'bonding';
- The process of 'bonding' is a result of/influenced by project work which deliberately encourages the acquisition of the different elements of IC.

Criticality

Here we can refer to Barnett, R. (1997) *Higher Education: A Critical Business* (Buckingham: Open University Press) – used by Etsuko in her PhD – which we have drawn on here.

Barnett identifies:

THREE DOMAINS

- propositions, ideas and theories – i.e. what learners learn about the world (in formal education what they learn in their 'subjects');
- the internal world, that is oneself, a form of critical thought that is demonstrated in critical self-reflection – i.e. what learners think about themselves as individuals;

- the external world, a form of critical thought that is demonstrated in critical action – i.e. what learners *do* as a result of their thinking and learning.

He also identifies four levels or degrees of criticality – increasingly complex/deep:

FOUR LEVELS:

- critical skills – reflexivity – refashioning of traditions – transformatory critique.

  At the first level the emphasis is on *skills* of learning how to be critical (and 'critical' of course does not mean 'being negative or attacking something/somebody – it means evaluating positive and negative).

  At the second level the skills are *applied* to the knowledge learners have acquired, to their own selves and to the world.

  At the third level, the criticality leads to *change* in the sense of modification of what has so far been accepted as 'common sense' in knowledge, in oneself, in what we do in the world.

  At the fourth level, the change is more *radical* and change is not just modification of what is 'common sense' or 'taken for granted' but is in fact overturning this and developing something new.

This is summarized in the table below adapted from Barnett (1997: 103)

	Domains		
Levels of criticality	Knowledge	Self	World
4. Transformatory critique	Knowledge critique	Reconstruction of self	Critique-in-action (collective reconstruction of world)
3. Refashioning of traditions	Critical thought (malleable traditions of thought)	Development of self within traditions	Mutual understanding and development of traditions
2. Reflexivity	Critical thinking (reflection on one's understanding)	Self-reflection (reflection on one's own projects)	Reflective practice ('metacompetence', 'adaptability', 'flexibility')
1. Critical skills	Discipline-specific critical thinking skills	Self-monitoring to given standards and norms	Problem-solving (means–end instrumentalism)
Forms of criticality	Critical reason	Critical self-reflection	Critical action

Therefore a good intercultural citizenship project will ideally have the following characteristics:

- create a sense of international identification with learners in the international project;
- challenge the 'common sense' of each national group within the international project;
- develop a new 'international' way of thinking *and acting* (a new way which may be either a modification of what is usually done OR a radically new way);
- apply that new way to 'knowledge', to 'self' and to *'the world'*.

As you work try to keep these abstract points in mind and find concrete ways of realizing them in practice.

As can be seen above, participants were also reminded that one of their number, Etsuko Yamada (2012), had drawn on Barnett in her PhD thesis and that an important reference was the report of a major research project examining the nature of foreign language teaching in universities and the degree to which it already introduced criticality into teaching and learning practices (Johnston *et al.*, 2011). This encapsulated clearly one of the purposes of our project: *Developing student criticality in higher education.*

Finally, in one of the messages that were frequently posted in the early stages of the project, participants' attention was drawn to a proposed framework and clarification of the competences of a global citizen by Reid and Spencer-Oatey (2013) where, again, the title was in harmony with our aims: 'Towards the global citizen: Utilizing a competency framework to promote intercultural knowledge and skills in higher education'.

Implementation of the Project

As mentioned at the beginning of this introduction, after Michael Byram proposed a collaborative project to teach and investigate intercultural citizenship education systematically, an online workspace on pbworks (pbworsk.com), organized and facilitated by Robert O'Dowd, was used to coordinate collaboration between a group of interested colleagues working in various educational environments (primary, secondary and post-secondary education) in 10 locations (Argentina, China, Denmark, Hungary, Italy, Japan, South Korea, Taiwan, the UK and the USA).

All members of this platform, except members in China, who could not access the platform,[4] were able to edit the pages, create new pages and communicate with each other through email and on asynchronous discussion boards. A background document described in the previous section provided information about the general theoretical framework that participants agreed to apply in their prospective projects.

As a first stage, anyone in the whole network interested in participating was invited to publish profiles of their classes or groups of learners for others to read. Information included age and level of learners, language being learnt and approximate level of proficiency, other languages present in the classroom (e.g. mother tongues and other foreign/second/third languages), any previous work done with this or other classes related to citizenship, access to online communication, any initial ideas about a citizenship topic/focus, and when the most convenient time would be for classroom work (bearing in mind that there would need to be a period (several months) for preparation) *and* how much classroom time, over what period of time, potential participants thought they could devote to this. Colleagues were invited to read the class profiles and comment on them with the goal of looking for potential partners with similar interests. From those initial interactions email communications ensued and project partnerships were formed. In the following weeks project partners co-designed their projects. They also shared their project descriptions on the pbworks.

All project partners engaged in what Byram referred to in a retrospective document – also uploaded to the wiki – as 'curriculum development', where we all started from theoretical principles and a philosophical rationale and designed our teaching and learning on that basis. The philosophical rationale was that we thought certain things *ought to* happen in language teaching: that there ought to be a content that gives learners a focus for their use/ learning of language; that the content ought to be linked to education for citizenship and its purposes and methods; and that the citizenship in the language classroom should be 'intercultural'.

The projects were planned to start in the fall/autumn of 2013, although they were in fact implemented at different periods depending on finding appropriate times in busy timetables. Finished projects were again shared on pbworks.

Further developments

As the first projects were completed, new questions arose and reach into the future, questions about sustainability, about formal evaluation of the projects individually and of the network of projects as a whole, and about modes of assessment of student learning.

If curriculum development is to become influential then it must be shown that it can be sustained by those involved and not just exist as an experiment on one occasion. It must also show that the principles and methods can be understood, absorbed and further developed by other teachers beyond those of the initial committed and enthusiastic group. It is one of the purposes of this book to start the second of these processes by making the ideas public and the procedures transparent.

With respect to sustainability for those involved, the first evidence for this came from a project that started earlier than most of the others. The project, between Argentina and England, was repeated with a new group of students in the following year and the two iterations are presented in later chapters (Chapters 8 and 9).

The question of evaluation of the success of the projects, of the ways in which, for example, students identify with the international perspectives of their projects, contrasting them perhaps with the national perspectives which they otherwise assume, was pursued in the analysis of data from students' interactions.

Overview of Chapters

The chapters have been arranged to lead the reader from research on how learners and teachers think about some of the key concepts of the project (Chapters 1–3) in Section 1, through two examples of how teachers can cooperate to work in parallel with their learners (Chapters 4 and 5 in Section 2) to Chapters 6–10 (Section 3), which describe how learners of different ages and different levels of linguistic competence can be taught on the basis of the principles of the project, including in particular how learners can be encouraged to take 'action in the community'.

In Chapter 1, Irina Golubeva, Manuela Wagner and Mary E. Yakimowski use a comparison and contrast between the USA and Hungary to characterize how university-level learners understand the concept of 'intercultural citizen'; they decided that the term 'global citizen' would be more accessible to learners replying to a questionnaire. Although they find some understanding of the concept among their two national groups, they conclude that it is limited and that a richer understanding needs to be developed.

Chapter 2 is also based on a survey of learners at universities, but this time in China. Han Hui, Song Li, Jing Hongtao and Zhao Yuqin decided to use the key term 'intercultural citizen' – and a translation – since it was familiar to questionnaire respondents. However, they also point out that terms transferred from Western countries to China are understood differently. Their analysis reveals how respondents characterize the 'intercultural citizen', but they conclude that, because of the social and historical specificity of education in China, respondents interpretations of, for example, obligations and responsibilities are much influenced by values present in Chinese society.

Chapter 3 addresses the question of teacher training and identity where Ulla Lundgren and her students write about a course in which both the form and the content were intercultural. The students came from different countries, working in international groups on issues that raised their awareness of interculturality and how it might impact on their work as teachers.

The analysis addresses the students' development of an awareness of their own stereotypes, a sense of international identification, an 'international' way of thinking and acting and an ability to apply the new way to 'knowledge' to 'self' and to 'the world'. The themes are thus those that have been raised in earlier chapters and illustrate how teachers too can be prepared to address interculturality in their work. Although Ulla Lundgren, like other authors in this book, does not hide the difficulties, her final optimism is one which we think runs through the book and we hope into further practice.

Chapter 4 is the first in Section 2 on 'Teachers cooperating' and involves two teachers, Etsuko Yamada and Jessie Hsieh, who worked together to develop ideas about teaching intercultural citizenship with learners whose language competence is very limited. In one case they were Taiwanese students learning English in Taiwan and in the other they were students from several different countries learning Japanese in Japan, and using English as a lingua franca in the classroom when their competences in Japanese were not yet adequate for their needs. Again, the authors describe their project in practical detail and show how their work was infused by theory, including Barnett's work which had been presented as a basis for projects (see above).

Chapter 5, by Stephanie Ann Houghton and Mei Lan Huang, also deals with the environment but the learners are this time at university, they too use English as a lingua franca. In this case, the two groups of learners followed a common online course. The project focused on a systematic process of the analysis of self and other, through criticality and evaluation of self and other, to reflection upon identity development. There is close analysis of the learners' products – worksheets for example – to analyse the impact of the project. As in Chapter 4, the cooperation here was between the two teachers, although they conclude that there is opportunity for cooperation between student groups in the future.

Section 3 begins with Chapter 6, which deals with younger learners. Melina Porto, Petra Daryai-Hansen, María Emilia Arcuri and Kira Schlifer cooperated in a situation where two groups of learners, one in Denmark and one in Argentina, were learning English as a foreign language and using it as a lingua franca. The learners were aged 11–13 and focused on a topic of common interest, the environment. They talked across the internet both synchronically and diachronically and compared and contrasted ideas about environmental protection, such comparison helping them to notice things in their own context which they had simply taken for granted. The teachers analysed data of interactions and established that an international identification took place, as was suggested by the theory described earlier in this Introduction. Learners began to acquire the skills of criticality and then took action in their own communities as a consequence of their work in the classroom.

Chapter 7, by Catherine Peck and Manuela Wagner, involves groups in the USA and Korea, with large distances of space and time between them, but also differences in terms of their studies, one group being undergraduates and the other graduates. The chapter describes in practical detail the stages of the project so that other teachers in other countries might be able to modify and replicate them for their own circumstances. This includes the difficulties as well as the successes because we want to remain pragmatic and honest. The focus of the cooperation was, as in the first two chapters, reflection on the key concepts but this time with interaction among the learners. They were asked to talk about their own language and culture learning and, because they were either future teachers or teachers already in activity, they prepared lesson plans for their own contexts. Here then we see an example of two groups working together on the same topic to gain new international insights, but then 'applying' their ideas to their own context.

With Chapter 8, by Melina Porto, we have another project that had university learners in direct contact with each other. In this case, one group, in Argentina, took their 'action in the community' to a further level by collaborating with a group of learners in a school. The topic was mural art and graffiti. Each group observed and analysed in their own environment and then, with the insights afforded by comparison in discussions with their partners in another country, produced their own art or graffiti in international groups of Argentineans and Italians. This created an identification that went beyond the national and into the international. Criticality was an important dimension of this project too, drawing on Barnett's work, and led to 'action in the community'. The chapter, like others, finishes with a discussion of difficulties and challenges so that other teachers can replicate the project, but also be aware of the problems that have to be overcome.

Chapters 9 and 10, by Melina Porto and Leticia Yulita, bring together learners acquiring each other's language – in contrast to the use of English as a lingua franca in earlier chapters – and show how a project can become embedded in practice. These authors describe a first project where their Argentinean learners of English and British learners of Spanish engage with a particularly sensitive topic – a war between the two countries – but manage to move beyond their national perspectives to one that is 'international' with a corresponding identification with an international group willing to take action in their respective communities.

The authors then describe a second project with new groups of language learners but with the same constellation of learners and languages. Again they deal with a sensitive historical topic, one which for the Argentinean learners defines their country's history. The interaction with British university learners helps the Argentineans to gain new perspectives and become engaged with their own community in ways that would not have occurred to them without the insights from their British partners. This second project will be followed by a third and so the experiment has become part of the routine; the teachers have 'trained' themselves and gained a new professional identity.

The purpose of the final chapter 'Reflections: Learning from the Challenges and Seeking Ways Forward' is to share the practicalities of our experience with our readers. We know that being involved in innovation is exciting. We know too the value of being part of a network of teachers. However, we also know that experimentation will not lead to real change unless it is repeated and becomes routine, and that it is not possible to transfer and apply what we have done to other situations in a simplistic manner. The Reflections therefore describes the challenges we met, how we tried to overcome them, and what we see as the ways forward into the future. We thus hope that our readers will be encouraged as much by our problems as by our successes, and make their own choices and decisions to introduce intercultural citizenship in a principled way into their own practice.

Michael Byram, Irina Golubeva,
Han Hui and Manuela Wagner

References

Agar, M. (1994) *Language Shock. Understanding the Culture of Conversation.* New York: William Morrow.

Alred, G., Byram, M. and Fleming, M. (eds) (2006) *Education for Intercultural Citizenship: Concepts and Comparisons.* Clevedon: Multilingual Matters.

Barnett, R. (1997) *Higher Education: A Critical Business.* Buckingham: Society for Research into Higher Education and the Open University Press

Byram, M. (1997) *Teaching and Assessing Intercultural Communicative Competence.* Clevedon: Multilingual Matters.

Byram, M. (2008) *From Foreign Language Education to Education for Intercultural Citizenship: Essays and Reflections* Clevedon: Multilingual Matters.

Byram, M. and Zarate, G. (1994) *Definitions, Objectives and Assessment of Socio-cultural Competence* (CC-LANG (94) 1). Strasbourg: Council of Europe.

Byram, M. and Zarate, G. (1997) Defining and assessing intercultural competence: Some principles and proposals for the European context. *Language Teaching* 29, 14–18.

Council of Europe (2001) *The Common European Framework of Reference for Languages: Learning, Teaching, Assessment.* Cambridge: Cambridge University Press.

Council of Europe (2010) *Guide for the Development and Implementation of Curricula for Plurilingual and Intercultural Education.* See http://www.coe.int/t/dg4/linguistic/Source/Source2010_ForumGeneva/GuideEPI2010_EN.pdf

Fleming, M. (2009) The challenge of competence. In A. Hu and M. Byram (eds) *Intercultural Competence and Foreign Language Learning.* Tubingen: Gunter Narr Verlag.

Guilherme, M. (2002) *Critical Citizens for an Intercultural World: Foreign Language Education as Cultural Politics.* Clevedon: Multilingual Matters.

Hermann, M.S., Hollett, N., Gale, J. and Foster, M. (2001) Defining mediator knowledge and skills. *Negotiation Journal*, April, 139–153.

Himmelmann, G. (2006) Concepts and issues in citizenship education. A comparative study of Germany, Britain and the USA. In G. Alred, M. Byram and M. Fleming (eds) *Education for Intercultural Citizenship. Concepts and Comparisons.* Clevedon: Multilingual Matters.

Houghton, S.A. (2012) *Intercultural Dialogue in Practice Managing Value Judgment through Foreign Language Education.* Bristol: Multilingual Matters.

Johnston, B., Ford, P., Mitchell, R. and Myles, F. (2011) *Developing Student Criticality in Higher Education: Undergraduate Learning in the Arts and Social Sciences.* London: Continuum.

League of Nations Union (1935) *Modern Language Teaching in Relation to World Citizenship.* London: League of Nations Union.

Løvlie, L. and Standish, P. (2002) Introduction: *Bildung* and the idea of a liberal education. *Journal of Philosophy of Education* 36 (3), 317–340.

May, S. (ed.) (2013) *The Multilingual Turn. Implications for SLA, TESOL and Bilingual Education.* London: Routledge

Reid, S. and Spencer-Oatey, H. (2013) Towards the global citizen: Utilizing a competency framework to promote intercultural knowledge and skills in higher education. In J. Ryan (ed.) *Cross-Cultural Teaching and Learning for Home and International Students. Internationalisation of Pedagogy and Curriculum in Higher Education.* London: Routledge.

Risager, K. (2006) *Language and Culture: Global Flows and Local Complexity.* Clevedon: Multilingual Matters.

Savignon, S.J. (2013) Communicative language teaching. In M. Byram and A. Hu (eds) *Routledge Encyclopedia of Language Teaching and Learning* (pp. 139–145). London: Routledge.

van Ek, J.A. (1986) *Objectives for Modern Language Learning.* Strasbourg: Council of Europe.

Warren, M. (2012) Professional and workplace settings. In J. Jackson (ed.) *Routledge Handbook of Language and Intercultural Communication* (pp. 481–494). London: Routledge.

Yamada, E. (2012) Fostering criticality in a beginners' Japanese language course. A case study in a UK higher education modern languages degree programme. Unpublished PhD thesis, University of Durham.

Notes

(1) This is inevitably a simplification to avoid many caveats and exceptions, which readers can add for themselves once the principles have been established.

(2) The fact that some languages are intercomprehensible because they are related, and speakers of one can to some degree, and especially with training, understand speakers of another, introduces a complicating factor to the discussion. For clarity's sake, we will not pursue this dimension in any detail here.

(3) We cannot here analyse the history of the relationship between foreign language education and citizenship education, but it is worth noting that in the years between 1918 and 1939 the League of Nations had an active education policy to bring the concepts of 'interdependence' and 'international co-operation into the thinking of young people'. In Britain the League of Nations Union had an active education committee and commissioned a report on how language teaching could and should be a location for education for world citizenship (League of Nations Union, 1935).

(4) The participants who were located in China had problems accessing the collaborative workspace throughout the project. Consequently, they had to receive documents via email and develop a separate though related project, described later in this book.

Section 1

The Baseline: Learners' and Teachers' Perceptions of Intercultural Citizenship

The first part of this book consists of three chapters in which the authors investigate students' perceptions of concepts such as 'global citizenship' or 'intercultural citizenship'. In order for educators to plan a curriculum that engages our students in intercultural citizenship, it is crucial for us to gain an insight into their perceptions of related concepts.

In Chapter 1, Irina Golubeva, Manuela Wagner and Mary E. Yakimowski investigate undergraduate students' perceptions of global citizenship. In particular they were interested in how undergraduate students at the university in the USA and in Hungary define global citizenship and whether or not language plays an important part in global citizenship in their opinion. Their findings provide some evidence that educators need to communicate to and negotiate with students why intercultural citizenship education can and has to happen at every level of their education as students tended to make connections between living in other countries and global citizenship rather than mentioning the role of education.

In Chapter 2, Han Hui, Song Li, Jing Hongtao and Zhao Yuqin explore how undergraduate students from two different educational backgrounds in China view citizenship and intercultural citizenship. Based on the students' answers the researchers draw conclusions about the role of culture and education in the students' perceptions. These results therefore highlight the importance of our understanding of different contexts for our curriculum planning while also showing the urgent need for education for intercultural citizenship, confirming findings from Chapter 1 in a different context.

In Chapter 3, Ulla Lundgren takes a different approach to gain insight into pre-service or future teachers' perceptions of their own intercultural development. Students who participated in a module called 'Intercultural Encounters' and taught by the author are at the same time co-authors of the chapter as Ulla Lundgren analyses their development of knowledge, skills and attitudes vis-à-vis intercultural citizenship and criticality through their own voices in the form of their reflections, which they shared throughout the module. As such, we experience personal accounts of the possible effects of intercultural citizenship education but also glimpse some struggles that the students experience as they are exposed to the intercultural citizenship curriculum.

1 Comparing Students' Perceptions of Global Citizenship in Hungary and the USA

Irina Golubeva, Manuela Wagner and Mary E. Yakimowski

Introduction

Throughout this book, the authors engage in transnational collaborations to teach intercultural citizenship in meaningful and systematic ways in a variety of educational contexts. More specifically, educators facilitate transnational communities collaborating on the development of intercultural competence (Byram, 1997). In addition, projects share a focus on action, combining 'critical cultural awareness' with 'internationalism' and 'acting in the here and now' (see the Introduction to this book). Gaining an understanding of what students believe it means to develop the knowledge, skills and attitudes that lead to intercultural citizenship can shed light on their perspectives before and during their engagement in such transnational projects. Of particular interest for us is whether students believe that foreign language plays an important role in their becoming an intercultural citizen.

The development of intercultural competence and foreign language education is important in both Hungary and the USA, despite the fact that these countries are significantly different in linguistic, economic and political matters, which could have an effect on learners' attitudes to foreign language education and global citizenship. For example, although in each country the school system endorses the learning of foreign languages, in Hungary the focus is having students learn more than one foreign language (see National Core Curriculum, 2012), whereas in the USA secondary students primarily learn one foreign language during their four years of high school. The increase in numbers of learners of English as a second language in the USA – nearly

60% between 1997 and 2007 (National Clearinghouse for English Language Acquisition, 2007) – has also led to an emphasis on pre-school to 12th grade (preK–12) 'emergent bilinguals' who will become approximately 40% of the school-aged population by 2030 (Thomas & Collier, 2002). In contrast to the situation in the USA, in Hungary the growing interest in learning foreign languages and especially English is also caused by an increasing tendency of emigration from the country to English-speaking countries like England, Ireland, the USA, Canada, Australia and outside the English-speaking world (see for updated statistics http://www.ksh.hu/ and also http://www.demografia.hu/).

One of the issues closely related to the question under discussion in this chapter – perceptions of global citizenship – is the issue of English as a language of international communication, especially with regard to the importance of English in a variety of contexts outside of English-speaking countries (see Kachru, 2005). There is a wealth of literature on English as an international language and as a lingua franca (e.g. Pennycook, 2004; Dewey, 2007; Blommaert, 2010; Seidlhofer, 2011; Cogo, 2012; House, 2011). Linguists and educators have also been studying the significance of globalization for the English language and its implications for language education (Kirkpatrick, 1991; Bauer, 1994; Crystal, 1997/2003, 2006; Jenkins, 2000, 2002, 2003; Holliday, 2005; Kachru, 2005; Gimenez & Sheehan, 2008; Saxena & Omoniyi, 2010; Schreier & Hundt, 2013). Less is written about perceptions of English as a global language (Maley, 1984; McKay, 2002; Georgieva, 2010; McKenzie, 2010). Finally, a growing interest in students' perceptions of global citizenship has emerged among researchers worldwide in recent years (Parmenter, 2011; Alazzi, 2012; Kilinc & Korkmaz, 2012; Morita, 2013; Han Hui, Song Li, Jing Hongtao & Zhao Yuqin's chapter in this book).

Another issue relevant here is the issue of terminology. While the authors are interested in a more complex view of intercultural competence or intercultural citizenship as outlined in the Introduction to this book, we also observe that a variety of terms is used to describe competences related to 'global' or 'intercultural' education. To understand what terms are currently used in the context of intercultural citizenship, we conducted a Google search (April 2014), which showed a number of related terms that might be difficult to differentiate. World citizen (978,000), global citizen (491,000) and international citizen (192,000) are the most frequent words, while planetary citizen (14,600), cosmopolitan citizen (8190), intercultural citizen (2300), multicultural citizen (1890) and supranational citizen (247) are seldom used. Although 'world citizen' resulted in the highest number of results in the search, the expression 'global citizen' has gained in importance (Olds, 2012; Abdi & Shultz, 2008; Bourn, 2010; Clark, 2010; Dower, 2003, 2008; Killick, 2011, 2012; Pike, 2008; Reid & Spencer-Oatey, 2012; to name just a few), and at universities (e.g. in academic institutional plans, in course and programme titles, and in curricular documents), 'global citizenship' has been used extensively (Olds, 2012).

However, there are also many definitions used in the various contexts describing what it means to be a global citizen (Oxfam, 2006; Schattle, 2006; Israel, 2013; Olds, 2012; Reid & Spencer-Oatey, 2012). Some universities have formed committees to define in their contexts what students need to do in order to become 'global citizens' (e.g. Frazier *et al.*, 2008).

Our decision to use 'global citizen' instead of the concept of 'intercultural citizen', 'world citizen' or any other of the above-mentioned terms is based on two considerations: first, the need to use a term with which our respondents (Hungary and USA university students) were likely to be most familiar; and, second, to make clear that the questions are linked to globalization and other related global issues. This led to the development of the overall research question, 'To what extent do university students' perceptions of global citizenship and the importance of languages differ in Hungary and in the USA?'

The Context

In Hungary, a small Central European country, intensive English as a foreign language education started in the early 1990s, after 40 years of compulsory learning of Russian (Enyedi & Medgyes, 1998; Terestyéni, 2000; Vágó, 2000). In the USA, although English is 'the language spoken by most people' (Ryan, 2013: 1), is not the official language throughout the country. According to Crawford (2012), 27 states in the USA have active Official English laws. Perceptions of English (and other foreign languages) in the context of globalization might therefore be quite different in these two countries. The majority of students in the USA sample are native speakers of this global language, while students in Hungary learn English mainly in school. That difference could impact students' views of relationships among languages, language learning and global citizenship.

In addition, it will be of interest to see what respondents consider to be the characteristics of and requirements for global citizenship and how far their conceptualizations differ from those of educators and researchers in the field. In particular, we will consider the conceptual framework for intercultural citizenship (Byram, 2008), which is applied to the various projects presented in this book, to understand which aspects of intercultural citizenship might be more intuitively understood by students and which might require more emphasis.

Methods and Data

To address our question, 'To what extent do university students' perception of global citizenship and the importance of languages differ in Hungary and in the USA?', we used a questionnaire with one section to gather background information about respondents, and four sections about global citizenship: respondents' definition of global citizenship; their belief about whether 'all' or 'some' are global citizens; their perceptions of themselves as global citizens; and their beliefs about languages.

The questionnaire (see Appendix A) included both qualitative and quantitative questions and was developed based on ideas from theoretical works on English in the global world (see references listed above in the Introduction to this chapter), and also on Dower's (2003, 2008) dilemma of 'all or some' people being global citizens and the list of characteristics of global citizen based on Logsdon and Wood (2002, 2005). The data were collected during the spring semester of the 2012–2013 academic year. In Hungary, students were given ample time to complete the survey, but some students might have felt limited by answering in a foreign language (English). To compensate for this challenge, they were given the option to answer in Hungarian. In the USA, students had about 15–20 minutes to complete the survey. In some cases, that might have prevented students from giving longer answers to open-ended questions.

We obtained a convenience sample of 127 university students in Hungary and 81 in the USA, a total of 208. Of the 208, 137 (66.2%) were female and 177 (85.5%) were born between 1990 and 1994, i.e. 22–26 years old.

Language competence

Of the 127 (60.87%) students from Hungary, 96 were female (76.2%) and of the 81 (39.1%) students from the USA about half were female (41, 50.6%). While 124 of the students in Hungary (97.6%) grew up speaking Hungarian in Hungary, the remaining three were English, German and Lithuanian native speakers. Among the students in Hungary, 63 (74.0%) indicated that they had at least an intermediate understanding of English. In contrast, 71 (87.7%) of the students from the USA grew up speaking English and seven (8.6%) Mandarin, and three students spoke Dutch, Korean or Thai as their first language. Of the USA students, 23 (28.4%) reported at least an intermediate level of understanding Spanish, a reflection of the fact that in the USA Spanish is the most frequently spoken language after English.

In terms of disciplines, the students in the sample from Hungary were mainly from Tourism Management, International Relations, International Business and Environment Engineering programmes. A substantial majority (111, 87.4%) had already been to another country, 42 (33.1%) for less than one month, 49 (38.6%) for a period of one to three months, and 15 (11.8%) for up to six months. A total of 95.3% reported that they spoke one or more foreign languages, the majority speaking either English (113, 89%) or German (81, 63.8%). Some 26.0% reported speaking three foreign languages, 18.1% reported speaking four foreign languages, and one person claimed to be able to speak 10 foreign languages. In addition to Hungarian, 11 languages were mentioned by students, namely: Dutch, English, French, German, Greek, Italian, Latin, Portuguese, Romanian, Russian and Spanish.

In the USA, the students were undergraduates in a general education humanities course. 50 (61.7%) respondents had been outside the States compared with 111 (87.4%) of their Hungarian peers. 15 (18.5%) had spent less than a month abroad, 13 (16%) between one and three months, and 13.6% (11) up to six months. 67 (82.7%) reported that they spoke a foreign language with the majority, 48 (59.3%), speaking Spanish at the elementary (25; 30.9%), intermediate (22; 27.2%) or advanced level (1; 1.2%). The range of languages mentioned by respondents in the USA was broader than in Hungary. Students reported 16 languages in addition to English, namely Arabic, Cantonese, Mandarin, Ebonics, French, German, Hebrew, Italian, Japanese, Latin, Mandarin, Russian, Serbian, Spanish, Urdu and Vietnamese.

Definitions of Global Citizenship

One hundred and forty of the total of 208 students (74 (52.9%) from Hungary, 66 (47.1%) from the USA) provided a definition of what is meant by a 'global citizen'. A thematic analysis yielded six themes, coded as: living/travel excursions; cultural awareness; equality; right of abode; inclusive philosophy; and multidimensional constructs.

Tied to the theme of living/travel excursions, there were 46 responses, 33 (71.7%) from Hungary (of 127, 26%) and 13 (28.2%) from students in the USA (of 81, 16%). Illustrations of definitions of 'global citizenship' in this theme are:

> A world traveller. Someone who belongs to more than one country across different continents. (USA)

> Someone who resides in or is travelling to a country other than their own. (USA)

> People who have experienced living in other countries. (USA; Hungary)

> A person who travelled a lot to different countries. (Hungary)

Cultural awareness linked to travel or to experiences from living in other countries with some reference to knowledge of foreign languages was mentioned in 26 (18.9%) responses. Of these, 17 (65.4%) were from students in Hungary and 9 (34.6%) from students in the USA. These responses typically went beyond merely travel. Some of the responses were:

> One who has a background in more than one culture, more than one citizenship of a country. (USA)

> The one who can travel without borders and is keen to know other countries and culture. (Hungary)

> A person who travelled/travels a lot, has been to many countries, knows about different cultures and their traditions. (USA)

> Speaks different foreign languages, lived in other countries, learned about other cultures and their traditions. (Hungary)

Another 18 (13.1%) students focused on right of abode. This theme had substantially different numbers of responses from students according to country as four (22.2%) were from Hungary and 14 (77.8%) were from the USA. According to these students, a 'global citizen' is:

> Someone who may either have multiple citizenships or visas to work and live in multiple different countries. That or having knowledge about the world around you.... (USA)

> A citizen that lives in or has citizenship in many countries. (USA)

> Cross-country nationality (*sic*) – especially in EU. (Hungary)

Issues of equality were mentioned by nine (6.6%) students, three from Hungary and six from the USA. There was contrast of equality with nationalism:

> Someone who recognizes humans as equal regardless of national origin. Global citizens do not consider citizenship a meaningful characteristic when making choices. Global citizens do not subscribe to nationalism. (Hungary)

There was also emphasis on ethics and responsibilities beyond one's own country:

> People across the globe whom (*sic*) respect ethical standards among the world. (USA)

> Someone who [has] responsibility to world as well as their country. (USA) (Word in square brackets added by authors.)

Another 35 (25.5%) students (14 (40%) from Hungary and 21 (60%) from the USA) had a broader concept which we labelled an 'inclusive philosophy'. They felt a 'global citizen' was:

> Citizen of the world, traveller of many places, person on Earth (USA)

> A citizen who is developing and who is open to the world (Hungary)

> I think the way to define this is a … hard thing to do. Being a global citizen means to me that the person is aware of the ongoing things around the world and knowing something about every culture, history, language. (Hungary)

> That person who is a global citizen often or always travels a lot, open to the world, he/she is interested in other cultures and also speaks different foreign languages. (Hungary)

In most of these it is noticeable that 'open to the world' recurs and seems to imply an interest again beyond the national. Of special note was that three students (two from Hungary and one from the USA, proposed a definition for 'global citizenship' that included responsibilities of the global citizen:

> A person who feels their societal responsibilities are more to all people on Earth than to just those in their home country (USA)

> The concept of an overarching one world government system in which all humans are joined as citizens of the earth such as to not replace but supersede current nation based government citizenships. This is the global citizenship. (Hungary)

Again, it is evident that there is a contrast between national and global citizenship where the latter is not 'replaced' but is of less significance, and responsibilities are to 'the world' or 'the Earth'.

A further group of questions had seven statements listed as possible contributors to global citizenship (Table 1.1). In Table 1.2, these results are provided in terms of the mean and standard deviation for the overall results, and for the disaggregated results by country. Using a five-point Likert scale examination of these seven characteristics, the item, 'Learn about other cultures' (mean = 4.14), was rated the highest overall.

We also compared whether there was a significant difference between the responses generated from the Hungary and USA participants. We found that two of the seven statements had no significant differences between countries: 'Travelling and getting experiences abroad are essential in order to become global citizens' and 'Learning about other cultures is important for becoming a global citizen' ($t = 1.633$, 1.204, respectively; $p > 0.05$). When examining results by country, the students from Hungary felt that English and other languages were very important for becoming a global citizen, as we have demonstrated in Table 1.1 by bolding the respective means and providing the calculated t-test where $p < 0.05$. In contrast, the US counterparts had higher results for believing it was natural that people in different countries speak with a different accent from English native speakers, and have different uses of grammar and/or vocabulary. Again, the respective means with significant difference are highlighted.

Table 1.1 Overall and factors impacting a global citizenship

	Total		Hungary		USA		t	d.f.	Significance
	Mean	SD	Mean	SD	Mean	SD			
Overall	3.82	0.528	3.87	0.465	3.74	0.609	1.665	201	0.098
Travelling and getting experiences abroad is essential in order to become a global citizen.	4.10	0.860	4.18	0.772	3.97	0.974	1.663	199	0.098
Learning about other cultures is important for becoming a global citizen.	4.14	0.851	4.08	0.717	4.23	1.025	−1.204	201	0.230
Speaking English is a prerequisite for becoming a global citizen.	3.53	1.210	**4.06**	0.843	2.72	1.250	9.072	200	0.001
Speaking other foreign languages is important for becoming a global citizen.	3.80	0.946	**4.08**	0.705	3.35	1.098	5.740	201	0.001
It is natural that people in different countries speak with an accent different from what English native speakers have.	3.89	0.866	3.76	0.830	**4.10**	0.886	−2.798	201	0.006
It is natural that people in different countries speak differently from native speakers in their use of grammar.	3.68	0.900	3.51	0.853	**3.94**	0.917	−3.334	199	0.001
It is natural that people in different countries speak differently from native speakers in their use of vocabulary.	3.64	0.942	3.46	0.850	**3.94**	1.011	+3.601	200	0.001

If we assume that intercultural competence would be a prerequisite for being a global or intercultural citizen, students' definitions covered only a small part of intercultural competence as defined by Byram's (1997) five competences. Analyses of students' definitions of 'global citizen' show that answers often revolved around 'knowledge': knowing other cultures and/or what is happening in the world – but not knowledge of social interactions.

Sometimes students also included knowledge of foreign languages. 'Curiosity' and having 'an open mind' were mentioned by some students. Quite often, global citizenship was seen merely as resulting from travel or from having the right to live in more than one country. However, it is possible that students had 'skills of interpreting and relating' in mind when they mentioned 'experience living in another country' or similar concepts. Few answers included a reference to anything which could be labelled 'critical cultural awareness', and even fewer to the 'action' component we consider a crucial element of intercultural citizenship (see the Introduction to this book).

Generally, responses tended to point to a vision of 'global citizenship' that happens, rather than one that is actively accomplished, and the implication is that we can only achieve global citizenship through travelling and having multiple passports and, more importantly, that nothing more is required. In other words, if educators do not facilitate awareness in students that in order to become a global citizen they need to actively work on related aspects themselves, they might wait in vain for the 'opportunity' to miraculously become a global citizen. Helping raise students' awareness that they can participate in their own development of global citizenship in a variety of ways and during their education could change their rather passive view of global citizenship. Considering that even in the literature it is quite difficult to find a comprehensive definition of global citizenship (cf. Olds, 2012), it is not surprising that students were unaware of the various components of this construct. However, as we saw earlier, the term is used widely in university policy-making and the lack of clarity in students' perceptions is a concern.

Participation in Global Citizenship

Also of interest in intercultural citizenship education is whether our students believe that 'all are global citizens' or 'some of us are global citizens'. Regardless of whether a definition of 'global citizen' was provided, students were requested to answer a dichotomous question to indicate whether *some* or *all* citizens were global citizens.

A total of 60 (29.8%) students indicated that they believed that *all* people are global citizens. A much higher and statistically significant different number and percentage of students from the USA than Hungary felt this way ($\chi^2 = 11.12$, d.f. $= 1, p > 0.001$; see Table 1.2). However, using a four-point Likert scale from 'always' to 'never,' a further analysis of the question to indicate the degree to which they considered themselves to be a global citizens revealed no significant differences (t-test $= 0.277$, d.f. $= 198, p > 0.765$). In fact, the mean was 2.44 Hungary versus 2.48 USA.

Dower (2003, 2008) elaborates on the 'all or some' dilemma. According to Dower, 'in some respects we are all global citizens, and in other respects only some of us are' (Dower, 2008: 46). In other words, both approaches can

Table 1.2 Student opinions regarding others and themselves as global citizens

		Total	Hungary	USA
Are all of us global citizens or are some of us global citizens?	Some (*n*)	148	101	47
	All (*n*)	60	26	34
Do you consider yourself a global citizen?	Mean	2.44	2.44	2.48
	SD	(1.1)	(0.87)	(1.21)
Total			127	81

coexist, or as Dower (2008: 39) explains, 'First, in some respects we are all global citizens, for instance because of a certain moral or legal status, but in other respects only some people are global citizens by virtue of their self-descriptions and/or active engagement with the world.' Dower (2008: 39) argues further:

> Insofar as we are all global citizens anyway, we are not educating people to *become* global citizens but rather educating them to *become aware of themselves as having this status* and of a set of opportunities that go along with this status. But insofar as being a global citizen is a matter of adopting a mode of self-conception and/or a manner of active engagement with the world, then the encouragement of this is an important aim of citizenship education and related programmes such as development education. (*Emphasis added.*)

The last point of 'active engagement with the world' as mentioned by Dower is in agreement with the goals of the projects presented in this book. However, as far as students' perceptions are concerned, this active engagement does not feature prominently in their definitions of global citizenship.

Responses to the question, 'Do you consider yourself a global citizen?' indicate that 13 (10.2%) of Hungarian and 23 (29.1%) of USA respondents answered that they 'never' considered themselves global citizens. In spite of the fact that only 53 (41.7%) respondents from Hungary, and 37 (45.7%) from the USA considered themselves 'often' or 'always' global citizens, all participating students had global concerns. They were asked to rank the issues they thought had the most impact on the world from '1' (most impact) to '18' (least impact). Our list included: poverty, famine, disease, charity, human rights, democracy, wealth, security, prejudice, xenophobia, discrimination, racism, sustainable development, ethical trading, peace-making/peacekeeping and environment protection, and we also invited students to add their own issues.

When asked to rank the most important issues, the respondents from both countries identified *human rights* and *poverty* among the three most important issues that impacted the world. *Security* was named as an additional important issue by Hungarian participants, while their peers from the USA marked *famine* as their additionally most important item. In both groups, students seemed to be less concerned with *prejudice, xenophobia, discrimination* and *racism*, which is of interest from an intercultural perspective and for further discussion of development of intercultural citizenship in our students (see the table in Appendix B).

There were a number of differences between responses on five of the 10 listed characteristics of being a global citizen (see Table 1.3). The Hungarian students rated two characteristics higher than their USA peers. These statements were 'Speaking English is a prerequisite for becoming a global citizen', and 'Speaking other foreign languages is important for becoming a global citizen'. The USA students rated three of the characteristics higher than their Hungarian counterparts. These statements were: 'It is natural that people in different countries speak with an accent different from what English native speakers have'; 'It is natural that people in different countries speak differently from native speakers in their use of grammar'; and 'It is natural that people in different countries speak differently from native speakers in their use of vocabulary'.

The fact that US students tended to be neutral, leaning towards disagreeing with the statement that 'Speaking English is a prerequisite for becoming a global citizen', while Hungarian students mostly agreed with the statement, raises questions. Maybe Hungarian students generally are more acutely aware of the importance of English as they are speakers of a less commonly spoken language. Hungarian students also agreed more strongly than US students with the statement that learning other foreign languages is important for becoming a global citizen. Did US students generally not make the

Table 1.3 Ranking of characteristics of a global citizen[a]

	Total	Hungary	USA
Learn about other cultures	85	54	31
Learn foreign languages	81	73	8
Learn to respect local cultural variations	66	33	33
Communicate with people from different cultures	63	48	15
Travel globally	52	35	17
Be an active member of community	40	19	21
Learn that among other duties we have as individuals we have responsibilities that are transnational	38	19	19
Learn to abide by universal ethical standards	35	9	26
Learn to reconcile local practice with hypernorms	28	20	8
Become politically involved	23	12	11

[a]Figures indicate the number of students placing the characteristic in the top or bottom five.

connection between speaking languages and being a global citizen? Since US students in this sample did not claim that English is important while other languages are not, we cannot assume that they believed that 'everybody should communicate in English anyway', an attitude often ascribed to those in the USA. Therefore, follow-up questions would be necessary to learn why these differences occurred in our data.

Another interpretation of the results is that students from Hungary emphasized linguistic aspects of global citizenship while US students focused on learning about other cultures (which was also considered important by students in the Hungarian sample). Both groups considered it crucial to learn to respect local cultural variations (scored as the second most important). However, if we compare the three most important and the three least important characteristics of a global citizen, we will discover some sharp contrasts in the perceptions of our Hungarian and US respondents. For example, while Hungarian respondents consider 'Learn to abide by universal ethical standards' the least important characteristic, US respondents reported it as the third most important. Additionally, 'Learn foreign languages', considered the most important characteristic by Hungarian respondents, is viewed as one of two least important characteristics by US respondents.

There could be a connection with another result in our survey. As indicated earlier, the data collected showed that, while 83.5% of Hungarian respondents spoke at least two foreign languages at elementary, intermediate or advanced level, only 54.3% of USA respondents reported speaking two or more foreign languages. The authors hypothesize that a major contributing factor is that there is currently no high school graduating requirement in world/foreign language(s) in the state in which the university is located. In contrast, in Hungary it is compulsory to pass a final Foreign Language examination for graduating from high school (see §6 (2) d, Act No. CXC of 2011 on National Public Education). Moreover, in Hungary, the knowledge of at least one foreign language at the intermediate level (B2 level according to the Common European Framework of Reference for Languages; Council of Europe, 2011) is required for achieving both academic and career goals. For example, those who apply for admission to a university are granted a high number of bonus points for language exam certificate(s) (see §20, Government Regulation No. 423/2012 (Dec. 29) on Admission Procedure in Higher Education); holding one or two language certificates at the intermediate (or in the case of some university programmes at advanced) level is an official requirement which must be fulfilled to get the degree (see §51, Act No. CCIV of 2011 on National Higher Education); and public and civil servants are paid a significant language allowance (see §74, Act No. XXXIII of 1992 on the legal status of public servants; §141, Act No. CXCIX of 2011 on Civil Servants).

Interestingly, the accumulated score for 'become politically involved' was similarly the lowest in both respondent groups. This reflects that the majority of the respondents in both Hungary and the USA viewed active engagement as less important, and compares with our findings earlier according to which, as far as students' perceptions are concerned, this active engagement does not feature prominently in their definition of global citizenship.

Conclusion and Further Perspectives

While our work is exploratory in nature, we found that the Hungarian and USA students are quite similar with respect to defining a global citizen. In our follow-up questions about whether students believe that 'all are global citizens' or 'some of us are global citizens', it is interesting to note that less than a third of all respondents from both countries and a significantly lower percentage of respondents in Hungary felt that 'all are global citizens'. When ranking the issues that have the most impact on the world, both groups of respondents marked quite similar ones as the most important (i.e. *human rights* and *poverty*) and, interestingly, the students from the both groups seemed to have less concern regarding such issues as *prejudice, xenophobia, discrimination* and *racism*. Finally, students were asked about the characteristics of a global citizen and ranked 'Learn about other cultures' and 'Learn foreign languages' the highest. When examined by country, the students from the USA selected 'Learn to respect local cultural variations' and 'Learn about other cultures,' while students from Hungary said 'Learn foreign languages' and 'Learn about other cultures'.

Given that the students in both Hungary and the USA view the definition of 'global citizenship' mostly from the perspective of knowledge and experience, how do we educate students about the multifaceted nature of intercultural citizenship?

The data in this study indicate that students have difficulty understanding global citizenship as a complex construct. Rather, respondents tend to make a connection between global citizenship and travelling. Although understanding other cultures is mentioned by some respondents in the sample, in general, answers point to a rather 'passive' conceptualization of global citizenship. If we compare this limited notion of global citizenship with the framework applied in this book according to which students are urged to act interculturally, often in transnational groups, the difference is obvious. Most of the components considered important in the framework outlined in this book are not featured prominently in students' perception of global/intercultural citizenship.

Implications for teaching

One implication for all educators then is to help students understand the multidimensionality as well as the importance of their active participation in the development of their intercultural or global citizenship. Additionally, it is important to clarify that we can and ought to develop competences related to global citizenship in the here and now rather than postponing it to 'when we travel'. The 'action' element does not require students to travel and live in other places, as will be evident from subsequent chapters that use the opportunities afforded by today's technologies. In other words, we need to move to the role of the educator being seen as one who facilitates students' awareness of the components of intercultural or global citizenship as well as students' role in their own education.

Another lesson we can learn from the responses pertains to foreign language education in particular. A huge shift has occurred in the fields of cultural studies to intercultural citizenship over the last 25 years (for an overview see Byram, 2014). Byram (2008) offered a new insight into the role of foreign language education in the globalized world. A deeper understanding of students' perceptions of global (intercultural) citizenship and the importance of language will hopefully contribute to the promotion of these ideas among foreign language teachers. How this approach can look in practice will be demonstrated in the following chapters. However, we also need to be aware that without changes in the minds of policy-makers it will be difficult to achieve a general change in foreign language teaching practice concerning intercultural citizenship education.

Implications for policy-making

Internationalization has globally become a buzzword in the context of education, and is mentioned in many university strategic plans as a main objective or task for university administrations. In addition to numerous other aspects, internationalization is associated with students' mobility (both outgoing and incoming). There is a wealth of research on the role of study abroad for intercultural citizenship as (see e.g. Byram & Rommal, forthcoming; Deardorff, 2009; de Wit, 2009; Hendershot & Sperandio, 2009; Lewin, 2009; Hanson, 2010; Killick, 2012; Wynveen et al., 2012; Tarrant et al., 2013; Streitwieser & Light, 2016).

The number of foreign students is one of the indicators through which the degree of internationalization is measured. However, practice shows that international exchange students create their own community and rarely 'mix' with the locals (see e.g. the surveys on the ERASMUS mobility students in Europe such as Brasoveanu, 2010; Alfranseder et al., 2011). Moreover, often the barriers that impede the contact between the two groups are created by the administration of universities, by offering different housing, classes, separate social programmes, etc. (see Lantz, 2014).

In order for study abroad to be fruitful for the development of intercultural citizenship, the task of the policy-makers and administrators is to find ways to create a truly international student community, which consists of both exchange and local students and has the atmosphere of active global engagement, collaboration and global responsibility.

Questions for further research

The current study represents a first investigation into the question of students' understanding of global citizenship in an opportunity sample in Hungary and the USA (for an investigation of student perceptions of global citizenship in two universities in China see Han Hui, Song Li, Jing Hongtao & Zhao Yuqin's chapter in this volume). Seeking answers from a larger sample in more contexts would offer a more reliable response to our questions. Also, more detailed questions about the exact understanding of global citizenship, the possible reasons for the rather 'passive' view of global citizenship, ways of enhancing active (political and social) engagement and how students think they can be prepared (in schools and at the university) to become global citizens would be important. Applying interviews as the method of qualitative research would definitely bring more detailed insights.

Acknowledgements

We would like to thank Yau Tsai and Michael Byram for their contributions to the development of the survey. We are also grateful to the participants of the survey as well as our colleagues in Hungary and the USA who facilitated data collection.

References

Abdi, A. and Shultz, L. (2008) Educating for human rights and global citizenship: An introduction. In A. Abdi and L. Shultz (eds) *Educating for Human Rights and Global Citizenship* (pp. 1–10). Albany, NY: SUNY Press.

Act No. XXXIII of 1992 on the legal status of public servants. See http://net.jogtar.hu/jr/gen/hjegy_doc.cgi?docid=99200033.TV (accessed 10 January 2015).

Act No. CCIV of 2011 on National Higher Education. See http://net.jogtar.hu/jr/gen/hjegy_doc.cgi?docid=A1100204.TV#lbj156param (accessed 10 January 2015).

Act No. CXC of 2011 on National Public Education. See http://net.jogtar.hu/jr/gen/hjegy_doc.cgi?docid=A1100190.TV (accessed 31 December).

Act No. CXCIX of 2011 on Civil Servants. See http://net.jogtar.hu/jr/gen/hjegy_doc.cgi?docid=A1100199.TV#lbj1param (accessed 10 January 2015).

Alazzi, K.F. (2012) Investigate Jordanian teacher candidates' views on global citizenship: Views from the classroom. *International Journal of Humanities and Social Science* 2 (1), 165–172. See http://www.ijhssnet.com/journals/Vol_2_No_1_January_2012/14.pdf (accessed 10 January 2015).

Alfranseder, E., Fellinger, J. and Taivere, M. (2011) *E-Value-ate Your Exchange: Research Report of the ESNSurvey 2010*. Erasmus Student Network AISBL, Brussels. See https://issuu.com/esnint/docs/esnsurvey2010_final (10 June 2016).

Bauer, L. (1994) *Watching English Change: An Introduction to the Study of Linguistic Change in Standard Englishes in Twentieth Century.* London: Longman.

Blommaert, J. (2010) *The Sociolinguistics of Globalization.* Cambridge: Cambridge University Press.

Bourn, D. (2010) Students as global citizens. In E. Jones (ed.) *Internationalisation and the Student Voice: Higher Education Perspectives.* London: Routledge.

Brasoveanu, A. (2010) ERASMUS – European Educational Mobility Program and cross-cultural shared experience and identity. *Studia Universitatis Babes-Bolyai, Studia Europaea* LV (4), 85–104.

Byram, M. (1997) *Teaching and Assessing Intercultural Communicative Competence.* Clevedon: Multilingual Matters.

Byram, M.S. (2008) *From Foreign Language Education to Education for Intercultural Citizenship: Essays and Reflections.* Clevedon: Multilingual Matters.

Byram, M.S. (2014) Twenty-five years on – From cultural studies to intercultural citizenship. *Language, Culture and Curriculum* 27 (3), 209–225; doi: 10.1080/07908318.2014.974329

Byram, M.S. and Rommal, L. (forthcoming) Becoming interculturally competent through study and experience abroad. In M.S. Byram, D. Perugini and M. Wagner (eds) *Teaching Intercultural Competence Across the Age Range: Theory and Practice.* Bristol: Multilingual Matters.

Clark, A. (2010) *The ABCs of Human Survival: A Paradigm for Global Citizenship.* UBC Press: Global Peace Studies.

Cogo, A. (2012) English as a lingua franca: concepts, use, and implications. *ELT Journal* 66 (1), 97–105.

Council of Europe (2011) *Common European Framework of Reference for Languages: Learning, Teaching, Assessment.* See http://www.coe.int/lang-CEFR (accessed 1 January 2014).

Crawford, J. (2012) Language legislation in the U.S.A. *Issues in U.S. Language Policy.* See http://www.languagepolicy.net/archives/langleg.htm (accessed 20 January 2014).

Crystal, D. (1997, 2003) *English as a Global Language – 1st and 2nd Edition.* New York: Cambridge University Press.

Crystal, D. (2006) English worldwide. In R. Hogg and D. Denison (eds) *A History of the English Language* (pp. 420–439). Cambridge: Cambridge University Press.

Deardorff, D. (2009) Understanding the challenges of assessing global citizenship. In R. Lewin (ed.) *The Handbook of Practice and Research in Study Abroad: Higher Education and the Quest for Global Citizenship* (pp. 346–364). New York: Routledge.

Dewey, M. (2007) English as a lingua franca and globalization: an interconnected perspective. *International Journal of Applied Linguistics* 17 (3), 332–354.

de Wit, H. (2009) Global citizenship and study abroad: A European comparative perspective. In R. Lewin (ed.) *The Handbook of Practice and Research in Study Abroad: Higher Education and the Quest for Global Citizenship* (pp. 212–229). New York: Routledge.

Dower, N. (2003) *An Introduction to Global Citizenship.* Edinburgh: Edinburgh University Press.

Dower, N. (2008) Are we all global citizens, or are only some of us global citizens? The relevance of this question to education. In A. Abdi and L. Shultz (eds) *Educating for Human Rights and Global Citizenship* (pp. 39–53). Albany, NY: SUNY Press.

Enyedi, Á. and Medgyes, P. (1998) Angol nyelvoktatás Közép- és Kelet Európában a rendszerváltozás óta. *Modern Nyelvoktatás* 4 (2-3), 12–32.

Frazier, D., Sanders, C., Kuker, G., Merkle, J., Haines, L. and More, B. (2008) Definition of 'Global Citizen'. See http://ns1.uiu.edu/strategic-planning/downloads/global_citizen_report.pdf (retrieved on 15 March 2014).

Georgieva, M. (2010) EFL: From 'You sound like Dickens' to international English. In M. Saxena and T. Omoniyi (eds) *Contending with Globalization in World Englishes* (pp. 113–136). Bristol: Multilingual Matters.

Gimenez, T. and Sheehan, S. (2008) *Global Citizenship in the English Language Classroom.* London: British Council.

Government Regulation No. 423/2012 (Dec. 29) on Admission Procedure in Higher Education. See http://net.jogtar.hu/jr/gen/hjegy_doc.cgi?docid=A1200423.KOR (accessed 10 January 2015).

Hanson, L. (2010) Global citizenship, global health, and the internationalization of curriculum: A study of transformative potential. *Journal of Studies in International Education* 14, 70–88.

Hendershot, K. and Sperandio, J. (2009) Study abroad and development of global citizen identity and cosmopolitan ideals in undergraduates. *Current Issues in Comparative Education* 12, 45–55.

Holliday, A. (2005) *The Struggle to Teach English as an International Language*. Oxford: Oxford University Press.

House, J. (2011) English as a global lingua franca: A thread to multilingual communication and translation? *Language Teaching* 47 (3), 363–376.

Israel, R.C. (2013) *Global Citizenship – A Path to Building Identity and Community in a Globalized World*. North Charleston, SC: Createspace.

Jenkins, J. (2000) *The Phonology of English as an International Language: New Models, New Norms, New Goals*. Oxford: Oxford University Press.

Jenkins, J. (2002) A sociolinguistically based, empirically researched pronunciation syllabus for English as an international language. *Applied Linguistics* 23 (1), 83–103.

Jenkins, J. (2003) *World Englishes*. Abingdon: Routledge.

Kachru, B.B. (2005) *Asian Englishes: Beyond the Canon*. Hong Kong: Hong Kong University Press.

Kilinc, E. and Korkmaz, U. (2012) *Turkish Graduate Students' Perception of Global Citizenship* (pp. 154–158). Orlando, FL: The International Society for the Social Studies. See http://files.eric.ed.gov/fulltext/ED531864.pdf (accessed 12 January 2015).

Killick, D. (2011) Seeing-ourselves-in-the-world: Developing global citizenship through international mobility and campus community. *Journal of Studies in International Education* 16, 372–389.

Killick, D. (2012) Global citizenship and campus community: Lessons from learning theory and the lived-experience of mobile students. In J. Ryan (ed.) *Cross-cultural Teaching and Learning for Home and International Students: Internationalisation of Pedagogy and Curriculum in Higher Education* (pp. 182–195). Abingdon: Routledge.

Kirkpatrick, A. (ed.) (1991) *The Routledge Handbook of World Englishes*. London: Routledge.

Lantz, C. (2014) Exploring the intercultural development of first year UK and non-UK psychology students. PhD thesis, University of York. See http://etheses.whiterose.ac.uk/6194/ (accessed 4 March 2015).

Lewin, R. (2009) Introduction: The quest for global citizenship through study abroad. In R. Lewin (ed.) *The Handbook of Practice and Research in Study Abroad: Higher Education and the Quest for Global Citizenship* (pp. xiii–xxii). New York: Routledge.

Logsdon, J.M. and Wood, D.J. (2002) Business citizenship: From domestic to global levels of analysis. *Business Ethics Quarterly* 12 (2), 155–187.

Logsdon, J.M. and Wood, D.J. (2005) Global business citizenship and voluntary codes of ethical conduct. *Journal of Business Ethics* 59, 55–67.

Maley, A. (1984) The most chameleon of languages. *English Today* 12 (1), 30–33.

McKay S.L. (2002) *Teaching English as an International Language: Rethinking Goals and Perspectives*. New York: Oxford University Press.

McKenzie, R.M. (2010) *The Social Psychology of English as a Global Language: Attitudes, Awareness and Identity in the Japanese Context*. London: Springer.

Morita, L. (2013) Japanese university students' attitudes towards globalisation, intercultural contexts and English. *World Journal of English Language* 3 (4). See http://www.sciedu.ca/journal/index.php/wjel/article/view/3474/2274 (accessed 10 December 2014).

National Clearinghouse for English Language Acquisition (2007) *The Growing Numbers of Limited English Proficient Students*. Washington, DC: National Clearinghouse for English Language Acquisition. See http://www.ncela.gwu.edu (accessed 11 January 2015).

National Core Curriculum (2012) *Government Decree No. 110/2012. (June 14) on the Issuance, implementation and application of the National Core Curriculum*. See http://www.ofi.hu/nemzeti-alaptanterv (accessed 12 January 2015).

Olds, K. (2012) Global citizenship – What are we talking about and why does it matter? *Inside Higher Education*, 11 March, 4:52 pm. See http://www.insidehighered.com/blogs/globalhighered/global-citizenship-%E2%80%93-what-are-we-talking-about-and-why-does-it-matter#sthash.tUNCeWqM.dpbs (accessed 15 May 2014).

Oxfam (2006) *Education for Global Citizenship. A Guide for Schools*. London: Oxfam. See http://www.oxfam.org.uk/~/media/Files/Education/Global%20Citizenship/education_for_global_citizenship_a_guide_for_schools.ashx (accessed 12 January 2015).

Parmenter, L. (2011) Power and place in the discourse of global citizenship education. *Globalisation, Societies and Education* 9 (3–4), 367–380.

Pennycook, A. (2004) The myth of English as an international language. *English in Australia* 139, 26–32.

Pike, G. (2008) Reconstructing the legend: Educating for global citizenship. In A. Abdi and L. Shultz (eds) *Educating for Human Rights and Global Citizenship* (pp. 223–237). Albany, NY: SUNY Press.

Reid, S. and Spencer-Oatey, H. (2012) Towards the global citizen: Utilising a competency framework to promote intercultural knowledge and skills in HE students. In J. Ryan (ed.) *Cross-cultural Teaching and Learning for Home and International Students: Internationalisation of Pedagogy and Curriculum in Higher Education* (pp. 125–140). Abingdon: Routledge.

Ryan, C. (2013) Language use in the United States: 2011. Report Number ACS-22. United States Census Bureau. See http://census.gov/library/publications/2013/acs/acs-22.html (accessed 9 September 2016).

Saxena, M. and Omoniyi, T. (eds) (2010) *Contending with Globalization in World Englishes*. Bristol: Multilingual Matters.

Schattle, H. (2006) Global citizenship in public discourse. *Reason and Respect* 2 (1), Article 6. See http://docs.rwu.edu/rr/vol2/iss1/6 (accessed 10 June 2015).

Schreier, D. and Hundt, M. (eds) (2013) *English as a Contact Language*. Cambridge: Cambridge University Press.

Seidlhofer, B. (2011) *Understanding English as a Lingua Franca*. Oxford: Oxford University Press.

Streitwieser, B. and Light, G. (2016) The grand promise of global citizenship through study abroad: The student view. In E. Jones, R. Coelen, J. Beelen and H. de Wit (eds) *Global and Local Internationalisation* (pp. 67–73). Rotterdam: Sense Publishers.

Tarrant, M.A., Rubin, D.L. and Stoner, L. (2013) The added value of study abroad: Fostering a global citizenry. *Journal of Studies in International Education* 20 (10), 1–21; doi: 10.1177/1028315313497589

Terestyéni, T. (2000) Az idegennyelv-tudás alakulása Magyarországon a kilencvenes években. *Educatio* 9 (4), 651–667.

Thomas, W.P. and Collier, V.P. (2002) *A National Study of School Effectiveness for Language Minority Students' Long-term Academic Achievement*. Santa Cruz, CA: Center for Research on Education, Diversity and Excellence, University of California–Santa Cruz.

Vágó, I. (2000) Az idegennyelv-oktatás fő tendenciái a 80-as és 90-es években. *Educatio folyóirat 2000/4 – Nyelvtudás, Nyelvoktatás* 668–690.

Wynveen, Ch. J., Kyle, G.T. and Tarrant, M.A. (2012) Study abroad experiences and global citizenship: Fostering proenvironmental behavior. *Journal of Studies in International Education* 16 (4), 334–352.

Appendix A: Survey Questions[1]

Part 1: *Definition*

How would you define 'global citizen'?

Part 2: *Beliefs regarding 'Some/All' Global Citizens*

Are all of us global citizens or are some of us global citizens?
- All of us are global citizens
- Some of us are global citizens

Part 3: *Perceptions regarding Oneself Global Citizen*

Do you consider yourself a global citizen?
- Always
- Often
- Sometimes
- Never

Rank the issues you think have the most impact on the world from 1 (most impact) to 18 (last impact). (You do not have to rank all of them, and you also may add yours.)
- poverty
- famine
- disease
- charity
- human rights
- democracy
- wealth
- security
- prejudice
- xenophobia
- discrimination
- racism
- sustainable development
- ethical trading
- peace-making and peacekeeping
- environment protection
- other (please specify).

Part 4: Languages and cultures

Please indicate your level of agreement with the following statements.

Travelling and getting experiences abroad is essential in order to become a global citizen.

Strongly agree	Agree	Neutral	Disagree	Strongly disagree
☐	☐	☐	☐	☐

Learning about other cultures is important for becoming a global citizen.

Strongly agree	Agree	Neutral	Disagree	Strongly disagree
☐	☐	☐	☐	☐

Speaking English is a prerequisite for becoming a global citizen.

Strongly agree	Agree	Neutral	Disagree	Strongly disagree
☐	☐	☐	☐	☐

Speaking other foreign languages is important for becoming a global citizen.

Strongly agree	Agree	Neutral	Disagree	Strongly disagree
☐	☐	☐	☐	☐

It is natural that people in different countries speak with an accent different from what English native speakers have.

Strongly agree	Agree	Neutral	Disagree	Strongly disagree
☐	☐	☐	☐	☐

It is natural that people in different countries speak differently from native speakers in their use of grammar.

Strongly agree	Agree	Neutral	Disagree	Strongly disagree
☐	☐	☐	☐	☐

It is natural that people in different countries speak differently from native speakers in their use of vocabulary.

Strongly agree	Agree	Neutral	Disagree	Strongly disagree
☐	☐	☐	☐	☐

Appendix B: Ranking of Issues Perceived to Most Impact the World

	Rank	Hungary Frequency	%	USA Frequency	%
Poverty	1	16	12.6	18	22.2
	2	10	7.9	13	16.0
	3	5	3.9	9	11.1
Famine	1	6	4.7	4	4.9
	2	12	9.4	14	17.3
	3	9	7.1	6	7.4
Disease	1	2	1.6	8	9.9
	2	6	4.7	9	11.1
	3	11	8.7	9	11.1
Charity	1	2	1.6	2	2.5
	2	5	3.9		
	3	4	3.1		
Human rights	1	18	14.2	11	13.6
	2	7	5.5	10	12.3
	3	10	7.9	11	13.6
Democracy	1	9	7.1	3	3.7
	2	9	7.1	3	3.7
	3	5	3.9	2	2.5
Wealth	1	11	8.7	5	6.2
	2	6	4.7	2	2.5
	3	11	8.7	5	6.2
Security	1	9	7.1	2	2.5
	2	11	8.7	3	3.7
	3	17	13.4	6	7.4
Prejudice	1	2	1.6	—	—
	2	6	4.7	3	3.7
	3	6	4.7	4	4.9
Xenophobia	1	3	2.4	—	—
	2	4	3.1	—	—
	3	1	.8	—	—
Discrimination	1	2	1.6	1	1.2
	2	5	3.9	—	—
	3	11	8.7	4	4.9

(*Continued*)

	Rank	Hungary		USA	
		Frequency	%	Frequency	%
Racism	1	2	1.6	2	2.5
	2	8	6.3	3	3.7
	3	5	3.9	—	—
Sustainable development	1	3	2.4	4	4.9
	2	7	5.5	1	1.2
	3	3	2.4	3	3.7
Ethical trading	1	3	2.4	—	—
	2	2	1.6	—	—
	3	3	2.4	—	—
Peace-making and peacekeeping	1	12	9.4	3	3.7
	2	7	5.5	1	1.2
	3	5	3.9	2	2.5
Environment protection	1	9	7.1	1	1.2
	2	11	8.7	3	3.7
	3	9	7.1	3	3.7
Other (education)	1	2	1.6	1	1.2

Reporting is the first three most important rankings.

Note

(1) This is a reduced version of the original questionnaire: only questions analysed in this chapter are included in Appendix A.

2 Exploring Perceptions of Intercultural Citizenship among English Learners in Chinese Universities

Han Hui, Song Li, Jing Hongtao and Zhao Yuqin

Introduction

This study explores perceptions of 'intercultural citizenship' held by Chinese university students of English. Terminologies like world/global/intercultural citizen have arisen in recent years for many different reasons, but global change and intercultural contacts may be the main reason. Intercultural Citizenship education has become a focus of educational research around the world with increasing waves of globalization, and a growing interest in students' perceptions of global citizenship has attracted researchers' attention worldwide in recent years (Golubeva, Wagner and Yakimowski's chapter in this book; Parmenter, 2011; Morita, 2013). Byram's intercultural citizenship theory (Alred *et al.*, 2006; Byram, 2008) has become known in European countries, the USA, etc., and implemented in practice by some language teachers (Porto, 2014).

However, 'intercultural citizen' is quite a new term for Chinese people. When we use terminology originating in Europe or North America in Chinese teaching contexts, learners naturally link the concept to the moral, political, and ideological education they received at different stages of their education, as we shall see in the research we are reporting in this chapter. We wanted therefore to explore in more detail how Chinese students perceive these notions and how they understand the meaning of 'education for intercultural citizenship' through English language teaching. As Chinese university teachers of English, we believe that intercultural citizenship education through education in foreign languages should cater to the students' needs and fit into the Chinese context. We assume that intercultural citizenship education cannot be separated from citizenship education and the latter serves as the base of the former. We also believe that, if the concept of citizen/citizenship is culture specific, intercultural citizenship education will also be culture specific. Furthermore, we assume that getting to know Chinese university students' perceptions of citizenship and intercultural citizenship education is essential for our foreign language teachers in the age of globalization. We hope too that our analysis provides a basis for future international comparative studies which could develop the concept and demonstrate the similarities and differences in varied educational contexts.

Driven by such assumptions and motivations, we conducted a questionnaire survey in two universities: University Z and University H with a total of 308 student respondents. These respondents' major subjects are various but all of them have taken a course in English, called 'College English', which is compulsory in China.

On the basis of our understanding gleaned from this survey, we also hope this research may help us to design a curriculum of intercultural citizenship for Chinese students in the future to prepare them to live in the age of globalization.

Previous Research

Intercultural communicative competence (ICC) was highlighted as a desired learning outcome in the National College English Curriculum in 2004 in China and in the National Curriculum for Secondary Schools in 2001 (Ministry of Education, 2001, 2004), and cultural awareness was introduced into this revised curriculum as one of the teaching objectives. Some researchers in China have previously investigated teachers' beliefs and practices regarding intercultural language teaching. Han (2010) conducted a quantitative study of EFL teachers' perceptions of culture teaching in secondary schools in Xinjiang in China. The findings showed that teachers are willing to teach culture as additional information to motivate students' learning and the time devoted to culture teaching is decided by individual teacher's preferences concerning knowledge of culture. Han and Song (2011) conducted a pilot study to investigate 30 university teachers' understanding of intercultural communicative competence in the Chinese English Language Teaching (ELT) context. The results showed inadequacy and vagueness in Chinese university English teachers' conceptualization of ICC and its relevance to ELT in spite of their strong desire to develop students' ICC. Jing (2013) explored the beliefs and reported practices regarding global awareness of EFL teachers at one senior high school in Henan province in China. His findings analysed teachers' beliefs about the concept and aim of global awareness, the purpose and importance of global awareness, the relationship with language learning, and teaching methods in the classroom. A framework of global awareness that includes knowledge, skills and attitudes emerged. Knowledge was found to be related to globalization, cultures, language, global issues and cultural self-awareness. The identified skills in this study include critical thinking, communication, language skills, self-cultivation and learning skills. Attitudes include responsibility, tolerance, openness, justice and respect.

In a study of teachers based on 720 questionnaires in Hong Kong, 561 questionnaires in Shanghai and eight rounds of focus group interviews, Kong, Lee and Leung (2006) showed that the reasons given for global citizenship education in Shanghai and Hong Kong in China are different. The top three reasons suggested by the Hong Kong interviewees are: 'to cultivate students' understanding and appreciation of diverse values', 'to broaden students' domains of knowledge' and 'to raise students' concern about world affairs'. For the Shanghai interviewees, the top three reasons are: 'to enhance the competitiveness of students in the future society', 'to broaden students' domains of knowledge' and 'to cultivate students' understanding and appreciation of diverse values' (p. 74). The findings also showed that Shanghai teachers were more interested in global issues, whereas Hong Kong's teachers were interested in local issues. Shanghai teachers emphasized knowledge and skills related to the concept of global citizenship, whereas Hong Kong teachers focused on values.

Teachers and researchers in other countries and regions have also considered global citizenship education in the context of English language teaching. In Europe, the British Council published the book *Global Citizenship in the English Language Classroom* (Gimenez & Sheehan, 2008), in which the seven chapters explored global citizenship with regard to curricula, materials, English courses, teacher and student attitudes, methodology, and activities. Parmenter (2011) investigated 642 university students' conceptualizations of global citizenship education and their views of themselves as global citizens. The participants were Arab, Chinese, English, French, Korean, Japanese, Russian, Spanish and Thai. The students' conceptions of global citizenship included four core concepts: human-beingness, connectedness, engagement and transformation. In another context in Japan, Houghton (2012), Houghton and Yamada (2010) and Yamada (2010) conducted action research to explore critical awareness in foreign language education. Their studies aimed to explore how critical cultural awareness can be taught in foreign language classes, and how critical cultural awareness emerges.

The comparisons of work in China and elsewhere suggest that there has not been enough detailed work on the understanding and applicability of global citizenship education and its concepts in China, and it was this specific research gap this exploratory study addressed.

Methodology

This study was conducted by analysing data collected through a self-designed questionnaire survey. A pilot survey with a list of 18 questions had been carried out among a number of students majoring in different specialties at the two universities, but all taking the required College English. According to feedback from the pilot survey participants and the analysis of the responses, we realized that the students had very limited understanding of the concept of intercultural citizen and intercultural citizenship education, and thus we decided to reserve questions about intercultural citizenship education in the foreign language classroom for future studies and leave out multiple choice questions that may affect students' free expression of their true understanding of the problems under investigation. The questions were then reduced to five and simplified for more effective data elicitation.

As Byram (2006) points out, linguistic complexities in communication should not be overlooked in discussions of complex concepts such as citizenship among people of different languages. When we designed the questionnaire we found that there are several Chinese equivalents to citizenry, and were aware that there were problems in translation, an issue which arises in multilingual research. Several terms can be taken as equivalents, like *gongmin* (the public people), *guomin* (literally, the people of the state), *shimin* (the city people) and *renmin* (the people), which all seem to refer to membership of the nation-state but each has its own intricate etymology and specific connotations in contemporary China (Feng, 2006), and Feng traces the historical evolution and development of all these terms. In this paper we will use the term *gongmin* because it has been much more commonly used to refer to general membership of the state in the last decades or so and has become more of an equivalent term than any others to the English 'citizen'. As for the term of 'world/global/intercultural/citizen', in Chinese we have different translations for 'world citizen' (世界公民)/'global citizen' (全球公民)/'intercultural citizen' (跨文化公民). We chose to use 'intercultural citizen' in our text rather than the others used in the questionnaire mainly because the questionnaire was designed with reference to Byram *From Foreign Language Education to Education for Intercultural Citizenship* (2008) and in order to keep consistency with the whole project.

The questionnaire was in Chinese, the participants' first language, in which both the questions and answers could be expressed most clearly and accurately by respondents. English versions of key terms, such as 'core qualities', 'intercultural citizenship' and 'duties and obligations', were also provided in brackets to help the participants understand the questions more precisely.

The questionnaire was to provide data to help us address the following questions:

(1)   What does 'citizen' mean to Chinese university students?
(2)   Are Chinese university students familiar with the concept of 'intercultural citizenship'?
(3)   What characteristics or traits do Chinese university students think an intercultural citizen should have?
(4)   What obligations and responsibilities/skills/attitudes do Chinese university students think an intercultural citizen should have?
(5)   What is the status of claimed intercultural contact by the Chinese students?

The first four questions relate to perceptions of citizenship and the last one is intended to look into the connection between such perceptions and students' intercultural contact.

The English translation of the questionnaire is provided in the Appendix.

Participants and Data

Two universities were involved in this project. University Z is an ordinary university that requires lower admission scores while University H is a key one that requires much higher admission scores. Thus the participants from University H were assumed to have both a high level of academic performance as well as overall high levels of the competencies required in formal school education. Although the participants in the two universities were from different parts of the country and had received their secondary education in quite diverse contexts, their education had taken place under the same national curriculum framework, including that for citizenship-related education. Citizenship education has been traditionally conducted in the form of moral education in Chinese schools, and political or ideological education with a focus on morality, social obligations, with patriotic ideology as the chief aim of general education (Gongmin Daode Jianshe Shishi Gangyao, 2001).

The participants included both English majors and non-English majors. All of the non-English majors at Chinese universities are required to learn College English. The participants from University Z were 150 second-year students majoring in English language. The majority were females (82%) and only 27 (18%) were males. Their age ranged from 19 to 20 years. Participants from University H were 158 first-year students (21.5% males, $n = 34$; 78.5% females, $n = 124$), 25 were English majors (16%) and the rest were science and engineering majors from 18 different schools and departments. Their age ranged from 18 to 21 years. The total number of participants from the two universities was 308.

Both groups of participants were selected through convenience sampling and the participants from the two universities were believed to be representative of students in other key or ordinary universities.

Frequency counts were made for answers to closed questions, i.e. Question 3 and the sub-questions of Question 5 in the questionnaire (see Appendix). As for responses to the open questions, we categorized the data through thematic analysis, grouping responses with same or similar meaning into sub-categories and the sub-categories into more general categories. The consequent groupings of responses were labelled with semantically consistent and distinctive terms. Following up the categorization of responses to open questions, a frequency count was also conducted of the number of responses under each identified theme.

Results and Discussion

RQ1: What does 'citizen' mean to Chinese university students?

The purpose of this question is to find out whether Chinese students know, or to what extent they know, about the concept of 'citizen'. The participants were expected to write out three items for 'core qualities' and 'responsibilities and obligations' of a citizen. The total number of respondents is 308 students and the percentages in Table 2.1 refer to the frequencies of themes analysed from the data.

It is interesting to notice that, among all the responses given by the 308 participants, 'rights' rank first, which probably reveals the growing awareness of individual rights among the Chinese, and also corresponds with the rise of individualistic values among the young Chinese, as has been observed in a number of studies by Chinese scholars. Jia and Jia (2006) examined the tension between emerging individualist identity and the more established traditional collectivist identity, and concluded that the former will be

Table 2.1 Core qualities/responsibilities and obligations of citizens

Traits/responsibilities and obligations	Frequency	Percentage
Rights	199	65%
Responsibilities and obligations	166	54%
Patriotism	160	52%
National identity	155	50%
Personal qualities	146	47%
Law and regulations	32	10%
Others	1	0.03%

$N = 308$.

maintained and develop through conflict and negotiation with the traditional collectivist identity in Chinese society at large. In the study based on a questionnaire survey among 1028 students from eight universities regarding individual dignity, independence/autonomy, privacy and individual development, Tang and Chen (2007) have also observed the co-existence of collectivism and individualism values and confirmed a strong individualist tendency among Chinese university student participants.

The interpretation of the citizen as someone who should have 'responsibilities and obligations' (166/54%), emphasizes the right of citizens to participate in the development of their country and their responsibilities towards their own country, and the similar position of 'patriotism' (160/52%), we believe, reflects the long-term effects of both formal school education and social political socialization in the Chinese context in which patriotism has a central role. 'Patriotism' is also emphasized as one the of core values advocated by the current leadership in the national drive for the realization of the China Dream.

Nearly the same weight was given to national identity, which suggests that having a legal identification and nationality indicates affiliation with country and a sense of belonging. We might interpret this as suggesting that the citizenship education that students have received could be viewed as focusing on moral standards and responsibilities, obligations and loyalty to the country that go with it. Social and political rights of citizens are permitted on condition that their commitments to the nation and the society are fulfilled and there exists no conflict between the national or collective interests and individual rights. When the Chinese communicate with people from other countries, many of them feel that they are expected to represent their own country with a sense of national pride and they will defend their national honour (e.g. Liu, 2008). The authors of this chapter have all had such experiences when living abroad.

Personal qualities as a citizen were also addressed. Qualities such as being respectful and unprejudiced, benevolent, morally and ethically sound, independent and having strong aspirations for life and for individual fulfilment were mentioned by students.

To our great surprise, the theme 'Law and Regulations' contained relatively few items and was given little attention. This is hard to explain. We may imagine that if citizens are without a strong sense of law-abiding awareness, the nation or country might not be advanced and civilized. If the younger generation, our students, only wants rights and place them at the top of their choice, without realizing the importance of laws and regulations, there might be a hidden danger that calls for our educators' urgent attention. Individuals are not only given rights and duties but should also abide by the country's law at the same time. The above identified traits and the ranking of the numbers for these traits offer interesting evidence for further study in this respect.

RQ2: Are Chinese university students familiar with the concept of 'intercultural citizenship'?

The purpose of this question is to find out whether students are familiar with the terms 'world citizen/global citizen/intercultural citizen'. The results of participants' familiarity with those terms is shown in Table 2.2.

It is evident from Table 2.2 that a clear majority of students had heard of the concept of 'world/global citizen', and this result matches a Google search done by Golubeva *et al.* in this volume. They found the most frequent used words are 'world citizen' (978,000), 'global citizen' (491,000) and 'international citizen' (192,000). This may also be explained by the fact that these two terms are frequently used in other areas, such as economics and social studies, so that students are accessing them often in various media. In addition to this, the development of globalization and frequent contacts across the world enables students to have easy access to public media such as the internet, TV, radio and newspapers, which expose them to these terms.

When it comes to the term 'intercultural citizen', only 21% of students had heard this term. This is not difficult to explain because this term is much less frequent (2300) in Golubeva *et al.*'s Google search. A further explanation may be that the concept of intercultural citizenship is a brand-new notion in China and the research on intercultural citizenship education has just started. Some scholars in China advocated this new research area of intercultural citizenship education in the Chinese context at an International Academic Conference held by Shanghai Normal University in 2012 and 2014 and some papers have been published related to this concept since then. For example 'Critical language–cultural awareness and intercultural citizenship awareness' (Song, 2012), 'EFL Education as Education for Global Citizens' (Jia, 2012), 'Intercultural citizenship: Foreign language teaching as an extension of national education' (Byram & Han, 2011) and 'Development of intercultural citizenship education in the language classroom and beyond' (Byram & Han, 2014), which may arouse some scholars' interest in research on this area in China.

Table 2.2 Familiarity with the terms of world citizen/global citizen/intercultural citizen

Terms	Frequency	Percentage
World citizen/global citizen	216	70%
Intercultural citizen	66	21%

N = 308.

RQ3: What characteristics or traits do Chinese university students think an intercultural citizen should have?

Students were asked, in Question 4, to write at least three items to show their understandings of the 'core qualities' of an intercultural citizen to parallel Question 2 about 'citizen'. Since only a minority, as was evident from the previous question, had prior knowledge of this word, the majority developed their ideas and connotations as they answered this question. There were, however, no noticeable differences between the answers of the majority and the minority and we analysed them together (Table 2.3).

It can be seen that students thought that the first core quality of an intercultural citizen should be the ability to visit or live in other countries as they wish and be familiar with foreign cultures (128/42%) if doing so. In addition to this, communicative competence in English was deemed important by a little more than a third of students (116/38%), which may imply that students see the linguistic and cultural knowledge of the individual as important. What is surprising is the emphasis on 'critical thinking and creativity' (106/34%) taken as one of the traits of intercultural citizens. This may, in part at least, be due to more recent discussion that the ability of criticality and analytical skills should be developed in foreign language education. Sun (2011) noted that 'critical thinking' has a long history in the West from ancient Greece to contemporary Western civilization and has been put as one of the core targets of university education in the USA. An often cited theoretical framework (Sun, 2011) classifies 'thinking' into six levels – remembering, understanding, applying, analysing, evaluating and creating – but foreign language teaching in China, Sun argues, mainly stays at the level of 'remembering and understanding'. This issue has aroused great attention and triggered many discussions, and this is probably why students mentioned this aspect.

Table 2.3 Core qualities of an intercultural citizen

Traits/characteristics	Frequency	Percentage
Ability to visit or live in other countries	143	46%
Familiarity with foreign cultures	128	42%
Communicative competence	116	38%
Abilities in critical thinking and creativity	106	34%
Understanding and respecting different cultures	74	24%
Promoting world peace	64	21%
Tolerance, convergence and adaptation	35	11%
Cultural awareness	31	10%
Inheriting and developing national culture	24	7%

$N = 308$.

However, though 'criticality' has been discussed by scholars and practitioners who intend to develop the ability of students through language teaching, the current situation of traditional ways of teaching focusing on language and grammar is not that easy to change.

It is also noticeable that students give some prominence to the purposes of intercultural citizenship: understanding and respecting different cultures (74/24%); and promoting world peace and knowledge of the world (64/21%). This may imply that in students' minds respecting the differences may reduce conflict and prejudice and maintain world harmony. The last three less mentioned items were: tolerance, convergence, and adaptation (35/11%); cultural awareness (31/10%); and inheriting and developing national culture (24/7%). As pointed out earlier, cultural awareness as a teaching objective was introduced into the reformed English curriculum at all levels of education in China. As a consequence, students know that language and culture cannot be separated and they understand they cannot learn a language well without culture learning (Han, 2010). Thus the possible explanation for this result may be that students think that an intercultural citizen should have this cultural awareness as a precondition to communicate with people from other cultures and this implies that critical cultural awareness should be extended to language education explicitly because critical cultural awareness includes a critique of our own cultures and societies as well as those of other countries (Byram, 1997).

From the diverse responses provided by students we concluded that they have gained some superficial understandings of an intercultural citizen, and they make a connection with travelling to other countries and knowing other cultures, etc. If we refer to the notion of intercultural citizenship applied in this book, it is noticeable that most of the components deemed important and outlined in this book are not in students' perceptions of intercultural citizenship, showing that there is a lack of systematic intercultural education in China.

RQ4: What obligations and responsibilities/skills/attitudes should an intercultural citizen have?

The previous question focused on the intercultural citizen as a person whereas this one explored the competences of the intercultural citizen. The participants were also asked in Question 4 to write three items each for what they believe to be the responsibilities, skills and attitudes that an intercultural citizen should have. A thematic analysis produced the results of Table 2.4.

Regarding the obligations of an intercultural citizen, it can be observed that students give priority to 'promoting communication' across different cultures (166/54%). Our interpretation of this result is that it is probably due to the introduction of the notion of cultural awareness into the English curriculum. This has stressed the importance of intercultural communication and

Table 2.4 Responsibilities/skill/attitudes of an intercultural citizen

Concepts	Items	Frequency	Percentage
Responsibilities	Promoting communication between different cultures	166	54%
	Promoting world peace and harmony	139	45%
	Patriotism	125	40%
	Protecting and promoting native culture	124	40%
	Observing laws and customs of both countries	115	37%
	Others	38	12%
Skills	Communication skills	303	98%
	Cultural knowledge and understanding of different cultures	205	67%
	Critical thinking and analytic skill	100	33%
	Adaptive skills	97	31%
	Survival skills	38	12%
	Others	26	8%
Attitudes	Learning from each other	249	81%
	Respecting others	142	46%
	Tolerance and acceptance	113	37%
	Equality and independence	90	29%
	Co-prosperity/common development	87	28%
	Friendly and seeking harmony	51	17%
	Protecting one's own culture	29	9%

$N = 308$.

had an effect on students' understanding. On the other hand 'patriotism' was also considered important (125/40%), suggesting that the obligatory education on national identity, morality and ideals which students had received in the education system was effective and could be justified in political terms.

'Promoting world peace and harmony' (139/45%) comes as the second obligation. Interestingly in the previous question on the traits of an intercultural citizen (see Table 2.3), as many as 64/21% also had 'Promoting world peace and harmony'. Such a response was not so much a personal trait in the common sense but it did reflect the value the participants placed on 'Promoting world peace and harmony', which was further demonstrated in their answers to Question 4. However when the word 'obligation' or 'responsibility' occurred in the question students placed more emphasis on this, which may suggest that in students' minds a peaceful and harmonious world is a universal goal the whole of mankind is pursuing, if they consider themselves to have this responsibility as an intercultural citizen.

Students, we noticed, gave some considerations to both their own culture and others' cultures. 'Patriotism' and 'Protecting and promoting native cultures' had the support of 40% in each case and this may suggest that students see these as synonymous. Only further research would be able to clarify this.

Other obligations include 'Observing laws and customs of both countries', where a little over a third of the students (115/37%), saw this as important. This contrasts with only 10% in Table 2.1 who mentioned 'Law and regulations' as important in defining the citizen. The difference is substantial and might suggest that the concept of 'intercultural citizen' has different connotations to that of 'citizen' and we wonder to what extent this result is linked to the idea of 'Respect and learn from other cultures' (74/24%); again only further research could clarify this, where perhaps in-depth interviewing might reveal the interconnections among students' concepts.

As for skills, it can be seen that students almost unanimously (303/98%) believed that 'communication skills' are important and they were probably thinking of the current teaching focus on foreign language with the five skills (listening, speaking, reading, writing and translating). This result was very similar to that obtained by a survey of teachers' perceptions of the importance of language and culture teaching. The teachers gave priority to the five skills of language teaching (Han, 2007). This was followed by 'cultural knowledge and understanding different cultures', chosen by about two thirds of the respondents (205/67%). There is substantial research (Hu, 1999; Hu & Gao, 1997; Jang, 2002), which shows that students are aware of the importance of culture learning in the language classroom, but it is also noticeable that 'Critical thinking and analytic skills' were suggested by almost the same figure (100/33%) as in the previous question, Table 2.3 (106/34%), which suggests a consistency in response on this topic.

As for the skill of 'adaptive capacity', slightly less than a third (97/31%) considered this necessary and this may imply that Chinese students do not realize the importance of this skill until they have had the opportunity to go abroad. To understand and be familiar with different cultures can enable them to improve their communicative competence or, the other way round, adaptive capacity may first develop when they have opportunities to talk to people from other cultures or to go abroad for study.

Although critical thinking is not identified as one of the teaching objectives explicitly in the curriculum, the realization of its importance has become ever more acknowledged and researched (Wen & Liu, 2010; Wen & Wang, 2010). It is encouraging to see that there are 33% of students who consider critical and analytic skills important since, as argued throughout this book, this is a crucial element of foreign language education, but this low percentage suggests the need to enhance such training in the curriculum and in practical classroom teaching.

When considering the role of attitudes, it can be observed that students put the item 'Learning positive things from each other' (249/81%) at the top, showing their knowledge-oriented attitudes. We can see that they want to learn something new and different. The concept of 'positive things from others' implies that they have to be able to distinguish what are the good points of others and what are not on the one hand, and on the other they have to be able to compare these with their own. 'Respecting others' was also valued highly by nearly half the students (142/46%). 'Tolerance and acceptance' took up 113/37%, and 90/29% of students choose 'Equality and independence' as one of the attitudes. Students also revealed some interest, as an intercultural citizen, in 'Co-prosperity and common development' (87/28%) and 'Friendly and seeking harmony' (51/17%), but 'Protecting one's own culture' (29/9%) showed a very low percentage. All of these results indicate a high degree of awareness and recognition as well as tolerance of the other, which seems to be in conformity with the collective value orientation of the Chinese culture on the whole.

RQ5: To what extent do Chinese university students say they have intercultural contact?

With this question, we wanted to find out what kind of activities students could get access to as a form of intercultural contact. Students were asked in Question 5 to mention whatever forms of activities they regard as intercultural contact. Table 2.5 summarizes the responses from the participants of the two universities.

From Table 2.5, we can see that the two major channels for students to have contact with other cultures are attending lectures or courses delivered by foreign teachers (233/76%) and using the public media such as the internet, TV and films (216/70%). This coincides with research in Japan in which Parmenter (2004) conducted a study to examine the perspectives of Japanese university students on issues related to intercultural citizenship. The

Table 2.5 Modes of intercultural experiences

Forms	Frequency	Percentage
Lectures and courses delivered by foreign teachers	233	76%
Public media (TV, internet, newspaper, films, etc.)	216	70%
Short-term visits abroad (such as studying, travelling, visiting relatives and friends overseas)	118	38%
Making foreign friends	100	32%
International communication experience	91	30%
None	58	18%

$N = 308$.

findings showed that the students' view of the intercultural citizen were influenced by their family, education and media like television and the internet. In China, Jing (2013) showed that Chinese high school students learned about culture and global issues from education in school and the media, and Han (2012) found that the most often used technique to teach culture by secondary English teachers was through textbooks. Short-term visits abroad and making foreign friends was an experience for about one-third of the students (118/38% and 100/32%, respectively). It can be seen that the percentage of intercultural communication experience (91/30%) is not yet high, but experience in other Asian countries such as Peck and Wagner (in this book) demonstrate that it is possible to develop this further.

For example, in Japan, the International Community Center of Waseda University organizes intercultural communication activities each year. The formal intercultural communication class can invite international students to join group discussions in English, and the Cross-Cultural Distance Learning course which has run since 1999 at Waseda University is considered to be a successful model to develop university students' intercultural communication competence (Nakano, 2014). At present, the two universities in this study do not have this kind of online intercultural exchange course, but it would be possible to design courses with partner universities in the future, and other chapters in this book describe online intercultural citizenship projects that have implications for Chinese universities.

In general, most of the students have experienced some form of intercultural communication, which is one of the necessary prerequisites to cultivate world/intercultural citizens. However, 58/18% of the respondents stated they had had no intercultural experiences. Although this may also reveal the respondents' confusion about what counts as intercultural experience overseas and at home, the lack of intercultural experience for almost one in five students is rather discouraging and poses a challenge for future work in intercultural citizenship education programmes.

Conclusion

Governments in many countries attach great importance to global citizenship education as a consequence of globalization. Since 2012, the Japanese Ministry of Education has promoted The Project for Promotion of Global Human Resource Development that aims to develop the Japanese younger generation's English abilities, intercultural competence and global perspectives in order to meet the challenges and succeed in the global field. In Japan too, the Second Basic Plan for the Promotion of Education in 2013 defined the educational policy of developing global human resources. Since 2010, the Chinese Ministry of Education has also included the development of global awareness and international talents in its 'Outline of China's National Plan for Medium-and Long-Term Educational Reform and Development 2010–2020'.

After reform and opening up since the late 1970s, China is blending into the global market actively with the economic boom, which demands a great number of talents. It is thus imperative to educate qualified intercultural citizens with professional skills to respond to the economic development in China. It has already become an important objective of English education for the current college students to integrate intercultural citizenship education into English learning and teaching in the university, improve abilities in critical thinking and creativity and cultivate high-quality international talents with knowledge of international issues.

The questionnaire in this study sampled Chinese university students, and though limited in the size of the respondent population and regional as well as academic background coverage, it offers data about these students' perceptions of the makings of a good citizen and a good intercultural citizen. The data suggest that there is a need for more systematic citizenship education and intercultural citizenship education among university students in China.

However, the Chinese context must be taken into consideration for such education as entailed by the differences in the foundations laid by historical as well as socio-political developments in citizenship education and differences in what is perceived as constituting intercultural citizenship in China and in other parts of the world. The influence of traditional Chinese cultural values and ideology promoted in the Chinese education system, the interpretation of obligations and responsibilities, the emphasis on harmony and mutual respect, etc., are important aspects of students' perceptions that cannot be neglected in the curriculum for intercultural citizenship education. The implications revealed in the survey data not only show the urgent need for intercultural citizenship education for Chinese university students but also point to the directions for our future efforts.

References

Alred, G., Byram, M. and Fleming, M. (2006) *Education for Intercultural Citizenship: Concepts and Comparisons*. Clevedon: Multilingual Matters.

Byram, M. (1997) *Teaching and Assessing Intercultural Communicative Competence*. Clevedon: Multilingual Matters.

Byram, M. (2006) Developing a concept of intercultural citizenship. In G. Alred, M. Byram and M. Fleming (eds) *Education for Intercultural Citizenship: Concepts and Comparisons* (pp. 109–129). Clevedon: Multilingual Matters.

Byram, M. (2008) *From Foreign Language Education to Education for Intercultural Citizenship: Essays and Reflections*. Clevedon: Multilingual Matters.

Byram, M. and Han, H. (2011) Intercultural citizenship: Foreign language teaching as an extension of national education. *Academic Research, China* 11, 128–135.

Byram, M. and Han, H. (2014) Development of intercultural citizenship education in the language classroom and beyond. *Academic Research, China* 13, 153–158.

Feng, A.W. (2006) Contested notions of citizenship and citizenship education – The Chinese case. In G. Alred, M. Byram and M. Fleming (eds) *Intercultural Citizenship Education: Concepts and Comparisons* (pp. 86–105). Clevedon: Multilingual Matters.

Gimenez, T. and Sheehan, S. (2008) *Global Citizenship in the English Language Classroom*. London: British Council.

Gongmin Daode Jianshe Shishi Gangyao (2001) [The implementation guidelines to construct civic morals of citizens]. *Renmin Ribao [People's Daily]*, 24 October.

Han, H. (2007) Teachers' perception of culture teaching in the EFL. *A Journal of Teacher Education* 3 (3), 45–52.

Han, H. (2010) An investigation of teachers' perceptions of culture teaching in the secondary schools in Xinjiang (Doctoral dissertation). See http://etheses.dur.ac.uk/109/1/HAN,_Hui_FinalVersion.pdf (accessed 6 July 2016).

Han, H. (2012) *A Study of Teachers' Perceptions of ICC Teaching in China: Teachers Perceptions of Inter/cultural Teaching in Chinese English Language Teaching Context*. Saarbrücken, Germany: LAP Lambert Academic.

Han, X.H. and Song, L. (2011) Teacher cognition of intercultural communicative competence in the Chinese ELT context. *Intercultural Communication Studies* XIIX (1), 175–192.

Houghton, S. (2012) *Intercultural Dialogue in Practice: Managing Value Judgment in Foreign Language Education*. Bristol: Multilingual Matters.

Houghton, S. and Yamada, E. (2012) *Developing Criticality in Practice through Foreign Language Education*. Frankfurt am Mein: Peter Lang.

Hu, W.Z. (1999) *Aspects of Intercultural Communication. Proceedings of China's 2nd Conference on Intercultural Communication*. Beijing: Foreign Language Teaching and Research Press.

Hu, W.Z. and Gao, Y.H. (1997) *Waiyu jiaoxue yu wenhua [Foreign Language Teaching and Culture]*. Hunan, China: Hunan Education Press.

Jia, Y.X. (2012) EFL education as education for global citizens. Paper presented at *SHSU International Conference of Intercultural Communication*, Shanghai, China, December.

Jia, Y.X. and Jia, X.R. (2006) The emergence and construction of individualistic identity in modern china: Negotiation and conflict between individualistic and the traditional ideological discourses. *Intercultural Communication Studies* XV (3), 89–109.

Jang, W. (2002) The relation between culture and language. *ELT Journal* 54 (4), 328–334.

Jing, H.T. (2013) Global awareness: Foreign language teachers' beliefs and practices. *Intercultural Communication Studies* XXII (1), 95–116.

Lee, W. and Leung, S. (2006) Global citizenship education in Hong Kong and Shanghai secondary schools: Ideals, realities and expectations. *Citizenship Teaching and Learning* 2 (2), 68–84.

Liu, Z.S. (2008) The current situation of contemporary Chinese citizen education and system construction. *Journal of South China Normal University (Social Science Edition)* 2, 23–28.

Ministry of Education (2001) *Jiaoyubu guanyu shiwu qijian jiaoshi jiaoyu gaige yu fazhan de yijian [Directive on Reforming and Developing Teacher Education in the 10th five-year Period]*. Beijing, China: Ministry of Education.

Ministry of Education (2004) *National College English Curriculum Requirements*. Beijing, China: Ministry of Education.

Morita, L. (2013) Japanese university students' attitudes towards globalisation, intercultural contexts and English. *World Journal of English Language* 3 (4), 31–41.

Nakano, M. (2014) Networked English language learning from English tutorials to cyber interaction at Waseda University. In R.C.-H. Tsai and G. Redmer (eds) *Language, Culture, and Information Technology* (pp. 1–32). Taipei: Bookman Books.

Parmenter, L. (2004) Interculturalism in Japan: An analysis of the negotiation of cultural citizenship among students in Japanese universities. Paper presented at *Interculturalism: 2nd*

Global Conference, Vienna, Austria. See http://inter-disciplinary.net/ati/diversity/interculturalism/ic2/parmenter%201.pdf (accessed 6 July 2016).

Parmenter, L. (2011) Power and place in the discourse of global citizenship education. *Globalisation, Societies and Education* 9 (3–4), 367–380.

Porto, M. (2014) Intercultural citizenship education in an EFL online project in Argentina. *Language and Intercultural Communication* 14 (2), 245–261.

Song, L. (2012) Critical language–cultural awareness and intercultural citizenship awareness in foreign language education. Paper presented at *SHSU International Conference of Intercultural Communication*, Shanghai, China, December.

Sun, Y.Z. (2011) English writing teaching and cultivating critical thinking. *Journal of Foreign Language Teaching and Research* 3, 126–132.

Tang, P. and Chen, Z.L. (2007) A statistical study on Chinese undergraduates' values of individualism /collectivism. *Journal of Sichuan College of Education* 23 (5), 13–22.

Wen, Q.F. and Liu, X.P. (2010) Woguo waiyulei daxuesheng sibian nengli liangju de xiuding yu xiaodu jianyan yanjiu [Revision of measuring tool on critical thinking ability of English majors and testing its reliability and validity in China]. *Foreign Language World* 4, 19–26.

Wen, Q.F. and Wang, H.M. (eds) (2010) Woguo yingyu zhuanye yu qita wenkelei daxuesheng sibian nengli de duibi yanjiu [A comparative study on critical thinking skills between English and other liberal arts majors]. *Foreign Language Teaching and Researching* 5, 350–355.

Yamada, E. (2010) Developing criticality through higher education language studies. In Y. Tsai and S. Houghton (eds) *Becoming Intercultural: Inside and Outside the Classroom* (pp. 146–166). Cambridge: Cambridge Scholars.

Appendix

调查问卷

首先感谢同学们参与此次问卷调查。本问卷调查是跨文化公民教育研究国际项目的一部分，调查数据将完全用于课题研究。本问卷为匿名填写，所有个人信息将严格保密。请根据提示如实填写有关信息并简短回答各项问题。

跨文化公民教育研究国际项目-中国项目课题组

2012年11月

1. 个人信息
   (1) 年龄:18–19 ☐ 20–21 ☐ 22–23 ☐
   (2) 性别: (a) 男 ☐   (b) 女 ☐
   (3) 专业:_____
   (4) 所学外语: 英语 ☐ 法语 ☐ 日语 ☐ 俄语 ☐ 其他 _____

2. 请从以下几个方面简要说明你对'公民'的理解:

   公民的特质 (Qualities of a citizen):
   (1) _____
   (2) _____
   (3) _____

公民的责任与义务 (Duties and obligations of a citizen):

(1) _____
(2) _____
(3) _____

公民的权利 (Rights of a citizen):

(1) _____
(2) _____
(3) _____

3. 你是否听说过下列词语 (在听说过的项目上打钩, 可多选):

全球性公民 (world/global citizen) ☐
跨文化公民 (intercultural citizen) ☐

4. 请从以下几个方面简要说明你个人对'跨文化公民'的理解:
跨文化公民的特质 (Qualities of an intercultural citizen):

(1) _____
(2) _____
(3) _____

跨文化公民的责任 (Responsibilities of an intercultural citizen):

(1) _____
(2) _____
(3) _____

跨文化公民应具备哪些技能 (Skills for an intercultural citizen):

(1) _____
(2) _____
(3) _____

对待其他文化和民族的态度 (Attitudes towards other cultures and people from other cultures):

(1) _____
(2) _____
(3) _____

5. 你是否有过与其来自他文化的人交流的经历? 如果有, 请注明具体情况。
(1) 有☐ 无 ☐
(2) 你的跨文化经历方式 (可以多选):
出国旅游 ☐ 出国学习 ☐ 出国探亲 ☐ 出国短期项目 (如国外冬令营、夏令营) ☐
结交外国朋友 ☐ 其他 ☐ (填写具体方式) _____
(3) 国内的跨文化接触 (可以多选):
(a) 参加外教讲座或课程 ☐
(b) 参与国际性交流活动 ☐

(c) 接触外国朋友或学者 ☐
(d) 担任对外交流活动翻译或志愿者 (如上海世博会、西湖博览会、哈洽会、冰雪节等) ☐
(e) 接触大众媒体 (例如: 网络、影视、报刊等) ☐
(f) 其他 ☐ (填写具体方式) _____

问卷结束, 谢谢合作!

Questionnaire

We would like to thank you for your participation in this questionnaire survey. As part of our intercultural citizenship education project, all data from the questionnaire will be used for research purposes only. The questionnaire is anonymous and all your personal information will be kept confidential.

Please give your answers for the following questions according to the instructions.

1. **Personal information (multiple answers allowed if applies)**
   (1) Age: 18–19 ☐; 20–21 ☐; 22–23 ☐
   (2) Gender: (a) Male ☐; (b) Female ☐
   (3) Major: _____
   (4) Foreign language(s) learned:
   English ☐; French ☐; Japanese ☐; Russian ☐; Other _____
2. **Fill in the blanks with brief answers for each of the given questions according to your own understanding:**
   Core qualities of a citizen include:
   (1) _____
   (2) _____
   (3) _____
   Most important duties and obligations of a citizen include:
   (1) _____
   (2) _____
   (3) _____
3. **Have you ever heard of the following terms (multiple choices allowed):**
   World/Global citizen ☐
   Intercultural citizen ☐
4. **Please fill in the blanks below to illustrate your own understanding of the term Intercultural Citizen:**
   The core qualities of an intercultural citizen include:
   (1) _____
   (2) _____
   (3) _____

The responsibilities of an intercultural citizen include:

(1) _____

(2) _____

(3) _____

The abilities and skills expected for an intercultural citizen include:

(1) _____

(2) _____

(3) _____

Expected attitudes towards other cultures and people from other cultures:

(1) _____

(2) _____

(3) _____

5. **Have you ever had any contact with people from other cultures? If yes, please specify.**

(1) Yes □; No □

(2) Mode of intercultural contact (multiple choices allowed): Overseas travel □; Overseas study programmes □; Visiting families and/or relatives abroad □; Short term international programmes (such as international summer camp or winter camp) □; Having international friends □; Other (please specify) □ _____

(3) Intercultural contact in China (multiple choices allowed):

(a) attending lectures and/or courses by international teachers □

(b) participating in international programmes □

(c) having contact with international friends or scholars □

(d) acting as interpreter or volunteer in international events (such as Shanghai World Expo, Harbin Trade Fair, Harbin Ice and Snow Festival) □

(e) intercultural contact through popular media (such as the internet, movies, TV programmes, newspapers and magazines) □

(f) Other (please specify) □ _____

End of Questionnaire

Thank you for your cooperation!

3 Intercultural Encounters in Teacher Education – Collaboration Towards Intercultural Citizenship

Ulla Lundgren and teacher students

Awakening! If I had to choose one word to describe my experience throughout this course, awakening would be it
(Mary, USA)

Introduction

This chapter focuses on a five-week teacher education module on 'Intercultural Encounters' at a Swedish university, which brought together student teachers of different nationalities, with different traditions of education, with the purpose of equipping them to teach in multicultural and internationalized societies. This was articulated in the aims for the module as developing the 'knowledge, skills and attitudes which are required to engage actively with people from other ethnic, cultural, religious and linguistic backgrounds'. The module, 7.5 credits in the European Credit Transfer and Accumulation System (ECTS; ec.europa.eu/education/tools/ects_en.htm), was a quarter of a full-time study course (30 ECTS).

Some of the students were attending a joint European Union and US Department of Education programme; others were Erasmus exchange students or 'freemovers', i.e. students who arrange their own international exchange. A few belonged to neither of these groups but were Swedish students who had opted to do an English-medium version of a compulsory module that they would otherwise do in Swedish. Most of the students had not deliberately chosen this specific module as it was part of an obligatory teacher education programme.

In the first part of this chapter the students are important co-authors, with their voices in italics. They were well aware that they were taking part in a curriculum development project and had given their written consent to their contributions within the project being used anonymously for scientific purposes, such as publications, teaching and research. I was actually encouraged by some students to write a paper about the module using their voices to illustrate their development. For obvious reasons I had to be the editor and make the selection of data. The first part of the chapter thus focuses on providing a description of the module as the students reported their experience of it and, to give this some structure, I have focused on some specific dimensions of the module design; their contributions have been selected to focus on the effects of collaboration and group dynamics. This means that other aspects of the students' experience had to be excluded, partly owing to length restrictions but also because an important purpose of this chapter is to suggest how other teacher educators might work in similar ways, and the focus is therefore on how students experienced novel approaches.

In the second part of the chapter, I focus on analysing what the students said as evidence of the effects and degree of success of the module. This means that there is a particular focus on questions of identification and critical reflection in relationship to that part of the theory of intercultural citizenship, which postulates that learners engaged in international groups will develop new insights and identifications, and that this kind of experience leads to critical cultural awareness (Byram, 2006) and re-assessment of assumed normalities. In other words, the students' development is addressed with respect to the characteristics of a 'good' intercultural citizenship education project as explained in the Introduction to this book. I was looking for an awareness of their own stereotypes, a sense of international identification, an 'international' way of thinking and acting and an ability to apply the latter to 'knowledge' to 'self' and to 'the world'. This last characteristic will be discussed in relationship to Barnett's (1997) theory as explained in the Introduction. I have focused elsewhere (Lundgren, 2014) on the part of the module that consisted of designing culturally responsive lesson ideas.

The module was taught three times and the data in the form of individual written reflections from the student teachers are drawn from the two last occasions:

Cohort 2: 26 students – UK, 3; Netherlands, 3; Hungary, 1; USA, 8; Sweden, 8; Spain, 3.
Cohort 3: 28 students – UK, 5; Netherlands, 1; Hungary, 1; USA, 10; Singapore, 1; Sweden, 10.

After the first time the design was considerably revised owing to the course evaluation by the first cohort. The main critique could be summarized as 'too theoretical and lack of practical implementation for our future profession'. The greatest change was the introduction of the ABCs model (see Appendix) as, at the time, I had been invited to take part in the US/European research project TRANSABCs (http://www.transabcs.org; cf. Schmidt & Finkbeiner, 2006; Finkbeiner & Lazar, 2014), with the aim of developing culturally sensitive teachers.

As it was against my conviction just to present ready-made lesson ideas and not to make the students aware of theory, the ABCs project seemed a good fit. In hindsight the model became the answer to turning theory into practice.

I had been given a free hand to plan the module and choose literature and lecturers. The design focused on intercultural citizenship and world citizenship education, which had been closely linked to my research interest for many years. Apart from a few sessions on religion, I did all the teaching myself. Teaching strategies included group discussions, oral and written assignments in groups or individually, and interactive practical exercises. The students often worked in groups of three representing different nationalities, which I had organized. A student's handbook with a set schedule for all lectures and the many activities and assignments was distributed at the module start. This was also available for the students at an electronic learning platform where *inter alia* assignments were submitted and web discussions took place.

Pedagogic Principles

The pedagogical bricks on which I tried to build the module were: participation, dialogic learning, student activity, involvement, experiential learning, connecting theory to practice, critical reflection, progression and relevance to future profession (inspired by e.g. Vygotsky, 1986; Bakhtin, 1986; Dysthe, 1993; Lave & Wenger, 1991), and some of these are the focus of the selections I have made from students' diaries.

Learning as a social activity, dialogic learning

In the very first lecture the underlying pedagogical theories were introduced to the students to help them make sense of the design and methodology of the module. As the students came from different educational cultures it was not obvious that everyone shared the idea of learning as a social activity through interaction with others, and in this respect, one student expressed her initial feelings about the module as follows:

When I first started this course, I was skeptical about the content and wondered how this course would help me as a future teacher. It wasn't until I started reading the literature, holding discussions in class, and meeting with students from other countries that I figured out just how helpful this content was going to be. (Linda, USA)

Referring to the theories mentioned above the students were encouraged to implement them during the module:

The course started up by teaching us about learning and how it is created in interaction and that everything we learn is based on the experiences we have with us from before. This was an interesting starting point because it became something we kept coming back to. (Pernilla, Sweden)

The theory that I believe had the most practical application for me and my peers so far in Sweden was the Socio-Cultural Theory. While the lectures and readings on Intercultural Encounters were strong and thorough, I cannot fully comprehend the theories until I have experienced them for myself. I need to build knowledge through my own doing. I need to make mistakes and learn from them. And I need to interact with other people to learn. (Nancy, USA).

Vygotsky's Zone of Proximal Development is completely in synch with my own beliefs of people needing others to go beyond a certain level of thinking and learning ... I could not have reached the level of learning that I achieved without learning from my partner and being aided in class support. (Laura USA)

One important principle throughout the module was that learning is social and that dialogue should be a fundamental part of the experience, and the theory of social learning was implemented as students worked together and learned in groups. An interactional learning environment was created for the whole student group but each student was also assigned to a study group of three different nations:

[W]orking in small groups in our class was an extremely effective way to learn from other people. For one, it gave everyone the possibility to speak what they were thinking, especially the ones who may be too shy to speak out in class. (Steven USA)

Working with people from other cultures, backgrounds and experiences was one of the most useful and interesting things we made, the fact that the working groups were mixed was a very good way of working because we could see and live what is real interculturalism. It made me realize the importance to understand the others and their own way of doing things. (Manuela, Spain)

These studies groups have really opened my eyes that sometimes you have to view situations from other people's culture perspectives rather than just assuming that my way is right. (James, UK)

To complement this social learning dimension, students were encouraged from the start to keep a personal diary to write down any observations and comments about their own reactions to what happened during the module. Keeping a dialogue with their own minds also created other opportunities to practice the theory of dialogic learning. To encourage them to do this task, which students often find a chore until it begins to work for them, they were made aware that there would be a personal reflection assignment at the end and that it is easy to forget small incidents which may be of use for the last assignment.

I took a look back through my journals and was very surprised to see how much I took notice to and learned every lecture. Even more of a surprise was how little I knew at the beginning. Truthfully, I do not think that I was completely ignorant to other cultures, but I never really gave it a second thought about how I would deal with it in my classroom or how I would teach others to acknowledge it. As my journals progress, I took more and more notice to everything and began to not only learn how to be aware and teach intercultural competence, but I also notice that I became aware of it out of the classroom. (Mary, USA)

Experiential learning in an intercultural learning environment

The great advantage of practising situated learning (Lave & Wenger, 1991) arose naturally as the students came from so many different countries which created an obvious intercultural learning environment.

To be able to discuss differences/similarities that exist among us instead of 'out there in the world' made everything feel so much more real and important somehow. To have these people in my everyday life did not only make the differences/similarities easier to see and real but also important to understand. (Karin, Sweden).

We had the possibility to interact with people from other cultures, that is to say, that we were in an intercultural context talking about interculturalism, and this fact helped me to work on.

Book knowledge is good, and in theory it will serve you well if you know the information and when it should be used. However, there is never any sort of substitute for the real thing. Learning about intercultural encounters in a classroom that is made up of a majority of American students who hail from, for the most part, the same general socio-economic backgrounds, is not the same as learning about intercultural encounters while you yourself are in fact living one. Before this class I knew that it was important to respect the cultures of others, but I was never able to really practice it as I have always studied in a relatively homogeneous environment. (Mark, USA)

I have been able to not only learn from my teacher, the assignments I was given and the experiences I have had, but I have become friends with my peers. Through these friendships I have learned more about intercultural encounters outside of the classroom then I could have ever imagined. I not only learned about it but I experienced it firsthand. (Laura, USA)

Participation, involvement and student activity

Apart from the benefits for learning there is another theoretical aspect to participation. Allport (1954) specified four conditions for optimal intergroup contact: equal group status within the situation, common goals, intergroup cooperation and support from 'authorities', e.g. in this case, the formal status of the module. All of these conditions were fulfilled in the module, and the students became aware of the significance of cooperation, participation, inclusion, common activity, involvement:

Another positive aspect on that activity (lesson plans) was that we were working cooperatively helping each other and trying to improve our activities all the time.

In my opinion, this is one of the best ways to work because it gives you the other's perspective and point of view and you are able to listen to it, think about it, make a reflection and change it. (Paloma, Spain)

I really enjoyed the methods of teaching and learning used in this module. I felt I learnt more through participation. (Anonymous evaluation)

Everyone was included, and no one was made to feel uncomfortable, participation was encouraged. (Anonymous evaluation)

Really good that we have been so active, this is what I have missed at other courses. (Anonymous evaluation)

I felt very involved within the class, and feel the presentations have raised my confidence considerably. (Anonymous evaluation)

Progression

The module was designed to create a progression through a variety of activities and the students gradually recognized this and the connection between learning critical skills and self-reflection resulting in critical action. One student, looking back at the assignments, reflects on his gradual insight into how easily we generalize and stereotype people without recognizing individual characteristics:

[My] initial reaction towards many of the assignments we have had during the course, (is) that they were a waste of time and that we discussed things that we already knew. Although, now that I have the whole picture and can look back at what we have done it feels like everything has been for a purpose. And I do not think that any of the assignments could be taken out of the course, because they all have their specific purpose. This purpose could be that we should learn new things, or merely that we as small groups with students from different countries should sit down and discuss in order to be more aware that the view we have as individuals might not be the view that a person from a different country has. Of course there are differences, but they have not been as big as I thought at the beginning of the course. (Karl, Sweden)

Some Teaching and Learning Procedures

One of the expected learning outcomes of the module was that the students would see their own knowledge and experiences as relevant to their future classrooms. The limited space of this chapter allows a closer look at only a few activities/assignments: the ABCs leading up to the cultural analysis, the mini ethnography, the school visits and the lesson ideas. These will be explained below. (For a list of all assignments and guidelines for a selection of them, see the Appendix). In the following sections, students talk about how they experienced these methods.

'This is me'

'This is me' was a student PowerPoint presentation to introduce oneself to the group (for guidelines see the Appendix). The activity was meant to serve several purposes: getting to know each other and bonding; becoming aware of what has had an impact on their lives and applying the theoretical concepts of ethnicity, social group and gender to something most people take for granted; illustrating similarities and differences within the group; and serving as the stepping stone to discussions.

This was a great activity to get to know everyone in the class on a deeper level. Everyone had such an interesting background. If it weren't for the presentations, we wouldn't have had the opportunity to know the class as well as we do now It made the class closer to each other and although we are from different cultures, many of us share the same experiences. It also showed the uniqueness of ourselves as well as others. (Carol, USA)

I was reflecting on my own ethnicity, social group and gender whilst completing my presentation and was unable to identify what these features had to do with me. Then it suddenly occurred to me that ethnicity, social group and gender has covertly played a very important part of my life. They have dictated how people treat me and how I treat other people. (James, UK)

Learning about yourself through the ABCs

The three steps of ABCs (Schmidt & Finkbeiner, 2006) are: (A) autobiography – writing an autobiography about yourself; (B) biography – interviewing the partner to write a biography about him/herself; and (C) cross-cultural analysis – comparing the autobiography of oneself with the biography about the partner. This last step entails exploring cultural differences and similarities (Finkbeiner, 2009) using a combination of the iceberg theory (Hall, 1981) and a Venn diagram displaying overlapping characteristics as well as differences. These and all other assignments were written at home and handed in during the module, and the guidelines for assignments mentioned in this chapter can be found in the Appendix (The ABCs Guidelines and Instructions).

Writing an autobiography opened my mind to how I actually live my life and how I perceive the world around me. I took time to look back at the paths I had taken leading up to this point and began to decode my decisions, this activity enabled me to evaluate what I have and why. (Alison, UK)

The autobiography made me understand more about my past. I found memories that I didn't know I had when working with that assignment. (Mark, USA)

This was a very hard activity because it required me to really dig down deep into my life. It was quite emotional thinking about the things I have been through already in my life. This activity really gave me a sense of who I am, both good and bad. (Carol, USA)

What I have learnt is that it does not matter if you know how others behave if you still do not know why or how to respond to it. I feel that I started there and that I am now slowly moving on a journey towards understanding. Parts of me just wish that the journey would have had started before my semester in England, since that would have made some things easier for me. … I guess I was aware since I noticed the differences and thought about them, but what I did not have was the tools to be able to understand them. To be aware of differences is not really worth much if you cannot understand them and still walk around looking like you have a question mark hanging over your head. The only thing the awareness created was confusion and cracks in my self-confidence. (Karin, Sweden) [This student was part of a two-year project, first one semester in England, then one in Sweden and finally two in the USA.]

The iceberg theory gave the students an analytical tool to understand things about themselves and others which at first sight are not obvious as they are 'below the surface', such as a person's values, beliefs and assumptions.

Mini ethnography

The aim of the mini ethnography was to find out what events 'are all about' from someone else's perspective rather than one's own. After a lecture and some reading the study groups spent half a day observing on a bus, in a coffee shop, in a library, at IKEA, etc. The choice was theirs. The expected outcome was to help them see the same events from different angles and thus make them aware of multiple perspectives.

Doing the ethnographic exercise early in the course, was for me a way of showing how to put theory into practice. I feel that this is not done often enough generally speaking. To me, not getting the chance to put words into practice will make them fall flat. Except for the pedagogic aspects of implementing theory, I hope I will carry the idea of note taking and note making into my profession. It is always easy to jump into conclusions on the grounds of behaviour of colleagues, pupils or a person you meet on the bus for that matter. (Olof, Sweden)

School visits

The students spent a whole day in small groups in a school, with one Swedish student in each group. They observed teaching in classes and interviewed teachers about the connection between theory and practice of democracy and internationalization in education.

Initially the Swedish students saw their role in this assignment as accompanying and helping the international students understand what was going on in the Swedish schools. They thought the visits would only benefit 'the others' as they themselves were so familiar with the educational system in theory and practice. However, they realized that their assumptions were wrong:

The school visit was a great experience in that my fellow students saw things from their perspective whereas I used my Swedish pair of glasses when doing observations.

Things that I took for granted, such as the very informal relations between teachers and pupils, were the focus of their attention. It is one thing to repeatedly discuss these differences in class, but another to actually have seen it in real life and experience it. (Olof, Sweden)

It was such a good experience to do the school visits with my international class-mates and it became possible for me to 'step out of my own shoes' and look at the Swedish school situation from an outside perspective. (Britta, Sweden)

Experiencing a familiar school situation together with a 'stranger' helped the Swedish students to de-centre and 'make the familiar strange'. They saw things 'from the outside' and from a different angle. In other words they used 'ethnographic eyes'.

Lesson ideas

The aim of this assignment was to promote the ability to apply intercultural competence theories in practice by developing practical ideas to implement in the classroom in interaction with colleagues. It was done in several steps: first, peer review of the lesson plans in study groups, then presentation in plenary with feedback from the whole peer group and the instructor and then individually writing up the plans and submitting them for assessment according to a rubric (see Lundgren, 2014).

One of the best parts of the course was when we all presented our lesson-plans and could inspire each other to work with cultural encounters and citizenship in our class-rooms. The practical tips that you collect as a teacher while you undergo your training is worth gold! (Britta, Sweden)

Doing this activity (it) was useful to be aware of what we had learnt during the course and it was a good way to put it into practice. (Paloma, Spain)

Evaluating the Effects of the Module

I turn now to an analysis of the effects of the module, to evaluation, by examining what students wrote for evidence of change, of learning, and how specific changes relate to the theories underpinning our project as outlined in the Introduction to this book.

Challenging common sense

Theories and models of intercultural competence refer to 'de-centring' and challenging the 'taken-for-granted' (e.g. Council of Europe, 2014), and to comparison and contrast in the sense of juxtaposition to highlight what is otherwise not noticed, and this was a fundamental aspect of the module. One such juxtaposition entailed comparing processes and conditions in society (attitudes to ethnic minorities) and in schools (teaching methods, ethos, teaching about world religions, language education) in students' different countries. Additionally, personal values such as attitudes to family, marriage, etc., were brought up spontaneously in seminar discussions, especially in connection with their presentations of the activity 'This is me' (see above). The students started to re-assess assumed normality and question what they earlier had taken for granted, at the same time as they began to indicate signs of 'respect for otherness' which is found in many models of intercultural competence (e.g. Council of Europe, 2014). The language they use often includes the key words and phrases which are frequent in the literature and which were part of the discourse of the module, a discourse which the students have adopted. From here I have highlighted the key phrases in the quotes and indented them to indicate that they are now being used as evaluation data:

> *I am seeing my whole concept of the culture I come from, including my traditions and how I perceive the world, changing as I go through this experience.* **What I once thought of as normal, I question**. *Being so far removed from my friends and family, I am also realizing what is most important to me.* (Barbara, USA)

> *During the course on intercultural encounters there have been many occasions where I have found out that* **what I take for granted may not be the same** *as what other people takes for granted.* (Karl, Sweden)

> *I have looked critically into my background and seen everyday values and traditions of my own that have been* **ingrained in me from such a young age** *that I didn't realise where I got them from.* (Jane, UK)

> *At first it was difficult not to dismiss the other group members' ideas in favor of my own, but I learned that I could actually learn from them and their ways of thinking. I really believe that this helped me develop a more thorough* **respect for the 'otherness'** *in my group and it helped me notice that my culture was not the 'natural' one.* (Steven, USA)

> *Participation in this course has allowed me to take a* **step back from what I consider normal** *and question all that makes me the person that I am. My culture, my religion, my morals are all definitions of who I am and where I come from. By discovering who I am through self-reflection, I can have a deeper* **respect for those of different backgrounds**. (Barbara, USA)

The quotes also serve to illustrate that students became aware of their own stereotypes and generalizations about others which are part of the relationship to otherness which, as Allport (1954) also pointed out, can lead to prejudice:

> *I think that those activities (ABCs) were the ones that made me realise most the importance to understand each other by means of dialogue and respect.*

Thanks to the interview with my partner I could **change some of the clichés** *that I had in relation American people and their culture and behaviours, and I am sure my partner learnt many things about Spain and our own culture and* **she changed her clichés too.** (Manuela. Spain)

I realised that I had a very closed perspective of the world and that only through meeting people in this manner was I **able to challenge stereotypes** *that I may have picked up during my life. In some way I feel that I have begun to use an ethnographic eye to try and question why I think in particular ways and for what reason do I believe things? This is a valuable tool for me to develop because it will help me as a student teacher.* (Eva. Sweden)

We can see then that students had not only begun to challenge some of their own assumptions but had also begun to think about the causes of this process. Eva for example refers to her 'ethnographic eye' and Manuela refers to the importance of 'dialogue and respect'.

Critical cultural awareness

Comparison and contrast lead to noticing and challenging what is taken-for-granted, and in Byram's model of intercultural competence this can and should lead to reflection in the evaluation which often takes place spontaneously, an evaluation of our own beliefs, values and behaviours, and the beliefs, values and behaviours of others. His definition of 'critical cultural awareness' emphasizes the importance of being conscious of one's own critical and moral standpoint (Byram, 1997). The following quotes indicate the stage of noticing and reflecting as a consequence of comparing, of 'listening to others':

I am an English citizen and am **now fully aware** *of traits in society that are unique to Britain. Many of these traits I* **was unconscious** *to as they are just part of everyday life, it is not until I left England that I noticed how different other cultures and customs can be.* **Through listening to others** *in my class I have learned so much about the differences in education systems around the world. This has encouraged me, as a teacher, to adapt my classroom in future to meet the needs of all pupils from all backgrounds.* (Jasmine, UK)

Mark takes the further step of a leap of imagination to consider the potential effects of the process of reaction.

It was interesting **to see how I behave** *and* **think about how I would have behaved** *if I lived in another country where attitudes, values and beliefs differ, and how they would have affected who I am as an individual.* (Mark, USA)

When Maria (Sweden) was interviewing John (USA), she learned that his family tried to discourage him from becoming a teacher at first. In the USA, it is a widely held belief that public school teachers do not make that much money in comparison to other jobs a person could get with a college degree. Maria asked why John's parents would discourage him from becoming a teacher, but if his sister wanted to, that would be fine. John now takes up Maria's perspective and sees his parents' actions as narrow-minded:

> *Looking back, this all seems so narrow-minded, but I never would have realized that if it had not been for Maria asking about how strange it was.* (John, USA)

In another exchange, Sandra analyses the origins of her beliefs and like John identifies the catalyst which created the new awareness:

> *This moment was another one of those times when I realized just how much my beliefs are **influenced by how my parents raised me**. … This way of thinking is **engrained in me** as a part of my culture, but I was not aware of this belief until **someone from outside** my culture discussed it with me.* (Sandra, USA)

'Critical cultural awareness' is one of the more difficult dimensions of intercultural competence to grasp but we see here how students see the significance of 'someone from outside my culture' as Sandra says, or 'listening to others', to use Jasmine's words, are the triggers for reflection on what is 'engrained'.

Developing new insights and identifications

One of the elements of the project as discussed in the Introduction to this book was to develop in learners an awareness of some of their social identities and the potential for adding new ones, in particular through international experience. A quotation from Alred *et al.* (2006: 234) was used to make this explicit on the wiki which guided the project: that education for intercultural citizenship should involve:

> emphasising becoming aware of one's existing identities and opening options for social identities additional to the national and regional etc. (e.g. the formation of perhaps temporary supranational group identities through interaction with others).

The following section reveals students' articulations in their reflections at the end of the course of how learners engaged in international groups develop new insights and identifications. The use of the ABC activity helped them think about the identification with family:

*This (the ABCs) has been the work which has tied me to the course and the course literature most personally since it involved a closer look at myself and my life. I must say that it has been an important part of the learning process and that the quote showed in the beginning when we talked about ABCs was something I got to understand the true meaning of: 'know thyself & understand others' – I have asked myself on numerous occasions 'why I am, like I am' thinking that it is because of the experiences I have had in my life. This is not wrong, but it was first when did my autobiography that I really sat down to think about the experiences I have had, especially my earlier ones. It **became so true, so absolutely obvious, that my family was the biggest and most important thing in my life** and that my vacation house has been and still is my 'happy place'. I just cannot see how I have missed this before, and for now having this insight I am thankful. I have learnt so much about myself.* (Karin, Sweden)

In the next quote, Rob links family and Christian values, and the metaphor of 'digging under the surface' is the indication of how his experience during the module had changed his understanding:

*My family was not really religious and I feel my life was not shaped by Christian values and the church played little part in my life whereas my interview partner had a deeply religious background and his life was shaped by Christian values and a connection with the church. **On closer inspection digging under the surface for the underlying cultural values** I discovered that the church did play a role in my upbringing and although unconsciously my life has been shaped by underlying Christian values. This was **a great surprise to me** but has made me more aware of looking at different cultures and backgrounds with a **more critical eye to find the underlying values beliefs and attitudes**.* (Rob, UK)

In the final sentence, we also see another example of critical cultural awareness. He has, like others, realized new things about himself with 'great surprise', and then goes on to see how this leads him to be critical (or analytical) in his experience of other people's values, beliefs and attitudes.

There is also an interesting further development. Because they will be teachers, they begin to think about the role of schooling in creating identities, and the example here is particularly revealing since James was led to deny one of his identities because of the teasing of other children who, he implies by his phrase 'which should have been expected', saw him as different as a consequence of their being schooled into an ethnocentric society and national identity, a widespread phenomenon which has been much analysed in the social psychological literature (Barrett, 2007):

Through listening to others people's presentations it made me aware just how much my culture has influenced my life and just how ignorant I was about other *cultures. … It made me **question why my own education** had not taught me about other cultures' traditions and celebrations. When I was younger I used to visit my dad's country, Malta, regularly. … When I was very young I remember telling my friends that I was Maltese and everyone would tease me **which should have been expected**. This teasing has lead me to deny my cultural heritage but as I am getting older I understand that being Maltese is not a negative but a really positive aspect of my life which I am starting to embrace with open arms. **I believe that classroom should embrace and celebrate other cultures, rather than being an ethnocentric society**. Although I do remember that we did learn about some cultures' celebrations the teacher should have utilised their biggest resources, the pupils. In our classroom we had pupils from Egypt, Italy, Poland, France and Maltese. I now understand that all pupils should be made aware and learn about other cultures and not just focused on England.* (James, UK)

The students acquired new insights about their own national educational values by critically evaluating their own and their classmates' experiences. As we can see in the comment below, this opened up the opportunity for students to re-evaluate their judgements and behaviours which might have been taken for granted before. Barbara criticizes her own society for lack of interest in global issues:

*Sweden, as well as Europe as a whole, realizes that internationalization is the solution for both global solidarity and international competition and this is expressed on a classroom level. I believe that **America should take note of these practices** … America's lack of interest when it comes to global issues not only reflects on its school systems but also reflects upon society as a whole.* (Barbara, USA)

James, quoted above with respect to his Maltese identity, takes the ideas further into the question of citizenship education and again it is evident how important juxtaposition and comparison and contrast is:

*[The course] 'Cultural encounters' has provided me with a new perspective of the current United Kingdom education system. I now believe that we should be constantly questioning and **changing not only the national curriculum but the schools in general**. I feel that **Citizenship should have a better position** inside our National curriculum and be embraced by the teachers. Every country has different values and views on education and **by constantly comparing and contrasting** ourselves to different countries can only provide us with a chance to improve our education system.* (James, UK)

It was this emphasis on citizenship which was fundamental to the project as explained in the Introduction to this book and it became evident in my work that the students began to see themselves as belonging to an international community, thinking critically and becoming conscious about working with people from other countries as we in the project hoped. One of the processes involved was the experience of multiple perspectives on their own countries and cultures, as can be seen in the comments below. It becomes clear that an 'international' community of communication was formed within the classroom, formulated with phrases such as 'global citizen' and ideas of shared global experience:

> *Intercultural Encounters not only allowed me to move outside my comfort zone, but it also **helped to grow as a global citizen**. No longer do I only focus on cultural aspects in the United States, but I also focus on cultural aspects from other countries.* (Margaret, USA)

> *Before this course, I had **never considered my role as a world citizen**. I defined myself as an **American college student from central Pennsylvania**. Looking at that now, that description is loaded with meaning. Cultural, moral, religious, ethical values and more are all aspects of who I am and where I come from. This is true of anyone, no matter where in the world they are from. Being taken out of my own culture to live in another has shown me the many different perspectives there are to have.* (Barbara, USA)

> *It was also good to see that **some things do not only happen to me** and that other people around the world regardless of where they come from still have to face **the same types of fears and challenges** throughout their lives.* (Mark, USA)

It is noticeable that these examples are from US American students, a point to which we shall return, but that Mark has his idiosyncratic view of this as a process of finding an identification which is a welcome alternative to identification with his own culture from which he felt himself to be an 'outcast'. His metaphor is of identification with 'family', an identity which had become salient in the ABC activity as we saw earlier, but is now re-interpreted:

> *Before this class I had friends from around the world. Now, because of the understanding of what it truly is to be multicultural and what the real meaning behind intercultural encounters is, this **class has given me family** from around the world. Before this class, I saw myself as an **outcast in my own culture**, but now I see myself just as someone who has beliefs that hold similar to those of another culture. Before this class, I could **analyze myself within my own culture but I had no idea how I would fit into other cultures**. These things are important, but they are not the most important thing this class has given to me. They are simply the building blocks. They have helped me grow.* (Mark, USA)

However, not all students cherished the idea of citizenship education beyond the national. A Singaporean student questioned the concept, and as he says there is a strong emphasis in education in Singapore on nation-building in a country which is only a few decades old. He sees the two identifications as mutually exclusive for the moment:

> Singapore **launched a national citizenship education** in December 2010 and to jump into world citizenship seems like a leap frog jump into the future. It may **be too hasty for us** to consider world citizenship when our national citizenship curriculum is not yet tested, isn't it? So it was not surprising that I was not very interested in what was being presented in the course, it all sounds so alien to me. Perhaps it's because **Singapore is a young nation**, still finding her footing in the world citizenship arena. We are still focused on creating Singaporeans who feel a sense of rootedness to Singapore and to **talk about world citizenship is premature**, at least that's my view. I guess Singapore will need world citizenship education, in time, and when the time is right, we will have to catch up with other nations such as Canada, which is well known for her curriculum. (Chay, Singapore)

The same student had a theory why citizenship education beyond the national is high on the agenda in Europe:

> I also learnt the difference between intercultural and multicultural, the former being a process and the latter being a state. It was something new to me. In Singapore, multiculturalism is the norm and we take it for granted. We are brought up in an environment, exposed to the different cultures and traditions; understand the difference and the reasons for those differences. However, I believe that intercultural(ism) is more **prominent in Europe because they are seeing a rapid influx of immigrants and minority communities.** I may be wrong, but that's my guess from what I have observed. Europe is still in a process of integrating their immigrants and many still have the stereotypes of their forefathers. **Whereas, in Singapore, we are exposed to friends and families from different cultures that we can be said to be 'colour blind' to race.** Although some may argue that Singapore still has some racist policies, such as tagging her citizens with 'race/ethnicity' on their identity cards, but I see this as a way for the government to ensure that we are all fully integrated and everyone is reaping the full benefits of the country's progress – by keeping a check on the different progress of her citizens by collecting racial-specific data. (Chay, Singapore)

His arguments are similar to those expressed in our study of educating for world citizenship in South Africa and India in comparison to Canada (Cappelle et al., 2011: 22), where we conclude that:

Education in general and citizenship education in particular has been invested with tremendous hopes. It is seen as a means to unite the disparate groups within the nation to address the social, economic and political challenges the countries faces and, importantly, to create a morally regenerated citizenry. Pivotal issues of national citizenship remain the top priority in these countries and until they are addressed wider questions of world citizenship will remain a less pressing concern.

Are Western educational aims (like those in Canada), such as intercultural citizenship education, considered a 'luxury' by countries who have to start by building a national identity? It is not possible to pursue this question here, and it is a different issue that cannot be dealt with in this chapter, but it has been introduced to show how a course like this can be interpreted differently depending on students' origins.

An international way of thinking and acting

The US American students especially seemed to undergo some sort of transformation of mind as was hoped in the project as a whole. One criterion in the documents provided on the project wiki states there should be 'emphasis on becoming conscious of working with Others (of a different group and culture) through (a) processes of comparison/juxtaposition and (b) communication in a language (L1 or L2/3/...), which influences perceptions and which emphasizes the importance of learners becoming conscious of multiple identities'. There was some evidence of the impact of the process of cooperative work and comparison and contrast as revealed by Mary and Mark, with emotive terms such as embarrassment and personal change:

> I am **embarrassed to say how little I knew** and how little I was aware of the rest of the world before studying abroad. I am scared to say that if I did not study abroad **I would still be ignorant** to the people of the world and how to deal with other cultures in class. (Mary, USA)

> In our class alone, there are six different nations represented. And because of that, since coming to University here, my own **personal knowledge** of intercultural encounters and what it really means to be a citizen of the world has **changed and grown drastically**, and with this knowledge, I have **changed as a person** as well. (Mark, USA)

One aim of the project was to encourage learners to become involved in their communities – both existing ones and those they might learn about through cooperative work – and to take action in the world as a consequence of citizenship education. In this case there is the extra dimension of the participants being themselves future teachers and they begin to think about their professional roles and potential influence on their learners:

> The assignment we had where we were to plan and present lesson activities was very helpful, both in aspects of getting inspiration and ideas but also in **realizing what citizenship education is and its importance in our society**. It not only helps the students increase their understanding, it also is a possibility to inspire them to make a difference! I find that very **encouraging for me as a teacher as well**. It brings another dimension of importance to the teaching job, **knowing what influence you have (or could have) as a teacher**. It is a thrilling thought that one can actually make a change. As James Banks (2001) put it: Multicultural citizenship education helps students learn 'how to change the world'. (Lisa, Sweden)

> I know that I have always had a strong personal interest in this area, but I haven't really regarded it as a responsibility in my future living up until now. I suppose one of the greatest things I have learned is the very fact that you will never be 'done' learning about yourself through others, and the other way around. Personally I find that to be one of the things that truly make life interesting! … As **teachers we have to raise an awareness of the fact that what we choose to do or who we choose to be, will affect people around us**. Not only people living in the same neighbourhood or going to the same school, but also worldwide. If I buy fair-trade coffee or any other product that isn't made in the local area, it will affect others than myself. (Lisa, Sweden)

As explained in the Introduction, this aspect of the project was based in part on Barnett's (1997) theory of criticality and action in the world, and aimed to put students in a position to act as an international group. The assignment at the end of the module, creating culturally responsive teaching plans, was as far as this five-week module could reach in terms of a new international way of acting. Ideally the students should have been given the chance to try out their ideas in real classrooms, then come back and discuss the outcomes. That was not possible, but it is clear that the students saw the potential for action and in some cases saw the relationship with citizenship courses which suggests that they were thinking critically about their discipline or, in Barnett's terms 'knowledge', and in particular how it can be mediated to children, i.e. the pedagogical task they have to change their university learning into what is accessible for young people:

> I have been able to **use my skills and theories to develop potential lessons** to show children how important diversity is in today's society. Not only did these lessons force me out of a comfort zone, creating plans for teaching a difficult concept to young children, but it also excited me about the future of my teaching. Knowing that through these lessons I could potentially make a difference in young children's perspectives of the world is **beyond anything I could have imagined for myself**. I anxiously **await the day I get to try out some of**

my lessons, and am convinced that by educating the young generation about global tolerance is a key factor in improving the world and how diversity is viewed. (Betty, USA)

*In the final part of the course we developed some culturally competent lesson activities. I really enjoyed this and **could connect them to my background of earlier Citizenship courses**. I developed five lesson activities with a citizenship theme. I was introduced to the concept of critical literacy. On reflection of this theory **I could connect it to many things I had learnt on my English module in my first year of University** in the UK. For example **I have learnt that it is important for children to develop a 'critical eye'** when they are reading any information whether it be in the media or books. My lesson activities included a lesson on stereotyping which shows how images and pictures can be seen in a certain light depending on what caption or what interpretation you have f the picture. **This will teach children not to stereotype individuals** and not to believe everything they hear about immigrants in the newspaper or other media. I have also learnt from the course that in my future teaching it is important to bring the children's lives, culture and backgrounds into the lesson. This will allow them to become more culturally competent and in doing so you are also teaching them to be responsible global and local citizens.* (Rob, UK)

The students' interest in critically reviewing their own knowledge is evident from their expressing a wish to learn more about intercultural issues and the implications for their professional lives. First they think about the academic treatment of the topic and how they need to expand their knowledge:

*I realized how interested I am in that subject area and I have recently decided that that is **going to be the topic of my thesis paper** for graduation.* (Laura, USA)

*And now I know what I would like to do later: **learn more** about different ethnicities, cultures and habits, discover the similarities and the differences. Lots of people think similarities that are good, but in my opinion differences are more exciting because if we meet people with different backgrounds we can **develop and learn new things** about the huge world.* (Emese, Hungary)

Then they go to the stage of critical thinking about the implications for their professional lives as Steven points out:

*I plan on working in an inner city American school and I know I will encounter students from a wide variety of cultures and I **will need an understanding of their cultures in order to hold cross cultural communications**. I plan on peeking my head off the side of Stier's Lighthouse and peering straight down in order to see the many cultures that I am surrounded in rather than looking elsewhere to find multiculturalism. I will also need to practice and maintain **intercultural** *competence in order to teach most effectively* and *if I want to learn from my students as well.* (Steven, USA).

The module also inspired students to do voluntary work and in this sense some reached the level of action in the world which Barnett posits as a desirable outcome of all (higher) education:

> *My group elaborated about unaccompanied asylum seeking refugee children, this is something I have found* **personal interest in since I started with homework for refugee children***. I come across an intercultural meeting there as well; these children are from Afghanistan and very new to the Swedish society. I think I can start see my progress more obvious now, some of the* **actions I have taken these weeks have a strong connection to intercultural,** *for instance the book Swedish, more Swedish, that I have joined Fair Trade group and* **started volunteering** *with them and then started having homework lesson with the refugee children. All this things have* **started during this course, and now I can see how this course has changed me***. (Ingrid, Sweden)

The question of 'acting' is important in this aspect of the course and its aims. What we see here is both an immediate action, such as Ingrid's volunteering and plans for future activities as teachers, to which Rob and Steven refer. The long term effects of the course cannot be all anticipated but there is certainly clear evidence of strong intentions

Analysing the relationship to criticality

In an attempt to apply a more systematic analysis of the way students were describing their course and how they responded to it, in terms of Barnett's three domains and four levels of criticality, I categorized some quotes from the students' reflections according to Barnett's grid – see below – and then asked other members of the Cultnet group (see book Introduction) at an annual seminar to do the same. Initially this was an attempt to carry out some testing of the rating in terms of inter-rater reliability. The result showed however that there was variation in categorization. Most quotes were highly complex, as in the following example:

> *Through the course the aspect I found most inspiring and potentially life changing was the study of Ethnography. I felt this topic made me see things from a completely different perspective, one I have never seen inside myself before. I had almost opened the glazed window that tainted my views and vision of the people and world around me.* (Alison, UK)

This was classified variously by the members of workshop as domain Knowledge (level 2, and 3). It was also placed under domain Self

Table 3.1 Alison's quote categorized according to Barnett's (1997) three domains and four levels of criticality

Levels of criticality	Domains Knowledge (Study of Ethnography)	Self	World
4. Transformatory critique		Overturning what has been taken for granted and developing something new: *'potentially life changing'* *'a perspective ... (which) I have never seen inside myself before'*	
3. Refashioning of traditions	Ethnographic method helps the student modify what she has accepted as common sense in knowledge	Modification of what has so far been accepted as common sense in oneself: *'made me see things from a completely different perspective'*	Modification of what has so far been accepted as common sense in what we do in the world: *'opened the glazed window that tainted my views and vision of the people and world around me'*
2. Reflexivity	Critical thinking	Self-reflection , the student has applied ethnography to her own life which makes her reflect on it	
1. Critical skills			Problem-solving
Forms of criticality	*Critical reason*	*Critical self-reflection*	*Critical action*

(levels 2–4). Finally domain World was referred to (levels 1 and 3), as can be seen in Table 3.1.

- *Domain Knowledge*: the student has learnt about ethnography which she applies to herself and to the world (second level) but doing this also leads to a change (third level).
- *Domain Self*: The student demonstrates critical self-reflection (second level), she modifies what she so far has accepted as 'common sense' in

herself (third level) and this change is radical and developing something new (fourth level).
- *Domain World*: The student evaluates the world around her (first level) and modifies what she so far has accepted as common sense in what we do in the world (third level).

The fact that some raters placed the quote in, for example, level 3 of the domain 'Self' while others put it in level 2, indicates agreement on the domain. What then seems to have happened is that some raters noted a phrase which they would categorize as level 3 and others did not pay attention to this. No doubt this was a matter of lack of time to train the raters in a short workshop, but it also raises the importance of teachers – in this case members of Cultnet – being able to realize the implications of what learners – the students in my module – are saying and doing.

The students in the module were themselves teachers who had, as we saw, the intention to bring their insights from the module into their lesson planning. What needs to be pursued in future modules or courses of this kind is how the students can themselves simultaneously think about how they as learners would categorize their learners' responses to their teaching.

Conclusions and Lessons Learnt

The purpose of this chapter, like others in this book, is to inspire and encourage others to develop similar approaches to their work, whether as teacher trainers as here or as teachers in different phases of education systems as in other chapters. In order to do so it is important to recognize the weaknesses and what needs to be developed in the future, and not to suggest that this module solves all the problems.

The main issues concern time, the previous disposition of the students, data collection and selection of data. The module was only five weeks. How much of a *sustainable* development can occur in such a short time that would last and not fade away? During these five weeks most of the students certainly seemed to have experienced how they learnt about ideas and theories that made them think about themselves and the world they live in. The data above prove that. Yet how much will remain in their minds when they are not required to apply this new knowledge to lesson activities and have left a mentored international peer group like this one?

Some students, as we have indicated in the analysis of their reflective texts, had already started their journey towards an intercultural mind, some had gone far and others had not even thought about intercultural competence and intercultural citizenship and the connection to their future profession.

Given that there is no such phenomenon as a complete and fully interculturally competent person, the move *towards* intercultural and international thinking and acting, which seems to have happened in the group, is a positive factor. I would claim that the students have increased this ability, each of them at their own level. On the other hand the data are drawn from assignments and 'required' reflections (handed in before grading) and the anonymous on-line course evaluation, and there may well be an element of 'social desirability' in their responses as well as a wish to give the teacher what she wants to hear. Furthermore, the quotes presented are inevitably taken out of their context as they have to be of a manageable size, and the selection has been made by the teacher and author of the chapter and it could well be criticized that there may be a personal interest in showing a picture of a successful course. This is a problem which all such curriculum development and action research has to face.

Perhaps more fundamental than these matters of methodology is the fact that the module also raised uncomfortable questions about values and identity where the teacher has to be aware of the risks she is taking. Some students were open about their feelings:

> *Living in a place that I am completely out of my comfort zone is **amazing, terrifying, exciting and humbling all at once** and I would suggest it to anyone. Personal experiences as well as taking classes such as this expand horizons.* (Barbara, USA)

However, we can take encouragement from Astrid who recognizes her insecurity but feels she is 'going forward':

> *The autobiography and the cross-cultural analysis helped me to take a look at myself and my values. But I still felt **insecure and uncomfortable**. Who am I really? What are my core values? What would I really be prepared to DO to defend these unprejudiced opinions that I so easily might express in words? What is my role as a teacher when it comes to questions about world citizenship and intercultural competence? These are **some of the questions that I have been forced to ask myself through the critical eye** during this course. I feel that I have some way yet to go before I can honestly pronounce myself a good world citizen, but this course has opened my eyes , and **I am going forward in a more aware state**, conscious of what I am doing and in which direction I want to go.* (Astrid, Sweden)

This suggests that, in spite of the challenge of uneasiness, uncomfortable feeling and self-criticism which follows from putting yourself and your values under the magnifying glass, this group of teacher students have given us some hope for future intercultural classrooms. I am extremely grateful to the students who gave me the opportunity to work with them. They created the combined conditions for dialogic intercultural learning: an intercultural learning environment, cooperation and reflexivity. Without their engagement, curiosity, openness and positive attitudes to learning more about the Other, themselves and their future work in the world, I would not have experienced that a course could open eyes.

References

Allport, G.W. (1954) *The Nature of Prejudice*. Reading, MA: Addison-Wesley.

Alred, G., Byram, M. and Fleming, M. (eds) (2006) *Education for Intercultural Citizenship: Concepts and Comparisons*. Clevedon: Multilingual Matters.

Bakhtin, M. (1986) *Speech Genres and Other Late Essays*. Austin, TX: University of Austin.

Barnett, R. (1997) *Higher Education; A Critical Business*. Buckingham: Open University Press.

Barrett, M. (2007) *Children's Knowledge, Beliefs and Feelings about Nations and National Groups*. Hove: Psychology Press.

Byram, M. (2006) Developing a concept of intercultural citizenship. In G. Alred, M. Byram and M. Fleming (eds) *Education for Intercultural Citizenship: Concepts and Comparisons*. Clevedon: Multilingual Matters.

Byram, M. (1997) *Teaching and Assessing Intercultural Communicative Competence*. Clevedon: Multilingual Matters.

Cappelle, G., Crippin, G. and Lundgren, U. (2011) World citizenship education and teacher training in a global context: Canada, India and South Africa. CiCe Guidelines, London Metropolitan University. See http://cice.londonmet.ac.uk (accessed 7 July 2016).

Council of Europe (2014) *Developing Intercultural Competence Through Education*. See https://book.coe.int/eur/en/pestalozzi-series/5872-developing-intercultural-competence-through-education-pestalozzi-series-no-3.html (accessed 7 July 2016).

Dysthe, O. (1993) Writing and talking to learn. A theory based interpretive study in three classrooms in the USA and Norway (Diss. Rapport no. 1APPUs skriftserie). Tromsö School of Languages and Literature, University of Tromsö.

Finkbeiner, C. (2009) Using 'human global positioning system' as a navigation tool to the hidden dimension of culture. In A. Feng, M. Byram and M. Fleming (eds) *Becoming Interculturally Competent through Education and Training* (pp. 151–173). Bristol: Multilingual Matters.

Finkbeiner, C. and Schmidt, P.R. (2006) Introduction: What is the ABC's of cultural understanding and communication? In P.R. Schmidt and C. Finkbeiner (eds) *The ABC's of Cultural Understanding and Communication: National and International Adaptations* (pp. 1–18). Greenwich CT: Information Age Publishing.

Finkbeiner, C. and Lazar, A. (eds) (2014) *Getting to Know Ourselves and Others Through the ABCs: A Journey Toward Intercultural Understanding*. Greenwich CT: Information Age.

Hall, E.T. (1981) *Beyond Culture*. Garden City, NY: Anchor.

Lave, J. and Wenger, E. (1991) *Situated Learning. Legitimate Peripheral Participation*. Cambridge: University of Cambridge Press.

Lundgren, U. (2014) ABCs as a tool for action in the world. In C. Finkbeiner and A. Lazar (eds) *Getting to Know Ourselves and Others Through the ABCs: A Journey Toward Intercultural Understanding*. Greenwich CT: Information Age.

Schmidt, P.R. and Finkbeiner, C. (eds) (2006) *The ABC's of Cultural Understanding and Communication: National and International Adaptations*. Greenwich, CT: Information Age.

Vygotsky, L.S. (1986) *Thought and Language*. Cambridge, MA: Harvard University Press.

Appendix

Learning 2 – Intercultural Encounters, 7.5 higher education credits

General information
The course Intercultural Encounters is given within the Teacher Education Programme, General Education Area, Learning 2.

The aims of the course are to equip the students with theoretical and practical tools for personal and professional development of competences demanded for teaching in a multicultural and internationalized society. Such specific competences are the knowledge, skills and attitudes which are required to engage actively with people from other ethnic, cultural, religious and linguistic backgrounds.

Intended learning outcomes
On successful completion of this module, the students will be able to:

- demonstrate their understanding of key concepts of the area;
- demonstrate respect for otherness;
- demonstrate acknowledgement of identities;
- demonstrate an ability to recognize different linguistic conventions;
- demonstrate an awareness of cultural specific and cultural general knowledge of their own culture and another culture different than their own;
- understand several theories related to intercultural competence;
- demonstrate the ability to utilize theories to analyse cultural differences;
- demonstrate the ability to apply intercultural competence theories in practice by developing practical ideas to implement in the classroom.

Course contents
This course will explore theoretical and practical aspects of intercultural understanding from an international perspective such as:

- The concepts of culture, multiculture and interculture; cultural awareness.
- The international and national basis for intercultural education.
- Ethnicity and identities.
- Attitudes, values, stereotypes and prejudice.
- Intercultural communication.
- Brief orientation about world religions and how values/believes influence behaviour, etc.
- Language and power, bilingualism and language support in schools.
- World citizenship education.

- Some political, economic and social issues related to ethnic minorities and refugees in a citizenship perspective.
- Cultural similarities and differences.
- Theoretical cultural models to analyse cultural differences.
- Cultural knowledge to improve classroom learning and communication.

Entrance qualifications
To be eligible for the course the student is required to have the equivalent of:

- 30 higher education credits in Learning 1 as well as in a subject area of 30 higher education credits or in equivalent courses.
- Good knowledge of written and spoken English (course language). For international non-native English speaking students a TEFL certificate is required.

Learning strategy
Individual and group tutorials and group discussions, practical exercises, seminars, lectures, independent and directed reading.

Assessment
The student is graded after Intercultural Encounters. The grades are based on continuous assessment of the active participation in discussions and group work as well as on written and verbal assignments.

As learning in the course is regarded as an interactive process together with peers the course activities are mandatory This means that student's absence from the studies has to be made up for after individual inquiry in negotiation with the course coordinator. The course coordinator is responsible for examination and grading.

Grading scale
The grades are Fail, Pass or Pass with distinction. For international students the Swedish grading scale will be transferred to ECTS (European Credit Transfer and Accumulation System).

Course evaluation
The course will be evaluated according to directions in The Education Plan for the Teacher Programme. The results of the evaluation will be communicated to student and will function as a guide for development of the course.

Students are required to fulfil the following activities and assignments as presented in seminars or submitted on Pingpong

No.	Title	Responsibility	Presentation	Date for presentation	Assessment
A1	**Autobiography**	Individual	Submitted on Pingpong (Pp)/ Contents	25 Jan	Presented according to instructions on Pingpong/ Contents = pass
A2	**This is me**	Individual	Presented orally in class and submitted on Pp/Discussion	27 Jan	See above
A3	**Biography**	Individually	Submitted on Pp/Contents	28 Jan	See above
A4	**Values in education**	In study groups	Seminar Submitted on Pp/Discussion	1 Feb	See above
A5	**Mini ethnography**	In study groups	Submitted on Pp/Discussion	2 Feb	See above
A6	**Ethnic minorities**	In groups	Seminar Submitted on Pp/Discussion	4 Feb	See above
A7	**Cross-cultural analysis**	Individually	Submitted on Pp/Contents	8 or 10 Feb	Graded
A8	**Intercultural communication**	In study groups	Seminar Submitted on Pp/Discussion	9 Feb	See above
A9	**World religions I**	In groups	Seminar Oral presentation	14 Feb	See above
A10	**Field study in schools**	In groups	Seminar Oral presentation	11 Feb	See above
A11	**World religions II**	Individually	Submitted individually on Pp/ Contents	22 Feb	Graded
A12	**World citizenship education**	In groups	Submitted on Pp/Discussion	15 Feb	See above
A13	**Lesson activities**	Individually and in study groups	Discussed in groups and submitted individually on Pp/ Seminar	23 Feb	Graded
A14	**Reflection on cultural encounters as a learning process**	Individually	Submitted individually on Pp/ Contents	25 Feb	Graded
A15	**Course evaluation**	Individually	Submitted individually on Pingpong	25 Feb	See above

Guidelines for activities/assignments mentioned in the chapter

The ABCs guidelines and instructions
1. Background Information
The ABCs Model of Intercultural Understanding and Communication (Schmidt & Finkbeiner, 2006) originally aims at exploring cultural and intercultural differences through a three-step process involving two individuals from two different backgrounds.

The ABCs involve three steps:

A: AUTOBIOGRAPHY
Writing an autobiography about yourself.
This is not shared with the partner but it is read by the professor/instructor only. The autobiography is an important step; however it will not be evaluated as we consider this part as an expression of your own self. It is seen as a piece of art you create about your own self.

You save it as AUTO-ULEUSEyour code number.

B: BIOGRAPHY
Interviewing the partner to write a biography about him/her.
The biography is another important step. It will be shared with the partner; it will be read by the professor/instructor.

The biography will not be evaluated as we consider this part as your expression about the other. It is seen as a piece of art you create about your unknown partner to better get to know him or her.

You save it as BIO-ULEUSEyour code number.

C: CROSS-CULTURAL ANALYSIS
Comparing the autobiography of oneself with the biography about the partner to explore cultural differences and similarities as well as self- and other-perception.
This is the academic part and this part will be 'evaluated' by the professor/instructor. Here you will also refer to the theories the ABCs are based on and to any further reading theories on the topic.

You save it as Ci and C2-ULEUSEyour code number. The last step (C3) is to produce five culturally responsive lesson ideas/activities which will be assessed according to a set rubric.

The ABCs Model in the context of our class
In this course we will explore intercultural similarities and differences in your life stories with respect to your everyday culture and life (both public and private). We want you to focus on life events that you remember and

that are relevant to you. Important: as soon as you remember these events they are relevant, otherwise you would not remember them.

GOAL: We would like you to become aware of your own background, and go back to earliest memories including family values, traditions, habits, religious beliefs, hobbies, vacations, successes and defeats, perceptions of your own self and of others, etc.

Using the ABCs Model in this way will aid you in better understanding yourself and the other (your partner, your students) as learner(s) as well as your colleagues and others. This will contribute to your development of strong diagnostic and intercultural skills, which will be an asset in diagnosing your future students' intercultural learning skills and difficulties.

GUIDELINES FOR A SELECTION OF THE ACTIVITIES/ASSIGNMENTS

Autobiography – writing about yourself. An individual activity (step A in the ABCs model)
Instructions
Before you start writing find a quiet place for yourself. Close your eyes for one or two minutes and try to remember your earliest childhood events. Focus on happy and positive events.
First make a list and write down the keywords that best describe your memories. Start with the earliest. You decide which ones you pick and which starting point you take. You do not have to start from birth. You start with the event you are most comfortable with writing about and sharing with your instructor.

Your stories can relate to your life as a small child or relate to later events. You only need to write down events you feel at ease with and you are willing to share with your instructor/professor.

You need to know you are safe as your data will be treated confidentially. The autobiography is only one step within your ABCs portfolio, and it will not be graded.

Expected length:
At least 3 pages one and half space Times New Roman but you can of course write more pages if you like.

Submit on Pingpong.

This is me – an individual activity. PowerPoint Presentation of Self

Aim:
Getting to know each other. To make a PowerPoint presentation of yourself is a follow-up on your Autobiography, which only the instructor had access to. Now you will introduce yourself to the group and be introduced to the others.

Instructions:
Try to analyse what has had an impact on your life, why you are the person you are. Of course it is up to you choose what you want to give away of your personal life. The presentation shall include:

- Maximum 7 slides.
- Oral presentation maximum 3 minutes.
- Cover 3 parts: ethnicity, social group and gender.
- Each category must reflect at least one personal experience:
  ○ Ethnicity – nationality-shared customs, beliefs, morals and traditions, personal experiences;
  ○ Social group – traditional heritage, socio-economic status, personal experiences;
  ○ Gender – (culturally constructed) roles, beliefs, personal experiences.
- You may include video, music, pictures, and narrative but feel free to choose.
- Videos can be captured on webcam.

Sources and presentation:
Your Autobiography.
Submit on Pingpong after oral presentation.

Biography – interviewing a partner to write a biography about him/her. An individual and paired activity (step B in the ABCs)

Aim:
The biography is the second step of the ABC model. This is a further step towards developing your cultural sensitivity after you have written A1, your Autobiography.

Instructions:
After three meetings with a person who is culturally different from yourself you will construct a biography from key events that this person has told you about her/his life. You will make two unstructured or semi-structured interviews and at a third session finally check it with your partner. In this course you will be allocated a peer as interviewee. In the future you may wish to interview a parent of a child in your class or let two students in your class interview each other. While interviewing take notes or if you prefer and if both of you agree it may be recorded. After the first interview you will start writing the biography, but will return to the interviewee twice more. For each time you will check with her/him things that you want to know more about, have missed out or are uncertain of to get a final product that the interviewee agrees to.

Try to think of this procedure as a cycle:

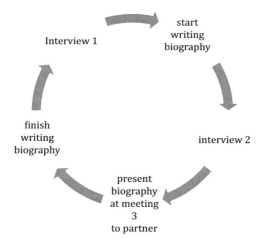

Our suggestion is as follows:

- Start by scheduling three sessions with your partner and decide if you shall use an audiotape or take notes.
- Meet in a neutral positive place; appreciate your partner's willingness to share his/her story.
- Start with some warm-up questions.
- Have more questions ready, but leave enough room for openness.
- Do not push, do not interfere, do not make your partner justify, just listen and be interested and friendly.
- Ask for example, this is really interesting, can you tell me more about this, how ….
- Once you have finished your first session, read your notes (or listen to the tapes and transcribe them or just most important parts); take the most important information, write down key words, and go through your notes (listen) again.
- Second session: Now follow up on the questions raised during the first session. The basic idea is to now have time for more substantial questions and answers, comments, reflections, and so on.
- After communicating with your partner as described above, you will write a biography about your partner based on the information he/she provided during the sessions.
- To conclude, you are going to review (check) the biography which you wrote about your partner. This will be done in the third session. Please follow these steps:
  - Provide your partner with the biography you wrote about him/her.

- ○ Ask: Does the 'life story' present his/her life in an appropriate way? Are there any misrepresentations or inaccuracies?
- ○ Ask: Are there any additional points that, from his/her point of view, that would be important or interesting to add?
- After communicating with your partner as described above, you will finish your biography about your partner based on the information he/she provided during the sessions. Save it on your computer. You will need the file for next step of the ABC's.

Expected length:
3 pages one and half space Times New Roman but you can of course write more pages if you like.

Cross-cultural analysis – Comparing autobiography and biography.
An individual activity.
(Step C in ABCs)

Aims:
- Performing a self-analysis of differences to become culturally aware of the connection between cultural expression versus values and attitudes.
- Creating a meta cognitive reflection of your own culture.

Instructions:
To start the comparison you need the following 'documents':
- Your own autobiography.
- The biography you wrote about your partner.

The actual assignment involves the following two steps:

Step I: Comparison
Compare your own autobiography with the biography you wrote about your partner.

Do you see any interesting similarities and differences in your partner's and your own life story? For example, are there similar or different experiences, events, or learning processes that were/are important in your lives? – Use the Iceberg Venn Diagram, two overlapping icebergs and write down **a list of similarities and differences**. Use this list for Step II.

Step II: Analysis
Now start thinking: in what respect, precisely, are these 'similar' experiences (really) similar, or how do they maybe differ after all?

On the other hand, are there any striking events or experiences ('critical incidents') in your partner's life story that would be unlikely to be part of your own life story? Or, are there any striking events, experiences or learning processes in your partner's life that, in all likelihood, would have a different meaning, relevance or impact in your own life? Do you see any connection to specific behaviour, values and believes.

Are there any differences or similarities which make you feel uncomfortable? Are there any similarities and differences that you admire?

Can you understand or explain why?
Refer to any relevant sources that you have come across in the course.

Expected length
Write down both steps and submit step C1 (about 2 pages) and step C2 (minimum 3 pages) on Pingpong.

Sources:
Finkbeiner and Schmidt (2006) What's the ABCs?
Iceberg Venn diagram in Finkbeiner (2009) Using 'Human Global Positioning system' as a Navigation Tool to the Hidden Dimension of Culture

Section 2

Teachers Cooperating

In Section 2 there are two chapters (Chapters 4 and 5) about 'Teachers cooperating', focusing on the introduction of intercultural citizenship education into the language classroom. Chapter 4 involves two teachers, Jessie Hsieh from Taiwan and Etsuko Yamada from Japan, who worked together to develop ideas about teaching intercultural citizenship. Two empirical studies in their own teaching contexts were conducted through action research. Learners with lower-level language proficiency participated in this project. In one case they were learning English (as a lingua franca in Taiwan) and in the other they were learning Japanese (in Japan, using English as a lingua franca when their competences in Japanese were not yet adequate for their needs). Again, the authors describe their project in practical details and show how their work was infused by theory, including Barnett's work, which had been presented as a basis for projects in this book.

Chapter 5 is also a cooperation project carried out by two teachers, Stephanie Ann Houghton from Japan and Mei Lan Huang from Taiwan, as in Chapter 4, but this time the learners at university level are using English as a lingua franca. In this case, the two groups of learners followed a common online course based on the Intercultural Dialogue Model, focusing on environmental action as one type of social action. The project focused on a systematic process of the analysis of self and other, through criticality and evaluation of self and other, and included reflection upon identity development. There is a close look at the learners' products – worksheets for example – to analyse the impact of the project.

In both chapters, the teachers conclude that there is opportunity for cooperation between student groups in the future after they have done the cooperation as teachers in their own context.

4 Beyond Language Barriers: Approaches to Developing Citizenship for Lower-level Language Classes

Etsuko Yamada and Jessie Hsieh

Introduction

An intercultural citizenship dimension in language education (Byram, 2008) can lead language education in a more suitable direction in accordance with contemporary changes in the world. However, there needs to be more discussion on 'how' to conduct such education in practice, and this chapter highlights the practical phase of the introduction of an intercultural citizenship dimension into language education. In particular, this study focuses on issues of citizenship for language learners/users with lower-level language proficiency (intermediate level at the highest).

One of the usual approaches to citizenship in language teaching is to introduce an intercultural citizenship dimension as a topic or content into language teaching, as is evident from other chapters in this book. However, such topics tend to become abstract, and suitable learners are assumed to be those who are already at a certain level of proficiency in the target language, such as intermediate- and advanced-level learners. For beginners'-level language teaching, it will be difficult to introduce this kind of topic unless a specific approach is taken, because of the level of grammatical structures and vocabulary required. So in this chapter effective intercultural citizenship education for beginners' level learners is discussed. It will lead to attention being paid to an essential concept of citizenship, 'social inclusion', which promotes the participation of learners in a community.

This chapter also expands the discussion to the issue of the ownership of languages. The goal of intercultural citizenship education in language education needs to be something that guarantees that anyone with any level of language skills can equally participate in a community. The disadvantage of 'lower language' skills can sometimes be a barrier and the right to participate should not be restricted by the language level he/she has.

Two empirical studies were conducted. The first was in a Japanese university for international students studying Japanese language, and the second in a Taiwanese university for local students learning English as a foreign language. Both groups of students were 'Basic Users' of their target language and would be described by the Common European Framework of Reference for Languages (CEFR) as learners at A2 level and below (Council of Europe, 2011: 24).

Transformation of Citizenship Education: From Exclusion to Social Inclusion

There are variations in citizenship education as a result of its transformation in the contemporary world and so, first of all, we need to make clear what kind of citizenship education was the aim of the two empirical studies in this chapter.

The origins of citizenship education, as described in Byram (2008), have been in various forms such as civic education in anglophone countries, or *politische Bildung* in Germany. The courses and purposes usually focus narrowly on the area and society they are based in, local and national. These kinds of citizenship education are particularly associated with national education that aims to foster national identification with a nation state. This also leads to a distinguishing inside–outside of the group and anyone outside of one's own group will be seen as alien.

However, we can see the transformation of citizenship education since the establishment of the European Union and after the Cold War. Instead of concentrating on each individual country, the focus has shifted to how to reinforce identification with a supra-national entity consisting of various countries and how to embrace people with different cultures and languages in a good balance. In a sense, the trend has shifted from 'exclusion' to 'inclusion'.

In accordance with global changes and the emergence of multicultural contexts everywhere, education for citizenship has thus become a focus in many countries and the traditional narrower focus on national education in each country needs to be revised with a new dimension in accordance with this tendency. The citizenship education developed in Europe, a transnational concept, offers a basis of citizenship education suitable for the globalized world (Byram, 2008).

Citizenships of a globalized world are named with nuances of difference, such as world citizenship, cosmopolitan citizenship and global citizenship. According to Oxfam (2006: 3), a Global Citizen is someone who:

- is aware of the wider world and has a sense of their own role as a world citizen;
- respects and values diversity;
- has an understanding of how the world works;
- is outraged by social injustice;
- participates in and contributes to the community at a range of levels from the local to the global;
- is willing to act to make the world a more sustainable place;
- takes responsibility for their actions.

Osler defines citizenship with an emphasis on democracy as follows:

Citizenship is essentially about belongings, about feeling secure and being in a position to exercise one's rights and responsibilities. Education for democratic citizenship therefore needs to address learners' identities and to promote and develop skills for communication and participation. (Osler, 2005: 4)

In a third perspective, Byram (2008: 157) also advocates that intercultural citizenship education be included specifically in foreign language education, 'by combining language education with political education as a response to internationalisation'. Foreign language education naturally needs to take into account a wider perspective than those which are assumed to be homogeneous entities such as schools, neighbourhoods or states/countries.

Furthermore, today's citizenship education can be more complicated in that the cultures and languages to be embraced in a society have diversity and the differences need to be respected. The sense of belonging of the people is not so clearly identified one-to-one as was assumed to be in nation-state based citizenship. A person can belong to more than one community or entity at the same time and can have multiple identities.

Inclusion is one of the key elements of the today's global citizenship; people are to be included in society. The Citizenship Foundation in the UK (2012) also asserts that 'citizenship education is about enabling people to make their own decisions and to take responsibility for their own lives and their communities' and the words 'action' and 'responsibility' are present throughout the literature, but above all, 'inclusion' in the society needs to be realized in citizenship education for a globalized world.

In Case Study 1 of this chapter, the small community in the classroom is a cosmopolitan space created by 'international' students – those who have come to Japan from many countries to study and are learning Japanese – and in this situation there are no native speakers of the language being learnt except the teacher. This reduces the power of the native speaker to a minimum since the teacher is aware of the issues and does not impose her native speaker authority. In Case Study 2, the target language, English, is not embedded in a particular national context used as an authority reference, and using English as a lingua franca puts the participants, the Taiwanese students, on an equal footing. Thus, the two empirical studies presented in this chapter were conducted as 'global citizenship education' in a context free of national or regional focus. The aim was inclusion in a globalized community and what is inferred from this study can provide an insight into the current discussion on global citizenship.

Citizenship and Language Education

Citizenship education that goes beyond national concerns was originally developed on the basis of the evolution of the community of the European Union (EU). It is interesting that the EU has stressed the importance of language issues in particular as a key to participate and to be included in the community.

> Proficiency in several Community [i.e. EU] languages has become a precondition if citizens of the European Union are to benefit from the occupational and personal opportunities open to them in the border-free single market.
>
> …
>
> Languages are also the key to knowing other people. Proficiency in languages helps to build up the feeling of being European with all its cultural wealth and diversity and of understanding between the citizens of Europe. (European Commission, 1995: 67)

Language means access to the community and therefore the European Commission decided to respect all the languages of the member states and to make all official documents available for people in the member states whatever their language. The Commission also set up the policy of 'one plus two' languages, which encourages everyone in the EU to acquire two languages of the community other than their own mother tongue.

The relationship between citizenship and language can also be seen in the following statement, where language learning for a globalized world is emphasized, not from the point of view of 'social inclusion', but as a marker for global citizens:

> Since these aspects of education are also central to language learning, language teachers are particularly well-placed to make a significant

contribution to education for democratic citizenship. Both language learning and learning for democratic citizenship within a globalised world imply openness to the other, respect for diversity and the development of a range of critical skills, including skills of intercultural evaluation. (Osler, 2005: 4)

It is interesting to see in Osler's definition that she mentions the importance of communication as well as participation and relates Education for Democratic Citizenship to language learning. In a sense, foreign language education has responded to the changing demands made by the global era such as the increased mobility of people and advanced technologies for communication. It is natural that the issue of Citizenship Education has been highlighted in relation to foreign language education, in which good communication and understanding of various values are essential in the interaction among people. As mentioned in the Introduction to this book, Byram's (2008) intercultural citizenship also overlaps with this point. Intercultural Citizenship thus cannot be separated from the issue of language education.

Language and Power

As mentioned above, EU policy tries to respect the languages of all the member states in terms of their value and equality. However, it is worth considering, how language users' equality can be realized in real contact situations. For example, it is doubtful if L2 learners of German language can discuss abstract topics with German native speakers without feeling a slight sense of being disadvantaged. It depends on the language level of the L2 learners, of course, but even if an L2 speaker of German has near-native proficiency level, s/he can still feel relatively powerless when interacting with native speakers. Thus, there can be a gap between policy documents and how they work in reality.

This challenge does not only occur between native speakers and non-native speakers. When participating in activities of a German-speaking community, for example, a beginner-level German language learner would usually feel more difficulty in participating in the life of the community than more advanced-level learners. Discussions of the different linguistic levels of the learners with respect to developing an intercultural citizenship dimension in language education need to be further developed than is often the case, and practical approaches suitable for each level need to be assured, so that the citizenship dimension introduced into language education realizes the principle of 'inclusion' of citizenship.

In addition, it can be helpful to think about the issue of English language teaching for non-native speakers (ELT), since English has established its position as the most useful language for communication among people with different backgrounds in this globalized world.

Hsieh (2009: 59) argues that ELT with an intercultural approach leads to the issue of language ownership/native-speakership. The question of who 'owns' English in the contemporary world where there are more non-native than native speakers (Crystal, 2006) cannot be decided on linguistic grounds. On the other hand, an intercultural perspective focuses on the use of English as a sign of willingness to develop relationships, and in that sense anyone who uses it 'owns' it. It is thus more than a medium for communication. This view leads to an appreciation of English language learners' authority in selecting, creating and re-creating in their use of English and Kramsch (1998: 31) refers to this as 'individual responsibility in the use of words and in the ownership of their meanings'.

If intercultural citizenship is the focus of language education, we need to examine carefully this question of ownership and the right of learners to use English for their own purposes. This leads to analysis of what approaches can be effective, how they can be dealt with in actual classroom teaching, and whether the approaches have to be different according to the learners' linguistic levels.

Language Education with Content or Content-based Education Considering Levels of Language Competence?

In the discussion of citizenship education in language classes, there often seems to be an assumption that the targets are to be intermediate- to advanced-level language learners. The approach becomes content-based and the learners need to have a certain level of grammar and vocabulary knowledge, in order to understand abstract issues and express their own thoughts in the discussion in a meaningful way. Indeed, if a citizenship dimension is to be introduced in language education, it will automatically be content-based teaching even if the language education has to follow a framework with the primary focus on linguistic aspects, such as a grammatical structure-based syllabus.

The question then arises with learners with lower levels of language competence, whether we can expect to follow the same approach. The outstanding feature of much beginners' level language study is the steady introduction of new grammatical structures in cumulative progress. Such is the tradition in the contexts of our two case studies with university students, i.e. adult learners. In intermediate and advanced levels, the clear cumulative progress of linguistic structures fades away and is replaced by the introduction of more advanced-level expressions and vocabulary related to the topic of materials being used. A topic-based approach can also be applied to beginners' courses but it is hard to deal with abstract social issues as is necessary for citizenship education. Topics for beginners usually tend to be confined to simple daily issues and therefore vocabulary and grammar structures are limited to concrete and non-abstract matters.

It is thus important to consider the role of content in the language education, particularly for beginners' levels, how 'content' should be located. What is the limitation of content for the beginners' level? Byram (2009) refers to CLIL (Content and Language Integrated Learning) developed in language education in Europe and suggests how to apply it to intercultural citizenship in foreign language education. CLIL puts emphasis on combining the four elements – content, communication, cognition and culture – and integrates them into language education. According to Byram, intercultural citizenship in foreign language education needs to include the following components:

- learning more about one's own country by comparison;
- learning more about 'otherness' in one's own country (especially linguistic/ethnic minorities);
- becoming involved in activity outside school;
- making class-to-class links to compare and act on a topic in two or more countries (Byram, 2009: 71).

In a sense, the above is a clue to aligning language education with intercultural citizenship. However, we can still see the assumption of targeting content-based intermediate- to advanced-level language education. How can this be integrated in beginner-level language teaching which is characterized by steady progression of grammatical structures? In practice, it is hard to draw a line between language teaching and content-based teaching, and it will be an issue of language first or content first.

In both of the case studies introduced here, we took the approach of 'content first' and we were interested in how to deal with the limitation of language within the content. This is then a kind of content-based language teaching of CLIL for lower-level language learners, although the two situations are different.

Two Case Studies

The two case studies were conducted separately in different countries but both of them sought the skills to manage education for intercultural citizenship for lower-level language learners. The first case study led by Yamada is the teaching of beginner-level Japanese language learners in Japan and the second case study led by Hsieh in Taiwan is for the local students learning English as a foreign language.

Both case studies were designed according to three points:

(1) intercultural citizenship (which is not embedded with a particular national context) was the focus;

(2)   a content-based approach for lower level language learners was taken;
(3)   the empirical studies were designed as Action Research.

We had a common agenda, and although the target learners and the countries of residents are different, we did not make any more adjustments than necessary, to follow our common agenda. The research was planned so that it fitted into the existing teaching environment that each of us had, since this natural setting is considered an important factor for Action Research with qualitative data (LeCompte & Preissle, 1993; Miles & Huberman, 1994).

The case studies set out to answer the following two research questions.

(1)   What approach is feasible to deal with citizenship for a lower level language class?
(2)   How can we allow learners, in particular, lower level language learners, to take 'ownership' of language?

Case Study 1 by Yamada in Japan

Context

This action research project was conducted in a mixed nationality class of a Japanese university from September 2012 to January 2013. The course, entitled 'Japanese Culture and Society', was offered for international exchange students from all over the world. In the semester of data collection, a total of six students from the USA, Indonesia, Spain and Brazil participated. They were studying in the Japanese university for one year, and were all aged 20 or 21. In this course, the principle of language use was 'beginner's level Japanese with a supplementary use of English'.

The course dealt with general topics in current Japanese society, such as education, environmental issues, family, geography, shops, etc. As the course was characterized as a content-based course and not a language class, communication through the target language was not the focus but the basic information on the above topics was presented in beginner-level Japanese that the learners could understand. Only when the communication became complicated did they tend to switch to English as the other lingua franca. This was often the case when it came to discussions.

The typical way of dealing with each topic was that the students were not only given information, but they were asked to consider the same topics as they occurred in their own countries, and to compare and contrast them with Japan. Through this process of objectifying the target information, they examined the reality in Japan more deeply. The goal was to help students to evaluate critically their own, as well as the target culture.

Although, the data presented in this chapter are all in English, the activities in the classroom were mostly conducted in Japanese. In other words, what the data in English show are the indications that many thoughts were developed in their mind while being engaged in the activities in beginner-level Japanese.

The data were collected from the students throughout one semester. They were the students' output type data (the reflection papers assigned after every session, projects and a follow-up group interview). These parts were conducted in English, as they were considered as the main source of analysis in this research and the priority was to gain outputs in a language in which they had high competence. Usual ethical procedures were followed and all the students provided their consent for the data to be used. A teacher's diary was also kept. The data were analysed using qualitative data analysis methods, as in Strauss and Corbin (1998, 12): 'Theory derived from data is more likely to resemble the "reality" than is theory derived by putting together a series of concepts based on experience or solely through speculation (how one thinks things ought to work)'. Distinctive keywords, i.e. words which appear repeatedly in the students' reflection comments, were the focus of analysis, as explained later.

A sample of the teaching design: Higher education in Japan

Although the data were collected from the students throughout one semester and several topics were dealt with, here, the focus will be mainly on one topic, *higher education in Japan.* The reason is, that in comparison with other topics, this one was an excellent opportunity to illustrate a clear transition from an 'intercultural dimension' to 'intercultural citizenship', and the data clearly indicated the difference between the two. Altogether, three sessions dealt with higher education in Japan.

The first session started with providing basic information about the general education system including compulsory education in Japan. The information on the countries where the students were from was also presented and compared by the students themselves. Then, the higher education system in each country was focused on, and entrance procedures, specializations, duration of the study, national/private systems, etc., were presented and compared between different countries. Through these comparisons, students did not gain simply information about the Japanese system but also knowledge about other countries and began to think about the assumptions behind these systems.

For the second session, students were asked to conduct a survey (as their homework assignment) among other students in the university about who pays the costs of education and how much. They were to ask two Japanese students and two international students of different nationalities. The purpose was to bring more cases to examine into the classroom, since, apart from Japan, there were only four country cases to discuss in the class. As a result of this homework assignment, we could add cases from Germany, France, Mexico, Finland, Vietnam and Spain.

In the third session, the education cost issue was the main focus and we tried to investigate the cause of differences in different countries' systems more deeply. The teacher introduced the case of the UK, where the gradual introduction of a tuition fee system led to a significant rise in fees in UK universities from the 1990s to the present. The educational statistics of OECD countries (OECD, 2011) on the proportion of GDP spent on education were also shown. The students discovered that the Japanese government's contribution to the education sector is actually the lowest among OECD countries. It was indicated as one of the causes of the high cost of education in Japan.

In fact, we were all surprised by the differences of various kinds among the countries. In Japan, students can usually take only one specialization (major) for a BA degree but in other countries, students can take three or four specializations and combine them. When the issue of tuition fees was investigated, we were all surprised by the difference between the very high tuition fees of private universities in the USA and the systems that do not charge any tuition fee at all, and where in addition, students can get grants to be able to concentrate on their studies, as for example in Finland and Brazil.

When the course was designed, it aimed to illustrate the differences among the situations in education and social problems related to education. By bringing in the issue of tuition fee system, the objective was to highlight the issue of 'equality of opportunity for education'. In fact, exactly as intended, the data gathered by students reflected the differences as we shall see below.

Data analysis

Students were asked to write reflections after every session. These reflections became the major source of indicating the differences which appeared in each phase of the teaching described above. During the data analysis process, there are specific keywords/expressions that students often use according to each stage.

After the first session:

Interesting that some new information I got from today's class is every country has their own management on educational system. (Data-1)

Today was somewhat different in that I learned something new about my own country. In comparing the tuition costs that we went over today, I was somewhat surprised to learn that within this group, the tuition costs in the US was most expensive. Going to class today, I was actually expecting Japan's tuition costs to be more expensive. (Data-2)

It is interesting to see the difference between the costs of public and private universities around the world, so that it brings out the problem of who has to be in charge of the payments: parents, university or government. (Data-3)

Keywords such as 'interesting' and 'surprised' appear frequently at this stage. However, from the next phase of the second session when tuition fee issues were introduced, other keywords started appearing. Words such as 'I wonder' and 'why' indicating that they are in the process of thinking, can be seen:

> It makes me <u>wonder why</u> we have to pay so much in America. I think because the school just wants to make money instead of focusing on education. (Data-4)

The above indicates that the student has not made a judgement on this issue, yet. However, maybe after this thinking process, they reach certain kinds of judgements.

> Maybe <u>UK system is good</u> in stimulating more students to be responsible for their education, instead of leaving all to the parents' effort. (Data-5)

> I don't have to pay for my education, as free education and health is the right for everyone in Brazil. It is a <u>good system</u> and I am proud of it. (Data-6)

Then, after the third session, they started searching for a better solution, which shows their belief that action in society is necessary.

> <u>The ideal system of</u> financial aid is grant because it will help the students completely, instead of worried about their education fees, they can focus on their studies in order to achieve the best result in their bachelor degree. (Data-7)

> <u>My country should change</u> their way of educational system, like make the tuition fee free and more helping the poor students, so everyone can have appropriate education. (Data-8)

In the next case, the student recognizes that action in society can follow from the insights they are acquiring:

> In terms of students' behaviour, many college students in the US are very opinionated and aware of the global issues. In this way, protests are very common in the US, especially about such issues (Ex. tuition costs rising) that directly affects the students. (Data-9)

The next two statements are from a follow-up interview after all the sessions were completed. In the data, it is clear that a 'sense of responsibility' towards their roles, an important element of citizenship, had developed:

> a lot of Americans don't think they have roles in the society – they think what can they do for themselves in the society – how can they use the society for themselves – now I'd like to have a role making a relation

between the countries – that more Americans are aware of the Japanese perspectives and the way of thinking so I like to educate them more about outside world. (Data-10)

my role – these exchanges of cultures – what other countries can learn from Japan and what Japanese can learn from other cultures – there is no better society – all of them have their positive and negative sides – these exchanges of cultures can be effective. (Data-11)

These data clearly indicate the change in the students' attitudes before and after the course. While the session was still dealing with the different situations of education in each country, their reactions were represented by finding something 'interesting' and being 'surprised', as if they were just spectators. But once the social contradictions were highlighted by the comparison of the higher education tuition fee systems, their critical thinking process was indicated by words such as 'wonder' and 'why'. Then, through the judgemental stage, they begin to search for an ideal way. Thinking back to the principle of citizenship, the basic concept is 'inclusion and participation', and they are followed by the concepts 'action' and 'responsibility'. We marked those expressions as the appearance of their intention to take action, although they did not reach the stage of taking real immediate action.

Case Study 2 by Hsieh in Taiwan

Context

In this case too, an action research project was conducted, this time in a semi-compulsory English class of a Taiwanese university in Taiwan from September 2012 to January 2013, during a total of 18 weeks in a three-academic-unit course entitled 'English for Graduate Students'. By referring to the course as 'semi-compulsory', we mean it was offered as a waiver for graduate students who did not meet the passing standard of the intermediate level of the General English Proficiency Test, which is one of the criteria for graduation. Students' level of English language in the course was thus beginner to lower-intermediate, as corresponded to CEFR A2 level and below. The class consisted of 41 graduate students with majors in different areas of Arts such as dance, drama, media, music, visual design; 40 were local Taiwanese students and one was from Malaysia. The average age of the students was around 25 and ranged from 23 to 45 years old. The ratio of female to male students was 3:1.

It is worth mentioning that English in Taiwan has long been regarded as a 'prestigious' foreign language and a passport to the world and economic competitiveness (Chen & Hsieh, 2011; Hsieh, 2009). According to Hsieh (2009: 28), under such circumstances, a fluent English speaker or a native speaker usually holds a superior image in the society. In contrast, people with low English proficiency, such as the students in this case, tend to regard themselves as 'inferior' or 'incapable' not only in English classrooms but also on occasions where English is used as a lingua franca. Thus, to achieve the goal of intercultural citizenship, the teacher deliberately taught 'English as an Intercultural Language' (EIcL). This means that English is not a language of a foreign (national) culture but a language to know about 'our' culture and 'other' culture. In other words, the language taught in the class was not native speaker centric but culture centred. We shall come back to this issue later in the language ownership section.

The course followed the same principle of focusing on content and CLIL (Byram, 2009) as that led by Yamada. A lower-intermediate level ELT textbook *Attitude 3* (Fuscoe *et al.*, 2007), published by Macmillan, was selected and used as a foundation resource book. The topics covered included peoples, cultures and world Englishes and touched upon issues related to groups, families, food and drink, social customs, festivals, traditions, cross-cultural awareness and world languages. The textbook was also useful for providing exercises and assessment of the selected topics in reading, writing, listening and speaking.

Both English and Mandarin Chinese were used for instruction and in-class communication. Although Mandarin Chinese was not necessarily the mother tongue of all students – some of whom had Taiwanese Chinese as their first language – it served as a lingua franca and a transitional language. In class, students were asked to use English for designated tasks or assignments, but were allowed to use Chinese for raising questions, explaining ideas and clarifying complex concepts, in short achieving efficient group discussions. As the semester went on, the teacher gradually increased the percentage of English usage from 50 to over 75%.

The course design

Taking Byram's (1997: 34, 73) intercultural communicative competence (ICC) model as the course design framework and assessment indicator, the course was divided into two main learning activities – 'language foundation build-up' and 'intercultural encounters' – which took place in the classroom and through fieldwork and independent learning. The course aims were explicitly introduced to the students as: (a) learning English through culture learning; (b) using English (EIcL) as a global lingua franca; (c) developing critical thinking skills through reading, writing and oral practices; and (d) developing characteristics as world/intercultural citizens.

Therefore, two domains of cultural content were deliberately brought into different learning locations. One included the introduction of principles and concepts of IC and EIcL. This domain of content was provided mostly through lectures and discussions on topics relating to IC and EIcL in the textbook and supplementary materials provided. The other domain of content was the 'organics' of all course activities, i.e. the content was not arranged in advance but expected to be generated 'organically' by participants in intercultural encounters and interactions.

The language foundation buildup was essential for providing the students with the required language skills and laying the ground work for their participation in later Intercultural Encounter Activities (IEAs). Four textbook topics were selected, namely 'People', 'Culture', 'Food and Drink' and 'World Englishes', as a means of preparing the students' knowledge of vocabulary, sentence usages, and grammar rules to engage in CLIL activities throughout the semester. In addition, the lessons were also intended to enable the students to acquire key concepts relating to IC and EIcL. Thus, the textbook was used as a medium/ guidebook to provide a foundation of the contents of the IEAs.

Two major IEAs were organized. The first was a visit to Ping-Ling, a renowned Taiwan tea production village near Taipei metropolitan area; this was our 'fieldwork'. It gave the students a chance to go out of the classroom and explore 'our/Chinese-heritage' culture of tea drinking, the local tea industry and people who make their living from tea. A group of 40 international students who were studying in an Executive Master of Business Administration programme of another Taiwanese University also joined this event. Thus, the students had opportunities to interact with 'others' using English as an International Language (EIL) and to observe how 'others' perceived the local culture. Although the students used the local language, Chinese, to interact with people in Ping-Ling, they were required to write their personal reflection about the trip in English. In this way, they had to process their thoughts in two languages and to strive to express their reflections in another language, EIcL in this case.

'Meeting Mena the Ghanaian' was the IEA implemented throughout the second half of the semester. It was a complete process of ICC learning in which the students got to experience and explore another culture in different learning contexts. It was, too, a continuous intercultural activity in the sense that they built up personal relationships with the invited guest speaker, Mena, who came from Ghana and had been living in Taiwan for more than 15 years.

The activity started with an independent learning assignment. In groups of five, the students were first given some weeks to investigate different aspects of the cultural background of their new friend-to-be Mena. Next, they were asked to present their research results and observations in the class. After the group presentations, all of the students had gained some general knowledge about Ghana, a place they had not been familiar with at all previously. They were asked to compare and contrast Ghanaian and Taiwanese culture. After that, they had to come up with questions for Mena regarding her home culture and her impressions and adaptation of Taiwanese culture.

Then it was time to meet Mena in person. Mena arrived in her Ghanaian traditional dress and brought her one-year-old baby girl, Ameera, with her. She used one hour each to tell about her own cultural background and her story of living in Taiwan. Afterwards, the students asked Mena either questions they had prepared earlier or ones that just occurred to them as they listened. Except for some specific Taiwanese terms, Mena and the students used only English as a lingua franca for communication.

The week after meeting Mena, the students were asked to compare what they had presented about Ghana with what Mena told them. The students were amazed by the gap between the two. A discussion of the causes of the phenomenon was then held. After that, they were asked to identify/recall challenges Mena had come across while living in Taiwan. As an African Muslim, she had come up against many difficulties and inconveniences in her everyday life. Amongst the various concerns, the students were concerned about new immigrant issues related to racism, access to childcare and children's education, health care, lack of social interaction and lack of equality of treatment in everyday living.

According to Byram (2003, 2008: 157), as a response to internationalization, instead of socializing people into an international identity, education for intercultural citizenship focuses on enabling learners to act sensibly in and across political entities, at whatever level. Hence, in groups, the students were asked to come up with their own problem-solving civic action plans for their 'new immigrant' friend, Mena, as the course's final project. This exercise was a thought experiment for the students but it was hoped that it would encourage them to carry out more 'actions' of intercultural citizenship/savoir s'engager (Byram, 1997) in the future.

The proposals made by the students addressed problems specifically relevant to Mena's everyday life challenges. The action plans covered issues of shopping for halal food, adaptation to Taiwanese food, acquisition of a local driving licence, intercultural communication and respect in the community, equal access to children's education and a need for a new-immigrant-friendly standard operating procedure in the healthcare system.

Data analysis

Usual ethical procedures were conducted at the beginning of the course: all 41 students provided their consent to their data being used. The data collected throughout the semester included students' learning journals, in-class assignments, anonymous post-course questionnaires and the teacher's diary. As the nature of action research is interpretive and qualitative, the data were analysed 'appropriately' (Holliday, 2002: 69) in attempts to answer the two research questions agreed between the two teacher-researchers and stated above.

The first research question – 'What approach is feasible to deal with citizenship for a lower level language class?' – requires evidence of feasibility by which we refer not only to whether the students achieve the goals set by the teacher but also whether they are positively disposed to the lesson content and purposes. The post-course questionnaires in Chinese and translated here for convenience, serve as the main source of indicating the desirability and feasibility of the teaching approach.

Generally speaking, the course received very positive evaluations from all of the students. The keywords that stand out are 'interesting', 'interacting', 'multiple means and methods' and 'practical/close to our daily life'. Some of the students explicitly expressed their appreciation of the cultural content and the two main activities provided in the course.

> The course not only provided language knowledge but also integrated cultural issues for discussions. I personally think the approach helped us not only to gain the language proficiency but also connect us to the world culture. (Data-12)

> This is not a regular English course. The teacher used the approaches close to our daily life, e.g. a field trip and an encounter with a foreigner. We were then given chances to deal with and investigate real problems. That is the key making this course much more interesting. We were also able to walk out of our comfort zone. (Data-13)

These data clearly indicate the change of the students' attitude and concept towards language learning and their increase awareness of becoming an 'intercultural speaker' (Kramsch, 1998). Moreover, 92% of the students agreed that the teaching approach helped them become more aware of self, others and the practice of citizenship. Although not every student would like to take an active role in civic actions in the future, they have their own ways of participating in the society. For example, in answer to the questions, 'After this course, would you be more active in civic engagement? If you would, in what ways?', the following responses were given:

> Yes. I think it is the most practical to just start being aware of and following civic issues. This is how I would like to participate in society at the moment. (Data-14)

> Well, yes. Though I am not that kind of person who is interested in politics/social issues. However, I think it is very important for citizens to take actions. I might start exercising my citizenship online. (Data-15)

> Maybe. In the past I used to understand some civic movements only with limited points of view, without investigating social issues in depth. Most of the time I just acted like a 'headless fly' and followed others like a blind person. In the future, I would like to learn more perspectives on issues. (Data-16)

> As an artist, I would like to think more proactively in how to participate in civic movement by applying art. (Data-17)

The above comments indicate that they did think thoroughly about citizens' participation, and made decisions on action based on their own circumstances.

The following two data were from the students amongst a few who kept most of their learning journals in English. In their journals, they illustrated how they used the language with confidence in recording classroom activities. Interestingly the passage below also illustrates how they form different identities of 'we' through recognizing self and other in different contexts:

> This week's article is interesting and easy to read. It's about social customs in Taiwan. In our group, we have someone came from south of Taiwan and someone is Hakka. We found that even *we all live in Taiwan*, but we have a little *but different social customs between us*. Because we come from the different area and different ethnic groups. It's very interesting to know many kinds of social customs. (Data-18; emphasis added.)

Here the distinctions are within Taiwan and 'we the Taiwanese', in 'our group' are seen to be much varied within the group, whereas in the following quotation, the presence of a Ghanaian means that 'we' refers to 'we the Taiwanese' because of the contrast:

> This class our teacher invited her friend Mena who from Ghana to make a speech. She introduced her country about geography, history, culture, food. We had a report last week so *we can understand what she said all of English*. But we still find a wrong information from Internet. Ghana is a beautiful place. It's very nature, simple. She said *Taiwanese* usually afraid of speak English because *we are scared to make a mistake*. I agree that. Before I went to 'Wall Street' (cram school) learning English, I also too. But when I grow I go abroad, meet a foreign friend, I have to speak a lot, so practice is very effect! (Data-19; emphasis added.)

The text below with { } shows an example of the words the student created and a sense of confidence and ownership of English, and an indication that this beginner learner was beginning to use EIL on their own responsibility:

> Every weeks write this journal. I feel {better than better}. But I still need the {'Google' help}. We talk about our social customs, it's interesting to talk over these {everyday around us}. We thought these {general} things but it's {uncommon} with foreigner. (Data 20)

Discussion: Sequential Stages Towards Action

We now turn to what can be inferred from the two case studies and examined in relation to academic theories.

One of the most widely referenced accounts of intercultural competence is that established by Byram (1997). The key element in his ICC is 'critical cultural awareness', which is defined as 'an ability to evaluate critically and on the basis of explicit criteria, perspectives, practices and products in one's own and other cultures and countries' (Byram, 1997: 53). The intercultural dimension provides the learners with opportunities to encounter 'otherness' presented by other, diverse cultures and also to reflect on themselves. It is, in a sense, a strategy to get to know 'yourself' better in the relationship with 'others' by interacting with various complex values. In other words, 'FLT should lead to cognitive and evaluative orientation towards learners' own society, a relativisation of the taken-for-granted, and consequently to an action orientation' (Byram, 1997: 44).

Baker (2011a, 2011b) makes a distinction between 'critical cultural awareness' and 'cultural awareness'. He also posits two stages of cultural awareness: the first stage is what is embedded in an understanding of cultures at a general level with a focus on the first culture. The second stage involves a more complex understanding of cultures and cultural frames of reference. The first stages are still based on 'cultures' but he characterizes ICC defined by Byram (1997) as in the second stage, beyond viewing cultures as bounded entities. In ICC, critical cultural awareness characterized by 'criticality' is the crucial element that underpins and expands the competence of dealing with specific cultures in Baker's second stage and the concept of being 'critical' needs to be addressed here in relation to criticality theory by Barnett (1997).

Barnett developed a theory of criticality to counter the current tendency to practical skills teaching in higher education, particularly in the humanities. Highlighting the importance of fostering 'criticality' and setting clear educational aims, Barnett proposed the two axes of domain and level, as shown in Table 4.1. The shaded parts indicate that related empirical data were gained from at least one of the case studies.

Compared with other critical theories such as Critical Pedagogy (e.g. Freire, 1972; Giroux, 1983) and critical thinking (e.g. McPeck, 1981; Siegel, 1988), Barnett's (1997), this conceptualization of criticality is similar to Critical Pedagogy, which is characterized by the ultimate goal of 'action in the world', aiming to foster those who can actively engage in transformative action in democratic societies beyond schools and universities. Critical thinking on the other hand is more focused on the individual and their development as thinking beings.

'Action in the world', which criticality development seeks as an ultimate goal, is also a crucial element for citizenship education. The task of citizenship education is to foster citizens who can take action with independent critical thought. Here, a discussion of criticality by Barnett (1997) can be related. Barnett suggested the concepts presented in Table 4.1 as a model of criticality. Following Yamada (2008), we can see the connection between citizenship and criticality by Barnett (1997) and they are both grounded by 'action'.

In Case Study 1, although some of the data, such as the ones with 'I wonder …' and 'why', can be comprehended as a form of critical thinking skill, because these keywords are indications of the start of their critical inquiry process (Houghton & Yamada, 2012; Yamada, 2008), there was no data relating to the domain of 'world'. In contrast, the two data with 'the ideal system is good' and 'My country should change' can be comprehended as indications of level 4, 'transformatory critique', the highest level in Barnett's table. Case Study 1 thus produced data that indicate students engaging in levels of criticality as shown by the shaded boxes in Table 4.1. Although no data reached into the domain of 'the world', if the study were extended to include work to be conducted outside of the classroom, such as fieldwork including collection of data from people outside the university, world-related data could be gained. In Case Study 2, there were some indications of 'reflection' and reconsideration of 'self', in particular in the data where students have different uses of 'we'.

What can be inferred from these case studies is the effect of the approach. The sequential stages of the development of 'intention of action' appeared in accordance with the change of the content of the sessions in Case Study 1. The students did not reach the stage of 'action' immediately but went through intermediate stages that can be important steps towards the development of an action mindset. As in Case Study 2, by arranging the activities to make the students conscious of 'self', it can lead them to 'reflection'. It is important for teachers to think about creating these stages in their planning.

As indicated by the data of the two case studies and Baker's (2011a, 2011b) theory, there can be sequential stages from basic cultural awareness, more advanced cultural awareness with criticality and intercultural citizenship with the emergence of intention to action. In a sense, intercultural citizenship can be based on the two basic stages of cultural awareness. There is then a difference between teaching for ICC and teaching for intercultural citizenship in language education, the latter being the higher stage based on developing ICC. During the three sessions about higher education in case study 1, the transition process from ICC building to the consciousness of citizenship can be seen – in other words, the transitional stage from intercultural education to intercultural citizenship education.

This is an important implication for education for citizenship: gradually sequenced stages need to be followed step by step, rather than aiming to bring the students up to the higher level of citizenship mindset from the start. Barnett's model in Table 4.1 can be a guide. His model implies that there are sequenced levels and stages to reach the ultimate form of criticality – transformatory critique in the domain of world – and we should take these steps into consideration when designing the teaching of citizenship. As shown in the data with the topic of tuition fees in Case Study 1, the upper stage of 'intention for action' can be created by focusing on social contradictions to make students think what ought to be.

Table 4.1 Levels, domains and forms of critical being (Barnett, 1997: 103)

	Domains		
Levels of criticality	*Knowledge*	*Self*	*World*
4. Transformatory critique	Knowledge critique	Reconstruction of self	Critique-in-action (collective reconstruction of world)
3. Refashioning of traditions	Critical thought (malleable traditions of thought)	Development of self within traditions	Mutual understanding and development of traditions
2. Reflexivity	Critical thinking (reflection on one's understanding)	Self-reflection (reflection on one's own projects)	Reflective practice ('metacompetence', 'adaptability', 'flexibility')
1. Critical skills	Discipline-specific critical thinking skills	Self-monitoring to given standards and norms	Problem-solving (means–end instrumentalism)
Forms of criticality	*Critical reason*	*Critical self-reflection*	*Critical action*

Practical Approaches and Skills of Teaching Citizenship for Lower-level Language Learners

As a consequence of these reflections, and based on the empirical studies and Barnett's criticality model, the following framework for teaching design with sequential stages towards citizenship awareness is suggested:

(1)   to bring 'otherness' into the classroom;
(2)   to compare and contrast properly;
(3)   to de-centre from what has been familiar and gain insights on self and others/to reflect;
(4)   to evaluate (examine) critically;
(5)   to engage in refashioning tradition;
(6)   to act in the world.

The major finding of this study is that the limitation of the language level does not necessarily constrain the teaching of an intercultural dimension leading to intercultural citizenship. However, measures which are not needed for more advanced level learners are needed for a teaching design with beginning language learners. Skills needed by the teacher inferred from the case studies include the following:

(1) *Content-based approach* – even at beginner stage, a 'content-first' approach is effective. In order to realize this, the following points also need to be considered. They are the difference from targeting more advanced-level learners.

(2) *Controlling the amount of reading* – reducing the amount of reading text in the target language is necessary if the aim of the activity is for the learners to focus on the content. The authentic extensive reading materials that can be very effective resources for upper levels are not suitable for lower-level learners. Simplified reading texts adjusted to the learners' level with controlled vocabulary and grammar structures can be produced by teachers themselves.

(3) *Mixed language approach: target language aided by a common language* – exchanging ideas/opinions using the target language for lower level language learners is difficult. Both case studies allowed the students to use their common language other than the target one depending on the occasion. In Case Study 1, although there were native speakers of English and most of the international students could manage English, whole class discussion in English was avoided, as studying contents through the limited Japanese language was the focus of this course. Instead, individual students were allowed to express their idea in any language in their reflections, which in fact had the advantage for us of gaining the data in languages in which they were able to express their thoughts more easily. In fact, in Case Study 1, all the participants used English in output type data. Also in Case Study 2, the students were allowed to communicate in their common local language but gradually it was shifted to the use of EIL. Data were also collected in their local language.

(4) *Arranging activities connecting the classroom and outside world* – this is not only the case with lower-level language learners but can be applied to intercultural citizenship education for all levels. As Case Study 2 arranged a visit to local tea industry and activities with a Ghanaian woman, it led to data indicating the activity in the domain of 'world' in Table 4.1. Activities connecting the classroom and outside world will be effective and are necessary to develop the dimension of 'action in the world', which is the ultimate goal of citizenship education.

Conclusion: Learners Have the Right to Participate

Ownership of languages and 'inclusion'

Hsieh (2009: 59) argues that EIL should be regarded as an intercultural language, which is used as a sign of willingness for relationship building, as well as a medium of making sense of something unfamiliar. Linguistically speaking, EIL owners do not have to be proficient English speakers. Teaching

EIL leads to an appreciation of English language learners' authority in selecting, creating and recreating in the use of English words. In other words, EIL users are in a sense privileged in the way that Kramsch (1998) views an 'intercultural speaker' who must have an increased sense of personal and individual responsibility in the use of words and in the ownership of their meanings.

Case Study 2 was designed to consider the above points. In Case Study 1 too, a space similar to Case Study 2 was created in the classroom; the participants were all non-native speakers of the language and not very proficient level speakers of the language, either. However, in the space created not only according to their linguistic level but also considering the kind of language, they shared the topics proposed. In this kind of space, the ownership of language of all the participants is secured and the realization of the citizenship education dimension of 'inclusion' is possible.

The right to speak

Global citizens today need to embrace diversities in both culture and language. They do not necessarily have a native-like level of language proficiency but a willingness and a right to participate in the society needs to be guaranteed equally to any member.

Introducing an intercultural citizenship dimension for lower-level language learners is not just a matter of adjusting the teaching according to their linguistic level. There are many other points to be considered as we discussed above. The concept of citizenship is not simple and a language can lead to the exclusion of someone from the classroom community. 'Responsibility' is an important element of citizenship and it is also crucial in 'ownership' of language. Thus, both concepts are connected and 'ownership' issues cannot be ignored in intercultural citizenship, in particular, for lower-level learners.

References

Baker, W. (2011a) From cultural awareness to intercultural awareness: Culture in ELT. *ELT Journal* 66 (1), 62–70.

Baker, W. (2011b) Intercultural awareness: Modelling an understanding of cultures in intercultural communication through English as a lingua franca. *Language and Intercultural Communication* 11 (3), 197–214.

Barnett, R. (1997) *Higher Education: A Critical Business*. Buckingham: Open University Press.

Byram, M. (1997) *Teaching and Assessing Intercultural Communicative Competence*. Clevedon: Multilingual Matters.

Byram, M. (2003) On being 'bicultural' and 'intercultural'. In G. Alred, M. Byram and M. Fleming (eds) *Intercultural Experience and Education*. Clevedon: Multilingual Matters.

Byram, M. (2008) *From Foreign Language Education to Education for Intercultural Citizenship*. Clevedon: Multilingual Matters.

Byram, M. (2009) Intercultural citizenship and foreign language education. *Syn-Thèses, Langue Interculture Communication, Revue Annuelle* 2, 61–73.

Chen, I.W. and Hsieh, J.J. (2011) English language in Taiwan: An examination of its use in society and education in schools. In A. Feng (ed.) *English Language Education Across Greater China* (pp. 70–94). Bristol: Multilingual Matters.

Citizenship Foundation (2012) *What is Citizenship Education?* See http://www.citizenship-foundation.org.uk/main/page.php?286 (accessed 5 September 2016).

Council of Europe (2011) *Common European Framework of Reference for: Learning, Teaching, Assessment.* Strasbourg: Council of Europe. See http://www.coe.int/t/dg4/linguistic/Source/Framework_EN.pdf (accessed 5 September 2016).

Crystal, D. (2006) English worldwide. In F. Hogg and D. Denison (eds) *A History of the English Language* (pp. 420–444). Cambridge: Cambridge University Press.

European Commission (1995) *Teaching and Learning: Towards the Learning Society.* Bruxelles: European Commission.

Freire, P. (1972) *Pedagogy of the Oppressed.* London: Sheed and Ward.

Fuscoe, K., Garside, B. and Prodromou, L. (2007) *Attitude 3.* London: Macmillan.

Giroux, H.A. (1983) *Critical Theory and Educational Practice.* Victoria: Deakin University.

Holliday, A. (2002) *Doing and Writing Qualitative Research.* Thousand Oaks, CA: Sage.

Houghton, S. and Yamada, E. (2012) *Developing Criticality in Practice through Foreign Language Education.* Bern: Peter Lang.

Hsieh, J. (2009) Reconceptualising English teaching in Taiwan: Action research with technical college students. Unpublished EdD thesis, University of Durham.

Kramsch, C. (1998) The privilege of the intercultural speaker. In M. Byram and M. Fleming (eds) *Language Learning in Intercultural Perspective: Approaches through Drama and Ethnography.* Cambridge: Cambridge University Press.

LeCompte, M. and Preissle, J. (1993) *Ethnography and Qualitative Design in Educational Research* (2nd edn). San Diego, CA: Academic Press.

McPeck, J. (1981) *Critical Thinking and Education.* Oxford: Martin Robertson.

Miles, M.B. and Huberman, A.M. (1994) *The Qualitative Researcher's Companion.* Thousand Oaks, CA: Sage.

OECD (2011) Chapter B: Financial and Human Resources Invested in Education, Indicator B4: What is the total public spending on education? In *Education at a Glance.* See http://www.oecd-ilibrary.org/education/education-at-a-glance-2011_eag-2011-en;jsessionid=7g1eab9cmjf1n.x-oecd-live-03 (accessed 5 September 2016).

Osler, A. (2005) Education for democratic citizenship: New challenges in a globalized world. In A. Osler and H. Starkey (eds) *Citizenship and Language Learning: International Perspectives* (pp. 3–22). Stoke-on-Trent: Trentham.

Oxfam (2006) *Education for Global Citizenship. A Guide for Schools.* See http://www.oxfam.org.uk/education/global-citizenship/global-citizenship-guides (accessed 5 September 2016).

Siegel, H. (1988) *Educating Reason: Rationality, Critical Thinking and Education.* New York: Routledge.

Strauss, A. and Corbin, J. (1998) *Basics of Qualitative Research* (2nd edn). Thousand Oaks, CA: Sage.

Yamada, E. (2008) Fostering criticality in a beginners' Japanese language course: A case study in a UK higher education modern languages degree programme. Unpublished PhD thesis, University of Durham.

5 Incorporating Environmental Action into Intercultural Dialogue: Personal and Environmental Transformation and the Development of Intercultural Communicative Competence

Stephanie Ann Houghton
and Mei Lan Huang

Introduction

The work described here is based on the Intercultural Dialogue Model (IDM) (Figure 5.1). The model helps teachers systematically to develop students' intercultural communicative competence (ICC) by building sequenced and staged learning objectives into materials design.

The model suggest a course of learning should be sequenced in five stages that lead students from the analysis of self and other, through critical analysis and evaluation of self and other, to reflection upon identity development. While it accords with Barnett's (1997) levels of critical reflection and Byram's (1997) ICC model, this model adds a further component of *savoir se transformer* to Byram's model to represent identity development as a form of personal transformation.

While past applications of the IDM (e.g. Houghton, 2010) emphasized the interface between self and other, Houghton (2012) suggested that student activity may shift to the interface between self and world to incorporate social action into the IDM framework: 'as learners go openly into the

Steps in the course of learning	Meta-levels
1	Self-analysis: student analysis of own value system (VS1)	
2	Analysis of other: student analysis of the value system of another person (VS2) having gathered information through empathy-oriented communication	**Development of awareness**
3	Critical analysis: juxtaposition, comparison and contrast of the two value systems (VS1 and VS2) to identify similarities and differences	Self-awareness Meta-cognitive awareness
4	Critical evaluation: student evaluation of the value systems of self and other (VS1 and VS2) with reference to a standard	Meta-affective awareness
5	Identity development: student orientation of self to others by selecting standards and evaluative tendencies	

Figure 5.1 The intercultural dialogue model

language and perspectives of others' (Houghton, 2012: 95). This might happen through dialogue that carries the potential to reform society corresponding to Barnett's (1997) notion of 'critique-in-action' and 'collective reconstruction of world'.

This chapter reports a 14-week action research study (April–June 2013) in which two groups of university students in Japan and Taiwan followed part of a course (available online) entitled 'Insights From the Field' (Coverdell World Wise Schools, n.d.) into which the IDM was integrated. Focusing on environmental action as one type of social action, both groups followed Unit 3 of the course (entitled 'Service: You Can Make a Difference') separately, in parallel, converging only at the end as we shall see. In this unit, students proceed through recognition of the overarching principle *Despite cultural differences, we are all united in a common bond of humanity* by exploring the concept of the common good with reference to the following enduring understandings: (1) there is such a thing as the common good, and individuals can strengthen the common good through various forms of citizen action; (2) service matters – people in our community volunteer to make a difference; and (3) you can make a difference in your community in a number of ways.

Having considered ways in which local Dominicans, Peace Corps Volunteers serving in the Dominican Republic, international agencies and the Dominican government worked for the common good in the aftermath of Hurricane

Georges in ways described in the 'Insights from the field' textbook, students went out into their own community and conducted interviews with community volunteers, exploring the ways in which volunteer community organizations work, identifying criteria for conducting service projects and using primary source documents to identify examples of various Peace Corps service projects. As a 'culminating activity', students then planned, implemented and evaluated service-learning projects in their own university or community.

The Course in Action

The Japan-based group consisted of 13 students (10 female, three male) majoring in Culture and Education, comprising nine Japanese students, one Malaysian student, two Chinese students and one Taiwanese student. The Taiwan group consisted of 14 students (10 female, four male) majoring in Nursing and Health Care, including Taiwanese students of different ethnicities: 10 Southern-Min students; three Hakka students; and one Aboriginal student.

An introductory lesson was followed by a series of six lessons that broadly followed Unit 3 of the textbook, although Lesson 6 ('Planning a service project') was taught before Lessons 4 and 5 to give students more time to plan their projects. After each of the first seven lessons, students were asked to write a learning diary reflecting on what they had learned in class and how they felt about it, raising questions and/or making comments. Students started planning their 'culminating activity' – group 'environmental action projects' (EAP) in week 3 – and were given time each week to develop them thereafter.

In weeks 8–10, the Japan-based and Taiwan-based students implemented their respective projects independently of each other at times convenient to them before submitting individually written project reports by week 10.

As the first six lessons followed the course of learning in an existing textbook, the syllabus was not directly structured around the IDM, although there are similarities. For example, students engaged in reflection upon their own values with reference to a given conceptual framework – stage 1 of the IDM ('Analysis of self') – in weeks 1 and 2 when they reflected on their concept of citizenship with respect to protecting the environment and, secondly, their experience of people putting aside their own needs to work together. Reflective self-analysis at both individual and group levels also characterized activities in weeks 4, 5 and 7 when students planned, implemented and reported on their environmental action project based upon group-based needs analysis and in the formulation of individually written project reports. Students also engaged in exploration of their interlocutor's values – stage 2 of the IDM ('Analysis of other') – in weeks 3 and 6 when they researched and reported on two community volunteers working for volunteer organizations, and reported on an interview with a local volunteer about environmental action in class. They engaged in critical evaluation with reference to an explicit standard – stage 4 of the IDM ('Critical evaluation') – in week 5 when they evaluated projects by applying evaluative criteria specified in Worksheet 6.

The IDM was used to structure the culminating activity EAP reports and EAP feedback reports. However, the EAP reports stopped at the critical evaluation stage rather than going on to have students systematically reflect and comment on possibilities for future change (stage 5 of the IDM; 'Identity development'). This would have involved students engaging in reasoned reflection upon whether or not to change in response to their interlocutor. Thus, in week 7, the EAP report was structured as follows:

Environmental Action Project (EAP) Report Structure

(1) needs analysis;
(2) project plan;
(3) project implementation;
(4) reflection;
(5) evaluation (applying the second list of evaluation criteria presented above).

Once students had submitted their EAP reports in week 10, the teachers exchanged reports and distributed EAP reports from the other group to their own students for consideration. Students were each asked to read one EAP report from a student in another country, and to reflect on their own EAP in its light before writing an EAP Feedback Report for that student. However, while students had been asked to evaluate their own EAP by applying the evaluative criteria specified above, students were also asked to think about those standards and decide whether or not they considered them suitable. In this way, students were encouraged to set their own standards for evaluation, and they were asked to explain why they chose them in a feedback report following the guidelines below:

Environmental Action Project (EAP) Feedback Report Structure

(1) Read and consider the EAP Report you are given.
(2) Critical analysis – compare and contrast it with your own EAP Report by identifying similarities and differences between them.
(3) Critical evaluation (standard-setting) – make a list of the standards for evaluation to apply when evaluating both essays. Describe each standard and explain why you think it is important.
(4) Critical evaluation (evaluation) – evaluate both essays by applying the standards you set in the previous stage. Identify both positive and negative points where possible, and justify your judgements by explaining your reasons clearly.

The EAPs are summarized in Table 5.1.

Table 5.1 Summaries of environmental awareness projects

Japan-based group

GROUP JBG1: LITTER PICKING PROJECT
- Three students (JS1, JS2 and JS3) wanted to pick up litter around the local train station → visited the station, looked around to see what needed doing and asked people there directly → however, when they checked the station, they found it to be quite clean, so they decided to try to clean the river on the university campus and planned to ask if they could borrow tools from the university → this later changed to a litter picking project on campus → students later discovered from a university officer that such voluntary student activity already took place on campus every fourth Wednesday (S1, S2 and S3 just did not know about it)

GROUP JBG 2: ARIAKE BEACH LITTER PICKING PROJECT
- Four students (JS9, JS10, JS11 and JS12) expressed concern about various (including some serious) environmental problems affecting the Ariake Sea coastline. They drove there on a rainy day to pick up litter along the beach, although it was not as littered as they expected.

GROUP JBG 3: FLOWER-PLANTING PROJECT
- Three students (JS4, JS5 and JS6) wanted to beautify the natural environment by planting flowers around the university campus → got formal permission from the Student Affairs office → bought the plants, soil and plant pots with their own money, and played with a cat that sat in a plant pot.

GROUP JBG 4: RECYCLING PROJECT
- Two students (JS7 and JS8) wanted to gather unneeded recyclable items from homes and take them to a recycling shop → tell friends about the project and get more people involved, research local recycle centres and what they need, etc. → however, when they checked at home, they found they did not have many recyclable items so they planned to contact a student volunteer group involved in recycling to ask for advice → took some old clothes to a second-hand shop and made 620 yen which they kept for themselves.

Taiwan-based group[a]

GROUP TBG1: RECYCLING PROJECT
- Five students (TS1, TS2, TS3, TS4 and TS5) wanted to promote the 3 Rs Action Project, that is, reducing (cigarette butts, plastic bags, batteries, aluminium foil bags, rubbish, etc.), recycling (glass/PET bottles, waste paper, etc.) and reusing (shopping bags, second-hand books, etc.) various items → tell patients' family in Chang-Gung Memorial Hospital, classmates and universities faculties to get more involved, make posters to raise people's awareness. However, they found that to be efficient and to get more people involved, they needed to be in collaboration with the volunteer coordinator of Chang-Gung Memorial Hospital, the dormitory superintendents (all the students of Chang-Gung University have to live in the dormitories during the weekdays) and the section leaders of Health-Care Section of CGUST and ask for their advice.

GROUP TBG 2: ENERGY-SAVING PROJECT
- Three students (TS6, TS7 and TS8) wanted to raise people's sense of responsibility to slow down the speed of global warming by carrying out an energy-saving action project → Installing the water-saving devices in faucets, turning off the corridors' light in the dorm after 10:30 p.m., no air-conditioning when the temperature is

Table 5.1 *(Continued)*

lower than 28°C, only one elevator at non-peak period, etc. → they found their action needed to be implemented not only in the school , but also outside the school campus, such as their houses, the public places, etc. So, they planned to seek the collaboration with the local environmental protection groups.
GROUP TBG 3: ANIMAL PROTECTION PROJECT
• Three students (TS9, TS10 and TS11) wanted to reduce the pollution from the stray animals on the campus and in the local communities and to promote 'No Animal Experimental Product in our daily life' to respect the right to life of each species → They posted the text on the FB, Plurk, Twitter and so on, put up posters in public places to deliver the concepts of concern for the animals, like 'Raise it, love it and don't abandon it'. However, they found that it was not enough to 'Be a volunteer one day', as held by Taoyuan County Animal Conservation Society, with actions such as delivering flyers, raising money, helping at the charity bazaar, caring for animals, keeping the stray animals' site clean. → They needed to collaborate with Animal Protection Association to get more volunteer groups involved to set up more stray animal shelters.
GROUP TBG 4: LITTERING PROJECT
• Two students (TS12 and TS13) wanted clean up the Aboriginal tribe community in Hua-Lieun city (eastern part of Taiwan) and the Zhi Qing Lake on university campus separately → they carried out inter-university collaboration, such as the volunteer student clubs of National Taiwan Sport University (a neighbouring university) and Tzu Chi University's Medical Service volunteering groups → they found that they needed to input more knowledge about how to clean up effectively, so the advice from the volunteering groups was required.

ᵃOne student did not submit the report.

Evaluating the Project: Analysing the Data

While students generated much written homework during the course, only the EAP reports and EAP Feedback Reports were used to investigate two questions that were a basis for evaluating the success of (some aspects of) the project. Each teacher analysed their own students' data, the dataset amounting to 14,544 words in total for the Japan-based group and 13,767 words for the group in Taiwan. Ethical issues related to informed consent, participant anonymity and the safe storage of data, for example, were duly followed. The purpose of what we called the 'Reflective Analysis' was to identify implications for modifications in any future replication of the project.

Coding of the data (Creswell, 2003; Hopkins, 2002) used the four stages of the IDM as codes:

- 'Analysis/Own' captured statements about their local environment.
- 'Analysis/Other' captured statements on another person's analysis of their own local environment.

- 'Critical Analysis' captured statements identifying similarities/differences between their own EAP project and that of another person.
- 'Standards' captured statements describing the evaluative standards they applied in critical evaluation.
- 'Critical Evaluation/Own' captured evaluations of their own EAP.
- 'Critical Evaluation/Other' captured evaluations of the EAP of another person.
- 'Personal Transformation' captured statements on ways they thought they had changed as a result of the experience.
- 'Environmental Transformation' captured student statements on ways they thought they had changed the environment as a result of the experience.

The EAP reports

The first four sections of the EAP Reports from the projects summarized above in Table 5.1 describe the needs analysis, project plan, implementation and reflection, generated statements about students' analysis of their own environment before and after the project and were coded 'Analysis/Own' accordingly. In the *needs analysis* section, students in the Japan-based group tended to highlight particular environmental problems such as students living alone near campus who drop litter without a care (JS3). Students sometimes commented upon what they had noticed when they had looked more closely at their environment, perhaps noting how it was not as dirty as, or dirtier than, they had expected. JS2 found fewer PET bottles caps lying on the ground than expected, while JS3 noticed that there were more cigarette ends than expected, for example. Students based at the university in Taiwan live in the dormitories during weekdays, so they pay attention to particular environmental problems such as rubbish recycling/reducing/separating to carry out their duties with regard to daily rubbish in their rooms, cafes and campus (TS1, TS2, TS4). TS6, TS7 and TS8 observed the waste of energy (electricity) by students not turning off unnecessary lights, air-conditioning, computers, etc. TS13 commented that people dropped litter without a care in her Aboriginal tribal community, and TS9 noticed that the stray animals caused disease, and their waste dirtied the campus and nearby streets.

In *project implementation*, all the situational-specific problems offered students the opportunity to carry out a project (an environmental action), which involved them in a purposive intervention and brought them into touch with Others. Some students started a connection with the volunteer groups of Chang-Gung Memorial Hospital (TS2 and TS5), Tsu-Chi Medical University (TS1 and TS12), or Tao-Yun County Animal Conservation Society (TS9) and Animal Protection Association (TS10). TS3 interviewed the Volunteering Environmental Housewives Association, and TS4 and TS7 asked for advice and help from the dormitory superintendents. TS6 and TS11 used social networking such as Facebook, Twitter and Plurk to ask for advice or exchange opinions on environmental action with social volunteers or friends. TS13 connected with Taiwan Environmental Information Center and was in collaboration with inter-university volunteers (National Taiwan Sport University).

Overall, most of the student groups reported willingness to step outside their own perspective to have dialogue or interaction with Others, although TS8 reported that she did not interview or collaborate with any local volunteering association. The experience of conducting the projects also seemed to have brought some Japan-based students into closer contact with people already involved in 'their' kind of environmental action, such as JS3 who established a connection with a university environmental officer, although JS9 reported noticing but not talking to a local environmental officer by the beach because he seemed to regard them 'with a suspicious eye'. JS9 regretted not interviewing the man when they had the chance, but also seemed sensitive to being watched 'wonderingly' by strangers during the litterpick. Some students seemed sensitive to other people's reactions to their project such as JS4's expression of disappointment that none of her friends had noticed the flowers they had planted on campus, which seemed to have triggered her recognition of the need to involve more people in such projects, a point echoed by JS7, JS10 and JS11. Further, while some students seemed quite motivated to finish the task, as evidenced by JBG2 conducting their litter picking project in the rain, and JBG3 making a return trip to the shop when they realized they had forgotten to buy something, the commitment to environmental protection of JBG4 seemed questionable as they kept the 620 yen profit made by recycling their old clothes for themselves, rather than donating it to an environmental charity, for example.

Reflection on the project also generated students' inner disturbance caused by unfamiliar social interaction and openly going into the perspectives of Others, such as wondering why other students didn't turn off the unnecessary lights on the corridor (TS7). TS3 also observed that many students were not in the habit of carrying recyclable tableware with them, thus piles of rubbish (used plastic dishes, spoons and chopsticks, etc.) were still observed inside and outside the university cafe or dormitory. In such ways, reflection on the project sometimes generated questions in students' minds such as to why the government does not set up smoking areas in small streets (JS2), why people do not carry small bags to collect cigarette ends (JS2) or why so many people drop litter (JS12), which led to JS12 observing the lack of bins available in the area. JS8 also noticed how many different products were available cheaply at the second-hand shop.

The fifth section of the EAP report described the students' evaluation of the project and produced statements evaluating the project positively or negatively by applying the evaluative criteria described above. These were coded 'Critical Evaluation/Own' accordingly. While seven students made general comments without applying the criteria, five students systematically applied (some or all of) the criteria point by point. The following is an example from the Taiwan group:

TS12 EAP Report (Part 5: Project Evaluation)

(1) *Meets actual community needs* → Good impact
    After visiting the local community social workers, we discussed where is the most dirty area in my Aboriginal tribal community and we need to clean it up most. So the action plan is determined appropriately.
(2) *Is coordinated in collaboration with community* → good impact
    We linked with the chief of [a] University's Medical Service Center – Ms Teng, Wei-Weng via the Facebook. She acted as our consultant in the project development. At last we worked together for this 'Clean-Up-Up' action project.
(3) *Is integrated into academic curriculum* → some impact
    Environmental Servical Learning is a good deed of serving learning projects, and is integrated into the academic curriculum of foreign language education course.
(4) *Facilitates active student reflection* → good impact
    I saw a lot of bottles, garbage, cigarette boxes and many, many cigarette butts on the streets of my Aboriginal tribal community. I hoped everyone can have a more civic-mind to care for the environment and to develop a good habit of not throwing rubbish casually.
(5) *Uses new academic skill/knowledge in real world settings* → minimal impact
    We remembered that we had to meet together to begin the clean-up activity on the streets at seven o'clock in the morning … and we sweated a lot under the sun and sat together to eat the delicious lunch, we had super good team spirit to carry out the action project, and didn't know what new academic skill or knowledge had to be used appropriately.
(6) *Helps develop sense of caring for and about others* → some impact
    The brooms in our hands were a little awkward, our non-professional cleaning skills didn't bother us, we tolerate and encourage one another … we recognized that happiness comes from helping/serving others.
(7) *Improves quality of life for person served* → some impact
    Though the process of action project was tiring and difficult, the most satisfying and happiest things are the environmental situation of my Aboriginal community becomes tidy and clean and the power of joint efforts to keep the community's environment clean.

Generally, students tended to evaluate their projects negatively regardless of the standards applied by assigning 'minimal impact' as illustrated in section (5) of the above example, although students sometimes noted positive aspects such as the value of the group planning process (JS10) and the benefit of trying to help other members of the public combined with an increased sense of personal dignity in doing so (JS1). In the Taiwan group 10 students made general comments without applying the criteria, three students consistently applied (some or all of) the criteria point by point. Generally, students tended to evaluate their projects positively, although they sometimes noted negative aspects such as TS2's expression of disappointment that some people in CG Memorial Hospital did not raise their heads and glance at them when they conducted their environmental action activity on 'No Smoking! Give the Clean Air Back to the Hospital'. The results of second-hand books recycling for the hospitalized patients were not so effective as expected in terms of the amounts of the donation of used books (TS5) and the long-term implementation of litter-picking/rubbish recycling action projects needed more available time to achieve the desired goals (TS3, TS4, TS7, TS12 and TS13).

The code 'Personal Transformation' captured statements on ways students thought they had changed as a result of the experience, and the code 'Environmental Transformation' captured statements on ways they thought they had changed the environment as a result of the experience. Although these components were not explicitly built into task design, examples did emerge in the EAP Reports. Examples of environmental transformation were few given that most students were dissatisfied with the impact of their projects for various reasons. However, numerous examples indicative of personal transformation did emerge in statements of what they had learned in the project (JS3), what they should have done differently (JS3 and JS4) and why problems arose, such as not having enough money to buy all the plants they wanted (JS5), increased awareness of local environmental issues (JS1, JS2 and JS10), increased self-awareness related to personal values (JS8) and, most notably, increased motivation to engage in environmental protection activities in the future, combined with the expression of concrete new ideas about how to conduct their respective project differently in the future (JS3, JS5, JS6, JS7, JS8, JS9 and JS11). In the Taiwan-based group too, students thought they had changed and/or they had changed the environment due to the experience of their environmental action project. Examples of the code 'Personal Transformation' and the code 'Environmental Transformation' focused on statements such as 'everyone has a responsibility to contribute to "the carbon reduction" action project' (TS6), 'the practice of environmental action project on [litter-picking] is not just a paper-work' (TS13) and 'the environmental action project is initially vague, but we come to know the direction [i.e. where to start and to go] in carrying out the energy-saving project next time' (TS6, TS8) in the following.

TS8 EAP Report (Part 5: Project Evaluation)

Though there are disadvantages we have to improve, for instance, the public lectures on energy conservation are lack of attraction so that maybe some people don't want to participate it! Moreover, not only dormitory superintendents but also all student residents should do the energy conservation. Also, actions speak louder than words, so the energy conservation project is not a slogan! We'll surely know how to combine with the new knowledge to carry out energy-saving project next time.

EAP feedback reports

In the EAP Feedback Reports, students critically analysed their own EAP reports and one from a student in the other country by identifying similarities and differences between them. In the Japan-based group, of the 11 students who submitted the EAP Feedback Reports, eight identified similarities and differences between the two reports without including evaluation of them in their writing, as illustrated in the following.

JS10 EAP Feedback Report (Critical Analysis)

I am going to compare and contrast the report of [my partner] with my own repot. First I would like to talk about similarities between us. We have the same theme, which is to solve rubbish issue. We both thought the improvement of the rubbish issue made the local environment and the global environment better. In addition, we thought how people disposed of rubbish. On the other hand, we have a lot of differences between us. Her group asked the organization doing environmental protection for help her, and they called out to everyone to do together environmental protection, but my group did the activity by only ourselves. Her group did the activity at two different places, which are the school restaurant and school convenience store, while we did only around Ariake Sea. And her group attached weight on 'Reuse' and 'reduce'. For example, they promoted people to reuse the plastic bags and bring their own tableware. However, my group attached weight to 'Recycle'. We picked up the rubbish and separated it appropriately. Additionally, the biggest difference is the way of thinking. They want the world to be better, and they want to stop the global warming while we want the local area to be better.

JS5's reports lacked a critical analysis section and two students mixed critical analysis with evaluation (JS9, JS11) as follows:

JS9 EAP Feedback Report (Critical Analysis)

In my opinion, first of all, I think they did it well. Implementing this project with students from National Taiwan Sport University, which is next to their school, makes this project's scale larger. And due to the distance problem, they chose to clean up a lake near them instead of beach, which saved more energy and avoided complicated works.

I appreciate that they planned to associate with Taiwan Environmental Information Center and wanted to spread this project on the Internet. However, they did not mention that if they really carried out. If they did, I would be very impressed. If not, I would feel pitiful, because this is truly a great idea.

Comparing with our project, we did the same picking thing, but I found they are greater than our project in many ways. At first, they conducted this project with other people willing to serve, and this makes the project larger and more effective. Second, they conducted their project by foot, which consumed less energy comparing to us. Moreover, according to their article, they said they planned it very carefully, asking for advice from others, modifying their project many times to make this project better. This is the most important thing that impressed me. Nevertheless, it is very pitiful they didn't mention that if they met the actual needs and how was the real situation.

There are also many same points between our projects. In good way, we did carry our projects out and make environment around us cleaner. And from this project, we do have our awareness of environmental protection roused. On the other hand, we don't know if we met the actual needs, and we only conducted it once and do not care what it may be after the day we implemented our project. We both did our project in a small scale instead of laver aquaculture pollution and beach cleaning. It is not bad though, we just did what we can do by our hands and in such a limited time.

In the Taiwan-based group, of the 11 students who submitted the EAP Feedback Reports, 10 students clearly identified similarities and differences between the two reports without evaluating them in their writing, while TS2's reports lacked a critical analysis section and two students mixed critical analysis with evaluation (TS1 and TS11).

Setting standards

In the EAP Feedback Reports, students set standards for evaluating their own and their partner's EAP Reports in the standard-setting section. A brief overview of the standards set by students in both groups is presented in Table 5.2.

Japan-based students tended to choose criteria from one of the worksheets, including:

- increases local capacity;
- addresses expressed needs;
- seeks sustainable results;
- uses local participants as partners;
- meets actual community needs;

- is coordinated in collaboration with community;
- is integrated into academic curriculum;
- facilitates active student reflection;
- uses new academic skill/knowledge in real world settings;
- helps develop sense of caring for and about others;
- improves quality of life for person(s) served.

Alternatively, they generated their own criteria for evaluation. Criteria sometimes focused on the planning stages (student-generated evaluation criteria 1–6 in Table 5.2), the impact of the project (criteria 7 and 8), participant response (criteria 9 and 10) and the sustainability and quality-development of the project (criteria 11–14). Almost all students justified their standard-setting by explaining why they considered the criteria they chose to be important, although JS5 did not.

Regarding the Taiwan-based group, the majority of students chose some criteria from worksheets and others generated their own criteria for evaluation, which sometimes focused on the planning stages (student-generated evaluation criteria 1–3), the impact of the project (criteria 4), participant response (criteria 5) and the sustainability and quality-development of the project (criteria 7 and 8). Almost all students justified their standard-setting by explaining why they considered the criteria they chose to be important, although TS2 did not.

Critical evaluation

At the end of the EAP Feedback Reports, students evaluated their own and their partner's EAP Reports by applying the standards they had described

Table 5.2 Students' criteria for evaluating EAP reports

(1) Whether the purpose is clear and has been attained
(2) How much research was done
(3) Knowledge about other projects
(4) Whether participants visited at least one environmental voluntary organization and what they learned from them
(5) Contact with an environmental organization
(6) Effective publicity
(7) Whether the environment was improved or not
(8) How much difference the project made to the environment and other people
(9) How much project participants minds changed through the activity
(10) The quality of students' own self-evaluation
(11) What was done after project completion
(12) Evaluations of others of the project
(13) Possibility of continuation
(14) Improvement of the quality of projects
(15) How to contribute to the environment

in their standard-setting section. While many students in the Japan-based group evaluated their partner's essay, they often did not evaluate their own. In both sets of data from this group, however, students always justified their judgements by giving reasons as illustrated here where the criteria are italicized:

JS9 EAP Feedback Report (Critical Evaluation)

(1) *How much it made different to environment/other peoples*
In the plan of donate second-hand books, we can see at last, they sent the books they collected to others who need. Such as hospital, it can helps the people in hospital have a good time. So I think it is very good. In our plan we put some flowers on school's street. They just a little. Sometimes it can be noticed but sometimes they are ignored.
(2) *How many research we did*
From the essay we can see they carried out this plan after visited they classmate. And in our group, we asked the teachers and get the promise of school. But I think neither of us made a full investigation. Such as to ask peoples in hospital what books they like, and to ask students in [the] university if we need do this.
(3) *What we did after complete the volunteer activity*
After planting flowers, we did nothing to take care of it, it's very harmful to our plan.
(4) *The opinions of result we get from others*
According to this essay, I see the plan of donate second-hand book get a high praise from others, so it is a good thing. But in our plan, someone say the flowers are beautiful and someone just ignored them.

Almost half of the Japan students clearly applied some or all of the standards they had selected systematically evaluating both projects, while others did not evaluate their own projects at all and only focused on their partners' projects. However, students sometimes could not find the information needed to perform the evaluation, sometimes admitting that they could not fully understand what particular standards meant. Further, an attempt to apply a standard sometimes indicated that the student did not actually understand the standard being applied. This may explain why some students did not apply all the standards listed in their standard-setting sections. Taiwan-based students mainly evaluated both their own and their partner's EAP Reports in terms of the standards selected under the two categories of 'advantages or positive points' and 'disadvantages or negative points' rather than applying the standards they had set in the previous stage. Fifty-nine examples of data were coded Evaluation/Other, while 48 examples were coded Evaluation/Own, but in both sets of data; however, students always justified their judgements by giving reasons.

Personal and environmental transformation

To establish whether and to what extent the project had been successful in the specific issue of personal and environmental transformation, the data from the two document types analysed above were reviewed.

In the Japan-based group, expressions of 'Personal Transformation' arose mainly in the standard-setting section of the EAP Feedback Reports in the form of increased recognition of something important such as community needs (JS6), the need to learn from others (JS3 and JS10), to research the project to develop knowledge about it (JS3 and JS4), the need for critical self-evaluation (JS2) and active reflection (JS11) in project evaluation. While one example was also found in JS9's critical evaluation in relation to sustainability, no examples indicative of personal transformation were found in any other sections of the reports. Few expressions of 'environmental transformation' arose in any sections of the reports, perhaps because students were generally disappointed in the impact of their projects as noted earlier. While the importance of environmental impact was recognized in standard-setting in two cases (JS4 and JS9), examples more indicative of actual environmental impact were found in the critical analysis section in two cases (JS9 and JS10) and in the Critical Evaluation/Own section (JS4) in three cases (JS2, JS4 and JS9). However, no examples were found in the Critical Evaluation/Other section, which is understandable as students were not in a position to witness any actual impact of their partner's project in Taiwan.

In the Taiwan-based group, expressions of 'Personal Transformation' arose mainly in the standard-setting section of the EAP Feedback Reports in the form of increased recognition of something important such as community needs (TS1, TS2, TS3 and TS4), the need of local environmental maintenance (TS5 and TS8), the need to learn from others (TS1, TS3 and TS6), and active reflection (TS6 and TS11) in project evaluation. One example was also found in TS5's critical analysis in relation to sustainability:

TS5 EAP Feedback Report (Critical Analysis)

Participation in this environmental action project allows us to better understand the sustainability development of the planet, and we all need to work together for it.

There were however no examples indicative of personal transformation in any other sections of the reports. While the importance of environmental impact was recognized in standard-setting in one case (TS3), an example more indicative of actual environmental impact was found in the critical analysis section in one case (TS5).

Evaluating the project

Two questions provided the focus for the evaluation:

- How does ICC (as defined in Byram's (1997) model) emerge when environmental action is integrated into the IDM (in the ways described above)?
- To what extent do personal and environmental transformation emerge from student activity and learning when they are not included in the course as potentially assessable learning objectives?

The first question was considered important to see how learning objectives might manifest themselves in ways that are potentially assessable, although not assessed in this study. The personal and social transformation elements of the second question were considered important partly because identity development is not included in Byram's model, and partly because it remains unclear how teachers should ascertain whether environmental transformation has occurred, or even what the learning objectives should be in this regard.

Data generated by the needs analysis, project plan, implementation and reflection sections of the EAP reports suggest that, although the group projects were conducted locally and independently of groups at the partner university, there were some common elements. Specifically, they included the identification of situation-specific problems in the needs analysis stage followed by observation, group discussion and planning that led to direct action upon the environment. All of this led to some environmental transformation and reflection on the project and social contact with people outside the classroom was also a form of social transformation. Inner disturbance caused by unfamiliar social interaction as students stepped outside their own perspectives by taking the perspectives of others seemed to generate further questions about, and observations on, the world.

In this sense, communication with unfamiliar others outside the classroom seemed to result from student attempts to change the world. Analysis of their local environments (stage 1: IDM) and interrogation of their understandings of the world around them engaged students in disciplinary and societal reflection on the world. This often presented contradictory, situation-specific problems susceptible to purposive intervention as academic themes discussed in class related to citizenship became inner dialogue within students as they considered how to act upon the world through environmental action (Barnett, 1997). This demanded curiosity, openness and readiness to suspend disbelief about the world around them (Byram, 1997) as they moved through action or reflection upon their project.

Data generated by the evaluation section of the EAP reports, in which students evaluated their own projects by applying evaluation criteria set by the teacher, suggest that, overall, fewer than half of the students across both groups were able to apply the criteria in practice when evaluating their own projects. This may be considered disappointing but if the development of intercultural communicative competence is considered an ongoing process, the outcome of which should be assessed over a period of time rather than at one point in time as in the snapshot view of the EAP report, then the fact that some students had begun to use the criteria is an indication of a foundation being formed, and that they are putting the criteria into effect. Byram (1997) defines 'critical cultural awareness' as learners being able to evaluate on the basis of *explicitly-stated* criteria. Evaluation based upon explicitly stated criteria is also an integral part of stage 4 of the IDM. This affects decision-making as students evaluate multiple options, selecting some and rejecting others as they attempt to bring order to chaos. Further, it nurtures self-realization in students in the form of identity development (stage 5: IDM) as they reflect upon personal experience, defining the self through personal projects viewing attempts to understand the world as projects of self-discovery using education as a vehicle for realizing their own projects.

Indeed, despite the fact that a self-reflection component (stage 5: IDM) was deliberately excluded from the EAP report for reasons explained earlier, some evidence of personal transformation did emerge in the data in student expressions of what they had learned (i.e. knowledge transformation): increased awareness of the world around them, self-awareness of values, increased motivation to engage in future action and the generation of new ideas about how to conduct such projects in the future. However, if asked to reflect upon this area more carefully, the quality of student self-reflection may be enhanced, so this component should be built into task design rather than excluded in future studies.

A further notable point about student evaluations is that, while Japan-based members tended to evaluate their own projects negatively, Taiwan-based members tended to evaluate their projects positively and – in their teacher's view – too optimistically. In a sense, it does not matter whether students evaluated their projects positively or negatively because, although student accounts and evaluations of their projects are accessible to the teacher, which renders them potentially assessable, the environmental action/impact *itself* remains inaccessible to the teacher, which renders it necessarily a non-assessable by-product of the project concerned. Thus, the fact that there was very little evidence of actual environmental transformation reported in students' EAP reports does not itself present a practical problem for the teacher.

Data generated by the critical analysis section of the EAP Feedback Reports suggested that most students succeeded in identifying similarities and differences between their own EAP Report and their partner's, taking a comparative approach (Byram, 1997) *non-judgementally*, although some did not, either because the section was completely lacking or because they mixed analysis with evaluation. This indicates that they did not understand the task, that they had difficulty exerting the meta-cognitive control over evaluative processes needed to enable them to suspend judgement in their written work or perhaps that they lacked the linguistic resources. Allowing students to jump to judgement in uncontrolled ways can be considered problematic insofar as it allows them to rest (and evaluate) based on current understandings, which places limitations upon the time and space reserved (in stage 3 of the IDM) for stepping outside their own perspectives to appreciate those of others, searching deeper and seeking breadth in the analysis of incoming information in the process.

Data generated by the standard-setting section of the EAP Reports suggested that students could not only set evaluation standards clearly but also generate their own, which seems to indicate that value-clarification processes were underway (i.e. students were deciding what was important to them), reflecting personal transformation. Byram suggests that *savoir s'engager*, or critical cultural awareness/political education is the most educationally significant of the *savoirs* because it fundamentally re-characterizes language teaching and learning as education for citizenship and democracy (Byram, 2008: 233–236), and this brings into question the relationship between teacher and learner values. While Byram recognizes that teachers may not want to guide learner evaluations in a particular direction for ethical reasons, he recommends teachers to at least encourage learners to make their evaluations explicit and to be consistent in their application (Byram, 2008: 233). However, data generated by the critical evaluation section of the EAP reports suggested that students seemed less able to apply the standards consistently to the evaluation of their own and their partner's project, if at all. While almost half of the Japan-based students *did* consistently apply the standards they had set, the others did not, perhaps because they only evaluated their partner's essay, they did not understand the meaning of certain standards or they could not find relevant information in the reports. By contrast, Taiwan-based students focused more on identifying positive and negative aspects.

Students in both groups did, however, justify their evaluations by giving reasons that may reflect tacitly held rather than explicitly stated standards. This suggests an alternative teaching approach with which to guide student exploration of their evaluative standards. Although standards may be set consciously before proceedings to apply them consciously in evaluative tasks (as in the standard-setting section of the EAP report), students may be allowed to judge freely in the first place as long as they give reasons, the plenary discussion and deconstruction of which in class may later reveal tacitly held standards potentially rendering them more explicit and allowing students to choose more consciously between them, a process that was also followed by Houghton (2012) in the development of the IDM. In such ways, teachers can have students 'make the basis of their judgments explicit' (Byram, 2008: 233).

A notable issue is that students in both groups tended to devote more space to evaluating their partner's project rather than their own. This suggests that they did not treat both EAP reports fairly by devoting equal attention to both, which may indicate biased (prejudiced?) evaluation as students were not 'consistent in their judgements of their own society as well as others' (Byram, 2008: 233). Students need to engage not only in reflection upon the project, but also upon self-reflection, with a view to making careful and informed decisions about future project and/or self-development. This is because evaluation seems to influence student decision-making through the evaluation of options and self-realization by engaging in projects in the world (Barnett, 1997). The main conclusion from this study is that reflective components need to be built more systematically into task design.

A process-oriented view

In addition to viewing the outcome of the EAP and EAP feedback reports on the stage-wise basis presented above, they can also be viewed and potentially assessed in terms of the process orientation that occurs between various stages of the study as a whole. In other words, to understand the outcome of ICC development within this study, we can focus on the movement from the shift within the individual with respect to frame of reference – such as empathy, flexibility, adaptability – to the focus on the external world, where a form of critique-in-action is developed that is realized in critical action. Three main shifts, illustrated diagramatically in Figure 5.2, seemed to result from the development of the EAP and EAP Feedback reports. First, SHIFT 1

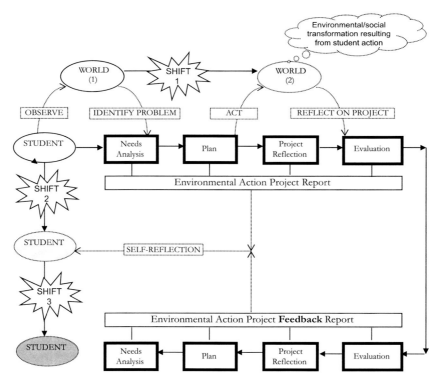

Figure 5.2 Dynamics and shifts in self and world evident in students' EAP reports and EAP Feedback reports

occurred (from WORLD 1 to WORLD 2) as the world was transformed environmentally and socially by student action. Second, SHIFT 2 occurred within a single student (STUDENT 1) to another position (STUDENT 2), as a consequence of observation of the world, problem-identification, project planning, implementation, evaluation and reflection (in the EAP report). Finally, SHIFT 3 occurred within the same student moving to a third position (STUDENT 3) through consideration, critical analysis and evaluation of their own and their partner's EAP reports (in the EAP Feedback report). Although self-reflection is located outside the EAP report and EAP Feedback report structures in Figure 5.2, this component could and should be added to the EAP report and EAP Feedback report structures in future studies.

Conclusion

Focusing on environmental action as one type of social action, this chapter reported on a 14 week action research study in which two groups of university students based in Japan and Taiwan followed a course into which the IDM was integrated. An overview of the course was provided, and two research questions were investigated to ascertain, first, how achieved learning objectives manifest themselves in written work in potentially assessable ways, and second, whether or not personal and social transformation can be considered potentially assessable learning objectives in their own right.

Although the projects were conducted locally in student groups separately from the groups at the university in the partner country, common elements emerged in the data generated by students describing their own projects in their EAP Reports, and social contact with people outside the classroom was also generated as a form of social transformation. Further, some evidence of personal transformation emerged in the data in student expressions of what they had learned (i.e. knowledge transformation): increased awareness of the world around them, self-awareness of values, increased motivation to engage in future action and the generation of new ideas about how to conduct such projects in the future. However, if asked to reflect upon this area more carefully, the quality of student self-reflection may be enhanced, so this reflective component should be built into task design rather than excluded in future studies.

Although there was very little evidence of actual environmental transformation reported in students' project reports, the environmental action/impact itself remains inaccessible to the teacher, which renders it necessarily a non-assessable by-product of the project concerned. Student accounts and evaluations of their projects are, however, accessible to the teacher, which renders them potentially assessable. However, data suggest that fewer than half of the students were able to apply the evaluation criteria in practice when evaluating their own projects, and students may tend to evaluate either too positively or too negatively, so teachers need to consider whether or not these issues matter, and why.

Data generated by the critical analysis section of the EAP Feedback Reports suggested that most students succeeded in identifying similarities and differences between their own EAP report and their partner's non-judgementally, although some did not either because the section was completely lacking, or because they mixed analysis with evaluation. This indicates that they did not understand the task, that they had difficulty exerting the meta-cognitive control over evaluative processes needed to enable them to suspend judgement in their written work or perhaps that they lacked the linguistic resources, so both of these issues need to be taken into greater consideration.

Data generated by the standard-setting section of the EAP reports suggested that students could not only set evaluation standards clearly but also generated their own, which seems to indicate that value-clarification processes were underway, reflecting personal transformation. However, data generated by the critical evaluation section of the EAP reports suggested that students seemed less able to apply the standards consistently to the evaluation of their own and their partner's project, if at all. A notable issue is that students in both groups tended to devote more space to evaluating their partner's project rather than their own. This suggests that they did not treat both EAP reports fairly by devoting equal attention to both, which may indicate biased or prejudiced evaluation patterns.

Students in both groups did, however, justify their evaluations by giving reasons which may reflect tacitly held rather than explicitly stated standards. This suggests an alternative teaching approach with which to guide student exploration of their evaluative standards. Although standards may be set consciously before proceedings to apply them consciously in evaluative tasks, students may be allowed to judge freely in the first place as long as they give reasons, the plenary discussion and deconstruction of which in class may later reveal tacitly held standards potentially rendering them more explicit and allowing students to choose more consciously between them

In addition to viewing the outcome of the EAP and EAP feedback reports on the stage-wise basis presented above, they can also be viewed and potentially assessed in terms of the process orientation that occurs between various stages of the study as a whole. In other words, to understand the outcome of ICC development within this study, we can focus on the movement from the stage of internal shift of self, which involves a shift in frame of reference such as empathy, flexibility, adaptability, to the stage of external world where a form of critique-in-action is developed that is demonstrated in critical action. Notably, a self-reflection component could and should be added to the EAP report and EAP Feedback report structures in future studies.

While the two groups of students based in Japan and Taiwan did not communicate directly about their projects, this may be a possible area for future development, technology and time permitting.

References

Barnett, R. (1997) *Higher Education: A Critical Business.* Buckingham: Society for Research into Higher Education/Open University Press.

Byram, M. (1997) *Teaching and Assessing Intercultural Communicative Competence.* Clevedon: Multilingual Matters.

Byram, M.S. (2008) *From Foreign Language Education to Education for Intercultural Citizenship: Essays and Reflections.* Clevedon: Multilingual Matters.

Coverdell Worldwise Schools (n.d.) Insights from the field: Understanding geography, culture and service. See http://files.peacecorps.gov/wws/pdf/InsightsFromtheField.pdf (accessed 13 March 2014).

Creswell, J.W. (2003) *Research Design: Qualitative, Quantitative and Mixed Method Approaches.* Beverly Hills, CA: Sage.

Hopkins, D. (2002) *A Teacher's Guide to Classroom Research.* Oxford: Oxford University Press.

Houghton, S. (2010) *Savoir se transformer*: Knowing how to become. In Y. Tsai and S. Houghton (eds) *Becoming Intercultural: Inside and Outside the Classroom* (pp. 194–228). Newcastle: Cambridge Scholars.

Houghton, S.A. (2012) *Intercultural Dialogue in Practice: Managing Value Judgment in Foreign Language Education.* Bristol: Multilingual Matters.

Appendix: Course Overview

Week	Teaching materials	Activities	Homework
1	• Introduction	• Self-introductions • Overview of key concepts: intercultural communication/citizenship/environment, developed/developing/third world country and hurricane/typhoon/cyclone impact • Discussion: How can people pull together to cooperate in natural disaster regardless of developmental level	• Learning Diary 1 • Paragraph 1: What is a good citizen? How can good citizens try to help protect the environment?
2	• Lesson 1: 'Working for the common good' (pp. 147–150) • Worksheet 1: 'In the aftermath of Hurricane Georges' • Worksheet 2: 'Working for the common good'	• The impact of Hurricane Georges on the Dominican Republic/working for the common good/how people worked together for the common good/why it mattered and what difference it made	• Learning Diary 2 • Paragraph 2: describe a time in your classroom, school, home and/or community when people had to put aside their own needs, think of the needs of others and work together
3	• Lesson 2: 'Who works for the common good in our community?' (pp. 151–152) • Worksheet 3: 'Presentations by community volunteers'	• Teacher report on (animal rescue) • Initial project planning in groups	• Learning Diary 3 • Paragraph 3: research and report on 2 community volunteers working for volunteer organizations
4	• Lesson 3: 'Service Projects in the Dominican Republic' (pp. 153–158) • Worksheet 4: 'Criteria for a strong service project'	• Review of Dominican Republic Peace Corps projects • Evaluating the success of a project: four given criteria • Read about individual projects/evaluate them by applying the four criteria (jigsaw reading) • Information exchange/discussion	• Learning Diary 4 • Paragraph 4: my ideas for a local environmental action project

Week	Materials/Lesson	Activity	Homework
5	• Lesson 6: 'Planning a Service Project' (pp. 164–170) • Worksheet 6: 'Service-learning rubric' (see Appendix 4)	• Plan a local environmental action project in groups • Evaluate the plan according to worksheet criteria for potential impact (strong/good/some/minimal)	• Learning Diary 5 • Paragraph 5: summarize the environmental action plan including a needs analysis
6	• Lesson 4: 'Conducting interviews in the community' (pp. 159–162) • Worksheet 5: 'Community service guide'	• Reading/discussion: World Environment Day (5 June) • Project development considering needs analysis	• Learning Diary 6 • Interview: interview one volunteer locally/by email and prepare a presentation
7	• Lesson 5: 'Why does service matter?' (p. 163)	• Presentations/discussion • **Environmental Action Project (EAP)** report development considering a specific report structure and sample essays	• Learning Diary 7 (week 7 only) • Project preparation/implementation (see Tables 5) • Deadline for written reports (week 10) • Japan- and Taiwan-based groups exchange project reports and give written feedback
8			
9		• Project presentations/discussion	
10			
11		• Japan- and Taiwan-based groups read each other's reports/discussion	• Japan and Taiwan-based groups prepare and exchange written feedback for each other following IDM
12			
13		• Presentation of feedback reports/discussion	
14			

Section 3

Learners Cooperating

The third part of this book consists of five chapters, which report in detail on learner collaborations across the internet. The authors share their experiences and demonstrate how meaningful interaction may influence the development of intercultural citizenship of both learners and their teachers.

The first chapter in this section, Chapter 6, written by Melina Porto, Petra Daryai-Hansen, María Emilia Arcuri and Kira Schifler, shows how young learners from Argentina and Denmark using English as a lingua franca begin to acquire the skills of criticality through being involved in the discussion of environment protection. As a result of internet collaboration, each group of 'Green Kidz' takes action in their own communities.

Chapter 7, by Catherine Peck and Manuela Wagner, echoes the first section of the book, dedicated to the understanding of the key concepts of intercultural citizenship, but this time university students from two different countries, Korea and the USA, are interacting. Being future teachers, or some of them teachers already in activity, participants are asked to prepare lesson plans for their own contexts. The authors describe in practical detail the challenges of such internet collaboration, and how the difficulties that the students encounter may provide excellent opportunities for intercultural learning.

In Chapter 8, Melina Porto reports on another project that involves university students. As in the case of other learners' collaborations described in this book, criticality is an important dimension of this project too. The participants observe and analyse mural art and graffiti, which leads them to 'action in the community'. Again, the author of this chapter discusses challenges and difficulties in order to help other teachers replicate this collaborative project.

The last two chapters in this section are written by the same authors, Melina Porto and Leticia Yulita. In Chapter 9, they show how a particularly sensitive topic of a war between two countries (Argentina and UK) can be discussed by learners from these countries in such a way that they move beyond their national perspectives towards an 'international' one.

In the final chapter, Melina and Leticia again report about a project that deals with a sensitive historical topic. This international collaboration between Argentinian and British university students not only shows how a meaningful interaction can help to gain new perspectives, but also demonstrates how working on such projects can become part of the professional routine for the teachers.

6 Green Kidz: Young Learners Engage in Intercultural Environmental Citizenship in an English Language Classroom in Argentina and Denmark

Melina Porto, Petra Daryai-Hansen, María Emilia Arcuri and Kira Schifler

Introduction

In this chapter we describe an online intercultural citizenship project about the environment in three English language classrooms, carried out in 2013/2014. In Argentina, 50 fifth- and sixth-grade primary school pupils (aged 10–11), took part, led by María Emilia Arcuri and Agustina Zoroza at Escuela Graduada Joaquín V. González, Universidad Nacional de La Plata. María Emilia Arcuri and Agustina Zoroza are English teachers and have been working at Escuela Graduada for five years. In Denmark, 20 seventh-form pupils participated (aged 12–13), led by Kira Schifler at Randersgades Skole, International Profile School of Copenhagen. Kira is an English, Danish and Drama teacher and has been working at Randersgades Skole for 17 years. The researchers in charge are Melina Porto in Argentina and Petra Daryai-Hansen in Denmark.

We begin by describing how the researchers established communication to set up the project and how they got in contact with teachers to start planning. Then, we draw up a list of aims and explain the way in which we met them, by providing a detailed description of our lesson plans and how they were carried out in the classroom. We also analyse extensive data that support our work and illustrate the merger between theory and practice. We end by considering the project's outcomes and some possibilities and challenges ahead.

Description of the Project

Antecedents and preparations

The project underwent several phases. The idea was first discussed informally between Melina Porto and Petra Daryai-Hansen in June 2012 and it developed gradually with continuous feedback from Michael Byram. It originates from the Green Kidz project carried out previously at Randersgades Skole, which had been selected as Copenhagen's International Profile School in 2009 by Copenhagen Municipality (2014). The school's goal is to 'educate school pupils to be innovative citizens of the world, and to communicate and develop intercultural competences through cooperation with international partners for both pupils and employees' (Randersgades Skole, 2012). After the United Nations Climate Change Conference in Copenhagen in 2009, which resulted in symbolic political statements that were not legally binding, a group of pupils from Randersgades Skole created the environmental movement Green Kidz because they believed that attention to the environment would disappear after the summit and that adults did not take their responsibilities seriously. The Green Kidz project is coordinated by Natural Sciences teacher Julie Svensson, in collaboration with pupils, who join the project. Financed by the Danish public television, a flashmob video was produced (http://www.youtube.com/watch?v=yVtZ6VBRvHk). Green Kidz also has a Facebook presence (http://www.facebook.com/greenkids2100) and has established bonds with other schools in Denmark and a school in South Africa.

We agreed to further develop the Green Kidz project, which until then had only been integrated in natural sciences classes, and as an optional subject, and to introduce it into the language classroom at Randersgade Skole and Escuela Graduada Joaquín V. González. We first designed a pilot study at Escuela Graduada Joaquín V. González, which was carried out by María Emilia Arcuri in a fourth form in 2012, prior to discussions with the head of the school, who welcomed the project. The school was particularly receptive in part because the project shared key theoretical tenets with other ongoing projects at the school, such as a conception of language as social and communicative practice and citizenship education. More specifically, since 2005 the school had been successfully implementing an environmental project called *Separación de Basuras* (Sorting Out Trash) that reaches all classrooms, not only the foreign language classroom. The pupils in the whole school had been introduced to recycling practices and were actively participating in small actions to take care of the environment. More globally, the school had also implemented a novel idea for a primary school in Argentina, which was to initiate pupils in participatory and civic practices intended to develop the skills of democratic life. A centre for democratic life (*consejo de convivencia*) was created in 2004 and each class has a delegate who voices the opinions of the pupils in that class in meetings intended to solve school problems that are important to the pupils, identify initiatives and make proposals to the school authorities. The school was therefore ready to welcome our project.

The pilot study in Argentina served to make adjustments to the final project. For instance, we agreed on the aims (linguistic, intercultural, citizenship and other) that we wanted it to accomplish and the stages the project would have; we made changes to some tasks that did not work well; we analysed the data to see whether there was a need to introduce any methodological changes. A lot of fine-tuning occurred in this phase, in particular because the Argentinean pupils were less proficient in English than the Danes. This difference was increased by the fact that Randersgades Skole had to include seventh-grade pupils instead of sixth-graders, because the project had to be postponed owing to a teacher strike in Denmark in spring 2013. Consequently we simplified some tasks for the Argentinean pupils and added more visual support. We ended up with a detailed weekly plan that comprised approximately 16 lessons spread over three months.

Another phase involved meetings and email conversations between researcher and teacher in each country, and then between both researchers.

Aims

The project team formulated linguistic, intercultural and citizenship learning objectives. Upon completion of the project, the pupils were to develop the following *linguistic competences* from Coyle *et al.* (2010) and *plurilingual competences* from Candelier *et al.* (2009):

- engage in a dialogue in English as lingua franca with Others;
- acquire, understand and use special language related to the environment; and
- acknowledge linguistic diversity in the English, Spanish and Danish languages.

Intercultural citizenship was developed from Byram (2008), proposing that the pupils would be able to:

- demonstrate a willingness to engage in intercultural dialogue with Others;
- allow Others to express their viewpoints, avoiding hostility and confrontation and resolving conflict when necessary;
- develop values such as respect, mutual understanding, social awareness and openness;
- raise awareness of the power of the media in creating stereotypical images of environmental issues that may influence attitudes and behaviours; and
- transfer knowledge to Others by engaging in civic participation locally.

With respect to what might be called *intercultural environmental citizenship* based on Byram's (2008) concept of intercultural citizenship, the pupils would be able to:

- understand environmental issues and how to recognize them in their own surroundings;
- challenge taken-for-granted representations of the environment;
- analyse critically (audio) visual media images, texts, practices, etc.;
- explore and reflect on environmental issues locally (in their community);
- develop rubbish sorting and recycling awareness;
- engage in rubbish sorting and recycling practices;
- encourage their extended network, i.e. their families, friends and other members of their community, to develop environmental awareness;
- contribute to improving the environment in their schools and their local communities;
- explore and reflect on environmental issues globally; and
- engage in research skills.

In order to meet these learning objectives, the project distinguishes between four levels of analysis (the school, the community, the family and media-analysis) and four levels of taking action (the extended network, the school, the community and the World Wide Web) (Figure 6.1).

Four levels of analysis: My school, my community, my family, media-analysis

In the first lessons, the pupils in each country recorded a video introducing themselves to the partner school, speaking in English. Furthermore, they became familiar with the virtual space *WorldGreenWeb*, a wiki that we created especially for this project, and they uploaded their videos there.

Analysis
(1) My school
(2) My community
(3) My family
(4) Media-analysis

Intercultural Citizenship Education in the Language Classroom

Taking Action
(1) My extended network
(2) My school
(3) My community
(4) The World Wide Web

Figure 6.1 Project design

The next step was to identify 'green crimes' in their schools and, later, in their communities after having been introduced to the notion of 'green crime' (i.e. a crime against the environment; see Figure 6.2) using a video produced as part of the Danish Green Kidz project that serves as antecedent (http://www.youtube.com/watch?v=EgmnQ3ELtV8&list=UUgwpj6gH0 eIM-3d8NGqNvrQ&index=5). In this video, a girl corrects her mother who wastes water. The pupils in both countries discussed how the girl feels about the situation and which character reflects their own attitude towards the environment. As a follow-up, they also drew green crimes to show their understanding of the topic and persuade people to change their attitudes towards the environment.

Since the video is in Danish, this was an opportunity for Argentinean teachers to raise language awareness by encouraging reflection with questions such as 'How does Danish sound to you?', 'What might *Spar på vandet* mean?' (It means *Save water*), 'How do you know?', 'What can you say about the writing system in Danish?' The pupils in both countries drew or video-taped the green crimes they identified in their communities and uploaded them to the wiki.

They then engaged in a rubbish analysis mini-project in their schools (Table 6.1), which involved them listing, classifying and sorting out the rubbish in the waste bins in their schools, and recording their observations with photographs and videos with the help of their teachers. They reflected upon the question: 'Are the pupils and teachers in our school committing green crimes?'

The pupils then compared and discussed the results in each country using the wiki. This was an occasion for the Danish pupils to discover the Argentinean 'Sorting Out Trash' project and to discuss the fact that, in this school, the waste was sorted in three different bins whereas there was no waste sorting in their own school.

In addition, the pupils carried out a survey among family members and friends about their environmental habits and also uploaded the results to the wiki. The results showed that the Argentinean pupils were more used to

What do you think this person is saying? (in groups)

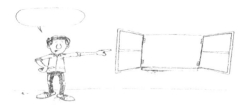

Now, draw a green **crime scene!** What do these people say? (individual work)

Figure 6.2 Pupils' worksheet 1: 'Toilet Green Crime'

Table 6.1 Pupils' worksheet 2: Rubbish analysis

What do you find?	How many items?	Could this item be recycled?
		yes/no/perhaps
		yes/no/perhaps

sorting waste, whereas Danish pupils were more used to buying eco-friendly products. Moreover, in their individual answers some Danish pupils pointed out that the waste sorting system in Denmark is quite limited.

Finally, the pupils in each country analysed critically (audio) visual media images and texts in order to gain awareness of the power of the media in creating stereotypical images of environmental issues that may influence attitudes and behaviours. This was done by exploring the following texts and videos from the Argentinean context:

- https://www.youtube.com/watch?v=EAQSlu2NLEs
- http://www.youtube.com/watch?v=eAn3jhn2_k4
- https://www.youtube.com/watch?v=mGLD813iQmM

The first link is a commercial which was made by the local government of Buenos Aires in order to raise awareness about sorting waste. The other two are commercials that were created by an important water company called Villavicencio as part of an environmentally friendly campaign to avoid deforestation and encourage people to recycle plastic bottles.

For Denmark, the following were chosen:

- a promotional music video about Copenhagen as City of Cyclists, that was made for the City of Copenhagen's Bicycle Office (http://www.you tube.com/watch?v=xsDxOx7PUP0);
- a video promoting putting shoe boxes in the rubbish can for cardboard, which was based on a collaboration between the franchise company Bianco shoes and the city of Copenhagen (http://video.kk.dk/video/8548433/genbrug-er-guld-reklame);
- and Copenhagen City Council's campaign video for Copenhagen as a clean city (http://www.youtube.com/watch?v=f7fcyyBJRvI).

If the previous videos are no longer accessible, any material that serves the purpose of triggering pupils' thoughts and reflections on such issues can be used.

The pupils made a comparative analysis and discussed who takes responsibility for the environment in the videos, and why that person takes responsibility. The media analysis was an opportunity to raise language awareness in both groups by (a) analysing some aspects of the Spanish and Danish languages in these videos and (b) discussing what strategies the pupils used in

Table 6.2 Let's share what we know: How are these languages similar and how are they different? (Extract)

	Green Kidz Argentina	Green Kidz Denmark
Hello!	¡Hola!	Hej, goddag!
to protect the environment	proteger el medio ambiente	at beskytte miljøet
Good Bye! See you!	Chau, ¡nos vemos!	Farvel! Vi ses!

order to understand a language they did not know. Most pupils agreed on the importance of visual support in understanding the different meanings involved in the dialogues. In the Danish class, one pupil was able to understand Spanish and he provided linguistic support for the class throughout the whole project. During the project, the Argentinean and Danish pupils developed with their teachers an overview comparing English, Danish and Spanish (Table 6.2).

Taking action collaboratively: Designing posters and slogans

On the basis of the critical analysis and evaluation of these media texts and the green crimes, rubbish analysis and survey tasks, the Argentinean and Danish pupils were ready to engage in the online collaboration phase of the project. The task set was to collaboratively design an advertisement to raise awareness of environmental issues. The teachers in each country brainstormed ideas and vocabulary with their pupils before both groups engaged in online communication using the project wiki and Skype. In both countries, the pupils reflected on communication strategies: how can you communicate in a foreign language with others who are probably less/more proficient in that language? The pupils adopted a number of strategies to cope with the different levels of language proficiency, such as using the chat function in the wiki and Skype, Google Translate and gestures, among other options. The Argentinean pupils needed the help of their teachers during all the phases of the project. Several Danish pupils also mentioned the problem that the Argentinian pupils were less proficient in English, but some other pupils emphasized that it was not an obstacle to communication: 'Vi snakkede engelsk med hinanden, der var ikke problemer, vi kunne godt snakke med dem' ('We communicated in English, there were no problems, we were able to talk to each other') (interview).

Considering the five-hour difference between the two countries, special arrangements had to be made for the Skype-session: the pupils in Argentina had to re-schedule their English class, and this required the consent from other teachers as well as the school head; the Danish pupils had to stay in the school after school hours and this also required the help of the school and of their parents. There were technical difficulties as well and therefore the online contact was not successful in all the groups. This led to a little frustration for some of the pupils, for which the teachers in each country found a solution. For instance, some of the groups chose to communicate in writing via the wiki and the Skype chat as an alternative.

With the aid of the teachers and the researchers, during the Skype exchange the pupils, in six groups (each group including three pupils from Denmark and eight pupils from Argentina), decided on the content of the advert (both linguistic and non-linguistic such as images and other resources), the languages to be included and the advert's purpose. In this process, an international identification emerged and we shall illustrate this later. Afterwards, the Argentinian and Danish pupils worked independently on the advert, which in all cases was a poster (Figures 6.3 and 6.4). For instance,

Figure 6.3 Posters: The Argentinian interpretation of the collaborative work

Figure 6.4 Posters: The Danish interpretation of the collaborative stage

the Argentinian pupils selected possible pictures for the poster, put them all together in a PowerPoint presentation and shared them with the Danish pupils in the wiki. Furthermore, some pupils were in contact outside the classroom on Facebook.

Four levels of taking action: My extended network, my school, my community and the World Wide Web

As a final step, the pupils in each country took action by carrying out some tasks in their extended network, their school, their community and the World Wide Web. For instance, the Argentinian pupils created videos and songs (http://www.youtube.com/watch?v=uysvpqx2vN0;http://www.you tube.com/watch?v=8zTlOCskmo8;http://www.youtube.com/watch?v= DjgTR6QeetQ;http://www.youtube.com/watch?v=nGE9oq3hTdo), which they shared in a Facebook group, designed by themselves (https://www. facebook.com/pages/Save-the-Planet-Argentina/603179783054514). They were interviewed by a local journalist and got the collaborative posters published in the local newspaper (http://www.eldia.com.ar/edis/20131121/ Alumnos-Plata-Dinamarca-abrazan-medio-ambiente-laciudad2.htm); they also printed the posters and distributed them in a kermes (a day when families gather at school to play games and share some time with their children, organized annually by the school); and they designed a street banner and

Figure 6.5 Street banner in *Escuela Graduada Joaquín V. González* in La Plata, Argentina

displayed it in the school street (see Figure 6.5). In addition, Radio Cool, a local radio in La Plata, shared information about the project.

In Denmark, the pupils put up their posters in the school and distributed them in their community. They wrote a letter to the local newspaper *Øbro Avis* and posted information about the project on the newspapers' Facebook page (https://www.facebook.com/osterbroavis). They also created videos and songs and uploaded them on Youtube (http://www.youtube.com/watch?v=LxR-9hNBG4k, http://www.youtube.com/watch?v=dlXLddVLdCs, http://www.youtube.com/watch?v=8usDFI6lEmA). A final Youtube video summarized the whole project and included the posters from Denmark and Argentina as well as other project products from both countries such as the surveys and photos (https://www.youtube.com/watch?v=3CRboXq2yZs).

Finally, the pupils informed Greenpeace Denmark (https://www.face book.com/greenpeacedanmark) and Greenpeace International (https://www.facebook.com/greenpeace.international) about the project and posted information about the project in the Danish Green Kidz Facebook group (https://www.facebook.com/greenkids2100). The video and the posted information represent an invitation to everybody to join the Green Kidz project and to save the environment.

Project Evaluation

We based the project evaluation on a mixed methods design (Punch, 2009). As one type of data collection, both the Argentinian and Danish pupils completed the written version of the *Autobiography of Intercultural Encounters for Younger Learners* (AIE, Council of Europe; Byram *et al.*, 2009a) individually in their classrooms, in Spanish and in English respectively. According to Byram *et al.* (2009b: 5) the AIE helps 'participants analyse and reflect on their participation in exchanges of any kind', focusing both on their 'personal development through the experience and, secondly, on the values, beliefs and behaviours of all involved'. In this way, the AIE contributes to developing the learners' intercultural competences and their intercultural citizenship (cf. Byram *et al.*, 2009b: 6; Muderrisgil & Barrett, 2011). In addition, semi-structured focus group interviews were completed at the end of the project. Focus group interviews are, as Punch emphasizes, 'data-rich, flexible, stimulating, recall-aiding, cumulative and elaborative' (Punch, 2009: 147) and, owing to the peer interaction and support involved, they are considered an adequate method to explore pupils' views (Hennessy & Heary, 2005). The AIE and three focus group interviews were carried out at Randersgades Skole on 7 March 2014. In Argentina the pupils completed their AIEs on 22 November 2013 and were interviewed one week later.

Findings

As explained in the Introduction to this book, an intercultural citizenship project should develop an international identification between the student groups involved, a set of specific skills such as de-centring, perspective-taking, etc., and criticality. We explain each aspect in turn, focusing on three sets of data: (a) the posters, which were developed collaboratively by the Argentinian–Danish groups in the wiki and in Skype sessions in order to engage pupils in intercultural dialogue, and were further designed within small groups in each country; (b) the AIEs, which described the reflections, thoughts, feelings, skills and experiences that the pupils developed individually during the project; and (c) the focus group interviews, which mirror these individual thoughts, feelings, skills and experiences, but set them in relation to those of other pupils by acknowledging or questioning them, thus developing values such as respect and openness as well as constructing and negotiating an individual and/or common understanding of the project and what it entails as a global concern. Pseudonyms are used here for both the Argentinian and the Danish pupils' names. Parents signed consent forms allowing their pupils to participate in the project and agreeing to have their work disclosed, suitably anonymized.

An international identification developed

The online communication stage involved the Argentinian and Danish pupils in a collaborative task, which was the design of a poster intended to raise environmental awareness in groups of mixed nationalities. During the process an international identification emerged. This means that the pupils temporarily abandoned their identifications as Argentinian or Danish and worked in cooperation with their international peers. We found evidence of this identification in the wiki and the posters as well as in the AIEs and the interviews, which we signal in bold here.

In the wiki, when the Argentinian and Danish pupils were asked to agree on the form and the content of their product, the pupils' use of first person plural or second person singular pronouns and verbs illustrates the construction of a common identification:

> Danish pupils: Do you agree about making a poster with two sides. One showing what **you** should not do and the other one showing what **you** have to do instead:). But what do **we** have to focus on?

> Argentinian pupils: We think **we** should focus on waste of power and destruction of forests. (Wiki conversation)

In the posters too, the first person plural was used. For instance, the first poster on the left in Figure 6.3a includes the following message: '**Hagamos** algo por el mundo este es **nuestro** deseo … **Cuidemos** lo que **tenemos**' ('**Let's do** something for the world this is **our** wish … **Let's take care** of what **we have**'). In addition, in the posters the pupils conveyed a 'green' message, that they made on their own, and spoke directly to their imagined audience. They addressed the readers of their posters as an international group: 'Ese es **nuestro** mensaje'; '<u>Hey you</u>!'; '<u>Use</u> it [water]wisely'; '<u>Usarlo</u>[a] sabiamente'; '<u>Stop</u> wasting water'; '<u>Spar</u> på vandet'; '<u>Don't cut down</u> the forest'; '<u>Think</u> about the environment', '<u>Piencer</u> a la klima' (cf. Figures 6.3a, 6.3b and 6.4). The use of imperatives (underlined) is worth noting because it is a direct address to the reader. The image of two hands holding each other in the first poster in Figure 6.3a may point to one of the key pillars in citizenship education, which emphasizes the commonalities that human beings share despite the many differences, for instance differences in the languages that the pupils speak, in the ways they handle rubbish at school, in their environmental habits, etc.

Furthermore, the international identification is mirrored in the image of the world: a globe surrounded by dynamic green arrows, which is at the centre of one poster and the world in the form of a drop of water, under which there is a green spot symbolizing the waste of natural resources (cf. Figures 6.3a and 6.4). In another poster, the Argentinian flag is placed in the right corner and the Danish flag in the left corner. An electric bulb is placed at the centre, between the two flags, nourishing a green tree, which symbolizes the common concern for the environment. This common interest is meant to go beyond national borders (cf. Figure 6.3b).

In addition, in the project, the proper name 'Green Kidz' was proposed as a collective identification. The Danish and Argentinian pupils acted on this suggestion in several posters, using either the logo or the name 'Green Kidz'.

Simultaneously, the posters include a comparative perspective, present throughout the project, which can be observed in the juxtaposition of (a) the three languages in some posters (Spanish, Danish, English), (b) the flags of Argentina and Denmark on the third poster in Figure 6.3b and (c) ideas. We shall describe this comparative perspective further in the following section, but for the moment it is important to say that it encouraged pupils to become 'intercultural mediators'.

In the Danish AIEs and interviews, the international identification (in bold) was emphasized in respect to the cooperation and communication between the Argentinian and Danish pupils: '**Vi** havde et samarbejde med at blive enige om hvordan posteren skulle se ud, og så skiltes **vi** ad' ('**We** worked together, deciding on how the poster should appear, and then **we** parted') (interview), '**We** talked English with **each other** and used **our** hands' (Kirse, AIE). Both successful communication and communication problems were represented as common experiences: '**we** couldn't really hear **each other**' (Mogens, AIE). In addition to verbal communication, also singing, dancing and laughing were used to interact and establish a transnational community: '**We** started with telling what **your** name was, and how old **we** were. Then **we** begun singing, I don't really know why, **we** just did' (Johanne, AIE), '**We** didnt talk much, just laughed and showed pictures to **each other** of 1D and Justin Bieber. **We** sang and danced' (Zoé, AIE). Laughter in particular helped overcome communication barriers: '**Vi** grinte meget fordi **vi** ikke vidste hvad **vi** skulle sige til hinanden' ('**We** laughed a lot because **we** didn't know what to say to each other') (interview).

The international identification (in bold), as well as the common message to foster environmental awareness (in italics), became evident in the Spanish AIEs and the interviews. For instance, in the interview Miguel said: '**estábamos los dos** [both countries] **de acuerdo** *en cuidar el medio ambiente*'; '**both of us** [both countries] **agreed** *on taking care of the environment*'. Similarly, Ramiro expressed: '**estamos** colaborando otro paises para *decirle no a los crímenes verdes y crear conciencia en todo el mundo*'; '**we are** collaborating [with] other countries *to say no to green crimes and raise awareness all over the world*' (Ramiro, AIE). He identified with Danish peers from the very beginning: 'El inglés fue **nuestro lenguaje** que **nos** sirvió de puente para **comunicarnos, vivimos** en el mismo planeta en el mismo en el que **estamos** en peligro'; 'English was **our language**, which worked as a bridge to help **us communicate, we live** in the same world, the same place where **we are** in danger' (Ramiro, AIE). He referred to English as '**our language**'. English for Ramiro was something that they shared as a community ('**nuestro lenguaje**'). The international identification is pervasive in this short extract from his AIE. At the same time, Ramiro shows different degrees of criticality. In saying, '**we live** in the same world, the same place where **we are** in danger' ('**vivimos** en el mismo planeta en el mismo en el que **estamos** en peligro'), there is an underlining process of critical self-reflection in order to modify what might be 'common sense': it's neither my fault, nor your fault; we are all responsible because we all live in this world. This is also revealed linguistically through word repetition ('mismo', underlined in the extract) and the phrase 'estamos en peligro' ('we are in danger'). This AIE extract shows Ramiro's intention to call for an immediate reaction in order to develop a new way of thinking.

Furthermore, some Danish pupils connected the universal engagement and responsibility for the environment (in bold) with their personal engagement and responsibility (in italics): 'But *I* discovered that the things **we do for the environment** are really important and *I* know that *I* will never stop doing it' (Zoé, AIE), '*Jeg* har altid sådan passet på miljøet. Det er jorden, det er jo de ressourcer **vi** bruger. **Vi** skal respektere det. Det er jo det **vi** lever af' ('*I* have always protected the environment. It's the Earth, it's the resources **we** use. **We** need to respect that. It's the resources **we** live on, you know') (interview). Several pupils emphasized their awareness of themselves as human beings consuming the world's resources and this being a common responsibility: 'Det er jo **menneskes** skyld at jorden bliver varmere og hvis det er **vores** skyld, så skal **vi** også tage ansvar og ikke bare skylde skylden på andre' ('The rising of the temperature on earth is caused by **human beings**, and if this is **our** fault, then **we** need to act responsibly, and not blame it on others') (interview). Both the responsibility and the threat are shared. It is therefore evident to these pupils that the Argentinian pupils shared their interest in the environment: 'Lige meget hvem **man** er, hvor **man** er fra, jeg tror at **de** tænker lige **så meget** på miljø **som vi** gør' ('No matter who **you** are and where **you**'re from, I think **they** care as **much** about the environment **as we** do') (interview), '**Vi** er jo på den sammen jord. [...] Hvis jorden springer i luften så dør **vi** jo **alle sammen**' ('**We** are all on the same planet. If the earth were to explode **we** would **all** die') (interview).

Overall, these examples show that the pupils learned to see themselves in relation to others and as they did, they developed an international way of thinking and acting that went beyond local concerns.

The skills involved in intercultural citizenship

It is possible to observe the skills involved in intercultural citizenship in all data types. As emphasized in the Introduction and in Byram (2012, 2014), these are the skills of observing, discovering, describing, analysing, comparing and contrasting, relating, interpreting, perspective taking, de-centring, critical thinking and reflexivity.

The possibility of working with pupils from another country fostered processes of comparing and contrasting. The Argentinian pupils saw their Danish peers in a positive light, understanding and valuing them ('Son *muy educados y amitoso*', 'They are *very polite and friendly*', Jorge, AIE and interview). The Danish pupils described the Argentinian pupils as 'kind and sweet' (Zoé, AIE), 'kind and fun' (Johanne, AIE), 'utrolig søde' ('extremely nice') (interview). Several Danish pupils discovered that the Argentinian peers wore a school uniform: 'They where all wearing a white shirt' (Ben, AIE), 'They [...] all wear the same uniform' (Mogens, AIE). Some pupils compared the Argentinian pupils with themselves or their peers and emphasized that the Argentinian pupils were younger and less proficient in English: 'They were smaller than us and don't speak that good English' (Mogens, AIE). In the interviews the Danish pupils discussed the Argentinian pupils' English accent. They compared different accents and agreed that the important question is where one comes from: 'Det er lettere at forstå, hvad kunne man sige ..., en dansk accent for os, fordi vi kommer fra Danmark, eller en amerikansk accent' ('It's easier for us to understand a Danish accent because we come from Denmark – or maybe an American accent'). Using this as a point of departure, the pupils emphasized that for instance the English-Irish accent is difficult for them to understand and they also compared linguistic varieties in Denmark: 'Vi kan jo heller ikke forstå jyder, altså sønderjysk er meget meget svært at forstå, for en Københavner som os, og Bornholmsk det er altså virkelig underligt' ('We can't understand some of our Danish accents either – e.g. if people come from the south of Jutland or from Bornholm [an island in Denmark]'.

In the focus group discussions related to the Argentinian school uniforms, the skills of observing, discovering, describing, analysing, comparing and contrasting, relating, interpreting, perspective taking and de-centring became strongly evident. Several pupils were surprised that the Argentinian pupils wore school uniforms and discussed their pros and cons. Most pupils emphasized that they were happy not to have to wear school uniforms, because people express themselves through their choice of clothes. However, all groups also formulated arguments in favour of school uniforms. For instance, some pupils said: 'Så skal man ikke gå op i hvad man tager på' ('Then you don't have to worry about what to wear') and 'Men hvis man er fattigt, så er det meget bedre' ('But if you're poor, it's much better'). Another group discussed whether bullying is related to clothes in their context, agreed that this is not the case, and wondered whether that is also the case in Argentina, thereby showing willingness to take another perspective:

Student 1: Jeg tror ikke at folk mobber folk på grund af deres tøj længere. Jeg tror at vores generation er sådan lidt ligeglad.
Student 2: Det ved du ikke om de er dernede.
(Interview)
Student 1: I don't think people are bullying each other because of the way they dress anymore. I think our generation doesn't care about that.
Student 2: You don't know whether they do down there.

Finally, the pupils de-centred and took the Argentinian pupils' perspective as they discussed why school uniforms are worn in the Argentinian context: 'Er det ikke for at man vise at man tilhører den skole?' ('Isn't it to show which school you belong to?') (interview).

The Argentinian pupils identified what made the Danish pupils different but they also appreciated their openness and cooperation to adjust to those cultural differences. In his AIE, Darío said: *'teníamos cosas en común. Recuerdo que ellos pusieron su buena voluntad en que se queden ellos en la escuela más tiempo del debido para poder hablar con nosotros'* ('we had things in common. I remember that *to be able to talk to us, they stayed after school in a spirit of goodwill'*).

Similarly, Lionel began by identifying differences but ended up finding what linked them together as a result of having participated in this project. We show evidence of the skills of comparing and contrasting (in italics) and the emphasis on becoming conscious of working with others through a process of bonding (in bold).

La verdad que si, ellos, su país y su escuela son muy diferentes a las nuestras obviamente también su lenguaje, **pero todos tenemos un mismo objetivo: cuidar el medio ambiente y eso es lo más lindo**. (Lionel, AIE)

Yes, the truth is that they, their country and their school are very different from ours obviously their language too, **but we all have the same objective: to take care of the environment and that's the nicest thing**.

Lo más lindo de todo es que **podemos**...**todos somos** *muy diferentes* **pero todos tenemos un mismo objetivo** que es cuidar el medio ambiente. (Lionel, interview)

The nicest thing of all is that **we can**...**we all are** *very different* **but we all have the same objective** which is to take care of the environment.

All the pupils underwent processes of this kind. In the process of becoming conscious of working with others, Eliseo, Carolina and Ignacio focused on emphasizing the differences between cultures, such as the linguistic competence involved in the encounter or time constrains (in italics). Others such as Valentina decided to focus on similarities by establishing a symmetrical relation between both cultures. This is revealed linguistically through sentence structure, in particular the use of parallel structure (underlined).

*Si nosotros hablamos en español y en inglés y ellos a parte hablan en inglés y danés*también las diferencias eran las edades eran diferentes otros tenían 13 o 14 y nosotros teniamos 10 o 11 yo tengo 11. (Eliseo)

Yes we speak Spanish and English. And besides, they speak English and Danish we were different ages too some of them were 13 or 14 and we were 10 or 11 I'm 11

Entre argentina y dinamarca era mucho la diferencia de horarioy los chicos de dinamarca ya salian de la escuela *y nosotros* todavia estabamos en clase. (Carolina, AIE)

There was a great time difference between Argentina and Denmark and when Danish kids were finishing the school *we* were still in class.

Ellos tenian un leguaje muy diferente al nuestro y había muchos rubios. (Ignacio, AIE)

Their language was very different from ours and many of them (pupils) *were blond.*

A ellos les gustaba One Direction a nosotros también les gustaba bailar a nosotros también. (Valentina, AIE)

They liked One Direction, and so did we, they liked dancing, and so did we.

These data simultaneously show evidence of other skills involved in intercultural citizenship such as observing ('las edades eran diferentes'; 'they were different ages'), discovering ('había muchos rubios'; 'many of them were blond'), describing ('A ellos les gustaba … a nosotros también'; 'They liked … and so did we'), analysing ('Ellos tenían un lenguaje muy diferente al nuestro'; 'Their language was very different from ours'), and relating ('A ellos … a nosotros'; 'They … we').

De-centring and perspective-taking allowed pupils to consider perspectives which were different from their own and this is fundamental in intercultural citizenship. De-centring began by noticing difference and acknowledging that it calls one's attention *'me sorprendí porque*teníamos que hablar siempre en inglés' (Marcos, AIE; *'I was surprised because* we had to speak English all the time'); *'Fue un día extraño*sólo porque saber que estar conectado con personas de otro país *ya es raro'* (Ramiro, AIE; *'It was a strange day because* knowing that we had to be connected with people from another country was weird enough'); *'Era como "wow", ibamos a hablar con los de otro país* (estaban, dice la profesora) … *como flasheados'* (Josefina, interview; *'It was like "wow", we were going to talk to those from another country* (you were, teacher said) … *like flabbergasted'.*

De-centring in turn led to perspective-taking. For instance, María explicitly put herself in the Danish pupils' shoes and attempted to understand their feelings in her AIE: 'No se como *se pudieron sentir ellos, yo creo que felices.* Me di cuenta porque se reian y sonreian'; 'I don't know *how they might feel, I think they were* happy. I realized that because they were laughing and smiling.' Andrea, by contrast, took the fact that they laughed as evidence of their nervousness ('Yo creo que *ellos se sintieron nerviosos por que* se reian de algunas cosas que decíamos'; 'I think *they were nervous because* they were laughing at the things we said'; Andrea, AIE). In her AIE, Carolina provided more details: 'Creo que ellos *se sintieron muy felices por* haber hecho algo por el mundo. *Me di cuenta por* todo el esfuerzo que pusieron en el poster y las ganas que tenían de hacer este proyecto' ('I think *they felt very happy about* having done something for the world. *I realized that because* of the great effort they put in making the poster and the engagement they kept throughout the project').

From stereotyping to the development of intercultural skills

Almost all the pupils mentioned at one point or another not knowing much about each other's country peoples and ways of life. In the Danish interviews, the pupils were explicitly asked to reflect on their preconceptions of Argentina. This was not the case in Argentina, where the teachers did not explicitly ask about preconceptions and the topic did not come up naturally during the focus group interviews. The Danish pupils said that before the project they did not know much about Argentina. They formulated stereotypical ideas about Argentina and Argentinians associating the country with football, heat, Hawaii, palm trees, beautiful colours and 'brune samba mennesker' ('dark-skinned samba people'). One student drew explicitly on exoticism describing Argentina as 'eksotisk, anderledes, fattig' ('exotic, different, poor').

As Stephan and Stephan (1996: 4) point out, stereotypes – as distinguished from prejudice – help organize and simplify the world, but stereotypes are primarily important for intergroup relations 'when they are negative, overgeneralized, or incorrect, because then they have detrimental effects on intergroup interactions' (Stephan & Stephan, 1996: 4). In Byram *et al.*'s (2002: 9) definition, 'the intercultural dimension in language teaching aims to develop learners as intercultural speakers or mediators who are able to engage with complexity and multiple identities and to avoid the stereotyping which accompanies perceiving someone through a single identity'. Representations of Argentina as warm and colourful are positive stereotypes about the *country*, while associations such as 'exotic, different, poor' tie *Argentinians* to a single identity and have a slightly more negative connotation.

In the Danish data, there is much evidence for negative, overgeneralized and incorrect stereotypes about both the country and its inhabitants. For example, most of the Danish pupils had stereotypical images of Argentina as being 'landsbyagtig' ('village-like'), 'lidt primitivt' ('a little primitive') and 'slumagtigt' ('slum-like'). The idea of poverty emerged forcefully and was contrasted to Danish economic wealth. Some associated Argentina with developing countries, Africa and mud houses. One student said: 'Jeg tænkte de var *megafattige* og *ikke havde computer og sådan noget*' ('I thought they were *very poor* and *didn't have computers and everything*').

Furthermore, the interviews showed that several Danish pupils had negative stereotypical ideas about discipline in Argentinian schools: 'Jeg troede at lærerne var ret *stramme* og at skolen var ret *disciplineret*' ('I thought the teachers were quite *strict* and there was a lot of *discipline* in school'); 'så tror man også at de *får tæsk* i skolen' ('then you also think they *get beaten* in school'). This idea was deconstructed during the Skype session, where most Danish pupils experienced that the Argentinian pupils were noisy: '*Man troede sådan rigtig*, at der var så meget disciplin, og at de skulle sidde på rækker, og virkelig holde deres mund når læreren talte, *men de var virkelig* ... hørte nærmest ikke efter, de løb rundt og skreg og alt muligt' ('*You thought there would be* a lot of discipline and they had to sit in rows and literally shut up when the teacher was speaking. *But in reality*, they didn't pay much attention, they were running around shouting and all'). In the interviews, the Danish pupils reflected on this discovery through relating, interpreting, de-centring and perspective-taking as they attempted several explanations for such observable behaviour. For instance, they hypothesized that the Argentinian pupils might have been excited about the Skype meetings and they attempted to understand such feelings by suggesting several possible causes for the excitement: the Argentinian pupils were meeting people from another country, they were younger, they could be less experienced in Skype meetings, they were less proficient in English and also there were technical problems. Furthermore, one student reasoned about the time difference: 'Det var *tidligt om morgen* for dem' ('It was *early in the morning* for them.').

Concerning the environment, several Danish pupils imagined Argentina as having severe environmental problems and not being interested in environmental issues:

Student 1: Jeg ved ikke så meget om Argentina, men jeg tænkte at de havde et *dårligt miljø*.

Student 2: Ja, *det tænkte jeg også.* (Interview)

Student 1: I don't know much about Argentina, but I expected them to have a *bad environment.*

Student 2: Yes, *I thought so too.*

Student 1: Jeg ved ikke hvorfor, men det kom bare sådan op til mit hovedet. At der *lugtede af benzin og der ligger skald, sådan urent, lidt slidtagtig over det hele.*

Student 2: *Ja* ... (Interview)

Student 1: I don't know why, it just popped up in my head. *The image of smelling gasoline, garbage and dirt everywhere.*

Student 2: *Yes* ...

The pupils contrasted this representation with their ideas about Denmark's environmental engagement: 'Jeg tror at DK er *førende*' ('I think Denmark is *in the lead*') (interview).

During the project, these stereotypical ideas were deconstructed. Through the above-mentioned media analyses and the 'Sorting Out Trash' project, the Danish pupils were surprised to discover that their Argentinian peers did show environmental consciousness. In the interviews they said 'Jeg blev ret overrasket over hvor dygtige de var til så noget med at sortere affald og det hele med miljøet' ('*I was quite surprised* how good they were at sorting their waste and everything'); 'Jeg var ... sgu forbavset over at de var så gode til at gøre rent og at recycle' ('*I was ... stunned* how good they were at cleaning up and sorting waste'). The words *surprised* and *stunned* are evidence of the skills of observing, discovering and de-centring that are necessary in intercultural understanding. The project also encouraged them to develop the skills of relating as well as comparing and contrasting, shown in italics in the interview extract that follows, in this case in relation to the environment-friendliness of the two schools as well as of the two countries (underlined):

Student 1:   Efter *det man så fra Argentina*, så så det ud som om <u>de er</u>...
Student 2:   ... <u>helt som Danmark</u>.
Student 1:   ... eller <u>mere</u>. (Interview)
Student 1:   After *what we saw from Argentina*, it looked as if <u>they</u> are ...
Student 2:   ... <u>just like in Denmark</u>.
Student 1:   ... or <u>better</u>.

Some Danish pupils concluded in the interview that environmental engagement is not bound to a specific country, but is rather a personal matter: 'Det er *forskelligt fra person til person*' ('It *differs from person to person*').

Many Danish pupils also stated that this insight is at the centre of what they learnt from the project through discovery skills: '*Vi kan lære at sortere vores affald lige som dem* i forskellige skraldespande og sådan noget. Her på skolen og derhjemme' ('*We can learn to sort our waste* in different litter cans *just like they do*. In school and at home'); '*Vi kunne lære* hvordan man sortere tingene fx det tror jeg egentlig *vi kunne lære meget af*' ('*We could learn* how to sort our waste for example, I think we could actually *learn a lot about that*').

Moreover, other stereotypes about Argentina were deconstructed by the activities carried out during the project and as a result of private communication using Facebook and the pupils' own research about Argentina. In the interviews the Danish pupils said: 'Det så ud til at de har *en ret moderne skole*, det blev jeg ret overrasket over' ('It looked as if they have *a fairly modern school*, I was quite surprised about that'); 'Jeg troede det var anderledes, der så rigtig *hyggeagtigt* ud' ('I thought it would be different, it looked *very cosy*'); 'Jeg så at der var *høje bygninger*' ('I saw there were *tall buildings*'). They concluded: '*Jeg har lært noget om Argentina*, om deres skole i Argentina, hvordan der ser ud, at de ikke bliver slået i skolen' ('*I have learned some things about Argentina*, about their school and how it looks and that they don't get beaten up'); '*Jeg er blevet meget overrasket, altså, jeg har fået et helt nyt billede på hvordan Argentina er* i det her projekt' ('I'm quite surprised, *I have built up a whole new image of Argentina* through this project').

Many pupils initially represented Argentina as being highly different from Denmark: 'Jeg tænkte på *fremmed* kultur, *andre* måder at være på, *andre* måder at se tilværelsen måske' ('I thought about a *foreign* culture, *different* people and *different* perspectives on life'). However, the project encouraged them to find the commonalities they shared, which brought them together:

Student 2:   Jeg synes det var godt med et land, der havde en *anden* kultur og at de levede på en *anden* måde *og så alligevel ikke*. (Interview)

Student 2:   I think it was good working with a country with a *different* culture and *different* lifestyle – *and then again, not so different*.

Several pupils emphasized how they discovered that the differences are in fact marginal: 'I saw how they live in Argentina. It is different from Denmark *but not that much*' (Zoé, AIE). Another student expressed: 'Altså jeg *kunne ikke se forskel* på kulturen.' ('Well, *I couldn't see the difference* between the two cultures') (interview).

The AIEs and focus group interviews show that the Danish pupils, inspired by the project, wanted to know more about Argentina, for instance about their religion and their social and economic conditions. Furthermore, they also wanted to discover what the Argentinian pupils knew about Denmark: 'I would ask about what they eat and how there life in Argentina is. I would also ask about *if they know something about Denmark and how we live*' (Mogens, AIE). Similarly, the Argentinian pupils were eager to keep in touch with the Danish pupils and learn more about their lifestyles, their country, and the impact of the project in their community. For instance, Azul wished to ask them 'que hacen cuando están aburridos' ('what do you do when you are bored', AIE). Laura said 'les querria preguntar como es vivir alli' ('I would like to ask them what is life like there', AIE). Carolina added 'Querria preguntarle si siguen reciclando' ('I would like to ask them if they keep on recycling', AIE).

Criticality and critical cultural awareness

The opportunity to participate in this international project encouraged pupils like Verónica to consider the possibility of creating a community of action outside school boundaries, which Barnett (1997) refers to as 'the external world domain'. After participating in this project, Verónica felt that she knew what was wrong and what was right, so she wanted people to cooperate (in italics). Prompted by a question in the AIE to say whether she would do something as a result of the project, she said: *'seguir hablando sobre el proyecto con los demás y tratar de cuidar el medio ambiente'*; '[I would] *keep telling others about the project* and try to take care of the environment'. Similarly, Laura and Magdalena identified very specific actions: *'Si, si, cada vez que vea a alguien tirar basura le exijire que la levante y que la tire al tacho'*, 'Yes, yes, *every time I see someone drop litter I will demand that they pick it up and throw it in a bin'* (Laura, AIE); *'ahora cuando veo una canilla abierta la cierro y le explico a esa persona que no tiene que desperdiciar el agua'*, 'now when I see that someone has left the tap running I turn it off and I explain to that person that wasting water is wrong' (Magdalena, AIE). A Danish student formulated in her AIE: 'It made me wanna *change the world to a better place'* (Emily, AIE).

Other pupils developed a new way of thinking through a process of critical self-reflection and evaluation, which motivated them to change their attitudes towards the environment. This is what Barnett (1997) identifies as 'reconstruction of self', and is revealed linguistically in the use of the following expressions of self-awareness in the following AIE extracts below (evidence in italics): 'tomé conciencia', 'me di cuenta', 'me cambio por completo la consiencia', 'me parecio' 'I became aware', 'I realized', 'It totally changed my mind', 'it seemed … to me'. Self-determination to change and help others change was also important as Constanza's AIE shows.

> Si *tomé conciencia*. **Porque *me di cuenta* que tan solo con un pequeño esfuerzo podemos mejorar el mundo.** (Jorge, AIE)

> Yes, I *became aware* (of the situation). **Because *I realized* that we can make a better world with very little effort.**

> Si. *Yo antes no reciclaba y esto me cambiopor completo la consiencia.* Porque al ver todo lo que cambia *me parecio* una gran causa. (Azul, AIE)

> Yes. *I* wasn't used to recycling and *this totally changed my mind.* Because when I saw the changes that can be made *it seemed* right *to me.*

> … *decidí que hay que cambiar y ayudar a las personas que conocemos a acerlo.* (Constanza, AIE)

> … *I've decided to change and help other people change too.*

At the same time, Jorge's AIE extract above shows that he was able to think critically about this issue and this involved him challenging the presupposition that being green takes a lot of effort.

It is also important to remember that critical thinking was an intended outcome of the project, because as Barnett acknowledges, this is generally reserved to higher education. This project shows that criticality can be an outcome too in the primary as well as lower secondary school context. For instance, the following interview extract shows Carolina engaging in complex hypothesizing as she placed herself in the Danish pupils' shoes and considered their perspectives when prompted by the teacher to say whether there was something else she would have asked Danish pupils: '*Si no hubiesen tenido* la oportunidad de estar … *ellos lo seguirían cuidando o empezarían a cuidarlo*' ('*If they hadn't* been given the opportunity to be there … *would they have taken care of the environment*'). When looking back on all the work done, Cora's simple words clearly summarize the transformatory critique process pupils experienced: 'Tiene razón el proyecto. A veces no pensas que vos abrís la canilla, la dejas abierta … mientras vos, no se, estás ahí, por ahí y no pensas que cuando no tengan agua, qué vas a hacer? Vas a pensar en eso' ('The project is right. Sometimes we don't realize that if you turn on the tap and leave it running … when you, I don't know, you are somewhere else and you don't realize that if you didn't have water, what would you do? You will think that'; Cora, interview).

In addition to the change in attitudes and beliefs described above, the result of this criticality and reflexivity was often a behavioural change. For instance, Eliseo, as a conscious intercultural citizen, decided to commit himself and start changing the way he treated rubbish at home. He explicitly referred to his private world (the family, underlined) but also to the universal when he explained why he made that decision ('para proteger el medio ambiente', italics added).

Si decidí hacer un proyecto de separación de basura en mi casa *para proteger el medio ambiente.* Porque esto te ayuda a proteger al medio ambiente en nuestras casas. (Eliseo, AIE)

Yes I've decided to carry out a waste sorting project at home *to protect the environment.* Because this helps you protect the environment in our houses.

In the Danish AIEs, a new way of thinking and acting became manifest too: 'Jeg slukkede for vandet lige *med det samme,* når jeg var færdig med det – *gør det stadig*' ('I turned off the water *right away,* when I was done using it – *still do*') (Kirse, AIE); '*I discovered* that the things we do for the environment are really important and I know that *I will never stop doing it*' (Zoé, AIE). In the interview, a student expressed his process of criticality in the following words: 'Jeg synes at jeg har lært at *vi egentlig godt kan gøre en forskel* her derhjemme, at *vi godt kan gøre det bedre,* fordi jeg tænkte at folk jo ikke gider skære ned for deres forbrug og alle tingene. Og det kan man faktisk godt, sagtens, altså man behøver jo ikke tage et bad i en time eller en halv time, også med bilerne, altså at man egentlig bare kan cykle. *Nogle gange skal man bare tænke over det*' ('I think we have learned that *we can actually make a difference* here, that *we can improve.* I thought people don't want to cut down on resources and all. But *you can easily do that.* You don't have to take long showers or drive a car. You can just use your bike instead. *Sometimes you need just to think about that*').

These extracts also show that, as a result of the work in their transnational groups, the pupils engaged in different forms of political action, described in the Introduction to this book as levels 1 and 2 of political engagement. These levels are 'pre-political' and mean in this case that pupils engaged with others (through different types of 'text' as well as 'in person' using Skype) and reflected critically on their own assumptions, and those of the others. We have seen how the project challenged Jorge's assumption that green changes have to be big. Moreover, the pupils also proposed and imagined possible alternatives and changes. For instance, in Argentina, Eliseo proposed separating rubbish at home and Laura, asking people to throw their rubbish in the bin. In Denmark, some pupils proposed an environmental project for younger pupils intended to raise awareness of their responsibility for the environment.

This project also provides evidence that higher levels of political engagement are possible in lower levels of education, in this case primary and lower secondary. This is important because this book shows that levels 3–5 definitely took place in projects in higher education contexts, and in particular in projects with a very specific political dimension such as the Malvinas project (Chapter 9) and the Football World Cup and Dictatorship project (Chapter 10). In our project, the Argentinian and Danish pupils engaged with one another, reflected critically on each other's perspectives and not only proposed change as we have just seen but also took action to generate change in their own society. This corresponds to level 3 of political engagement and is illustrated in the active steps that Laura, Eliseo, Kirse, Zoé and other pupils took to protect the environment.

This level became level 4 when pupils made their voices heard: the moment that change was proposed by the Argentinian pupils as a group and the Danish pupils as a group and when that change was carried out in each country. The civic actions that we described at the beginning of this chapter correspond to this level (designing and hanging a street banner, being interviewed in a newspaper, participating in a radio programme, sharing the project with Greenpeace Denmark, etc.).

Finally, level 5 of political engagement means that learners acted upon a certain issue as a transnational group. For instance, in one of the Skype conversations one group said: 'We could start hanging them [the posters] around the school or around some streets … in our communities'. During the collaborative work process, some pupils participated in the following exchange:

Danish pupils: What should the movie be about [Danish pupils initiated the interaction]
Argentinian pupils: See our film about wasting paper. We will do that in Spanish and English [Argentinian pupils suggested what could be done]
Danish pupils: We thought about filming clips of trash in our own language? [Danish pupils replied]

Argentinian pupils: Okay but use English too. We can put the video together, do you agree? [Argentinian pupils commented on what Danish kids said and invited them to join in the making of the final outcome] (Online worksheet, wiki, October 2013)

The pupils engaged in this transnational collaboration asking each other for help (in italics) and providing help (in bold):

Danish pupils: We suggest the poster should be about recycling. *If you've any ideas please send them to us.*
Argentinian pupils: **We can show people wasting paper and people recycling paper.** (Wiki conversation)

These online exchanges in the wiki provide evidence of level 5 of political engagement. There is a transnational group of pupils formed by Argentinian and Danish kids who have the task of identifying green crimes within their local contexts (classifications/causes/consequences). In this process, they recognize this problem as a universal concern and they choose to act upon it together, as a group. In this case, we consider the term 'action' as involving the different tasks pupils performed when using the wiki to communicate, such as suggesting a course of action, making decisions and agreeing on procedures and ideas in order to produce similar outcomes. In other words, from the moment pupils started interacting, they agreed on joint action to protect the environment and they followed their own 'transnationally' agreed upon guidelines to pass on this message, for example, the use of local newspapers to call for collective action in their local communities.

Challenges

Throughout the project, we of course also experienced challenges. The project was not perceived positively by some Danish pupils. Some of them said that the Skype meeting – owing to technical problems or communication problems – was a disappointment. For instance, one student answered the question about what he had learned in the project by saying: 'At man ikke skal Skype med Argentina' ('Don't Skype with Argentina') (interview). Other pupils wrote in their AIEs: 'I haven't met anyone' (Emma, AIE), 'All I remember is screaming … and about 4–5 persons' (Rose, AIE). In the interviews too, some Danish pupils said that their attitudes, knowledge and skills had not changed. One student emphasized: 'Mit blik på Argentina har ikke rigtig ændret sig. Jeg ser det stadigvæk som en eller andet gård med en ged der går' ('My impression of Argentina hasn't really changed. I still picture a farm with a goat walking'). Another student emphasized, in the name of her peers: 'Vi er meget dovne, vi orker ikke at finde en skraldespand' ('We are very lazy, we don't bother to find a dustbin'). She later stated: 'Det sker om mange år, så er jeg væk og mine børn er væk, og det kan godt være at jeg virker egoistisk' ('It won't happen in many years, then I will be gone and my pupils will be gone. Maybe I appear to be selfish'). Furthermore, attitudes were not always followed by actions. The student who wrote in the AIE that she wanted to change the world to be a better place admitted that she did not act differently as a result of the project after all.

The project also produced feelings of disorientation and fear on occasions. For example, some Argentinian pupils expressed having felt 'rare', 'timid', 'uncomfortable', 'nervous' or 'fearful'. Three pupils said they did not speak at all during the Skype conversations because they did not want to; and one mentioned that he felt sad because his mother had not signed the consent form and consequently he was not allowed to participate. Clearly this is an aspect that deserves more attention when teachers plan a project of this kind. Yet even those pupils who felt awkward about having to interact with pupils from a different country agreed on the fact that the experience was worth having in the end.

The fact that the Danish pupils were older and more proficient in English than their Argentinian peers was a source of concern for the teachers and the researchers. Almost all the Argentinian pupils mentioned this difference at some point and expressed having felt timid, concerned and even 'intimidated' by it. Hagen et al. (2006) recommend the following criteria when choosing a partner for international school projects: partners should ideally be similar ages, have similar proficiency levels and be equal in number. Even though it was not possible to meet these criteria in our project, we believe that this limitation posed challenges to the pupils, which most of the pupils were willing to solve. For instance, both the Argentinian and Danish pupils adjusted to the situation and found strategies to encounter the 'Other'. In this project at least three types of encounters took place: between different ages, between different proficiency levels in English and between Argentinian and Danish pupils.

Conclusion

In our analysis, we have shown that our project opened up new possibilities for pupils to develop an international identification and the skills involved in intercultural citizenship, to deconstruct stereotypes and to develop criticality and critical cultural awareness. Despite the challenges illustrated above, most of the pupils within the framework of the Argentinian–Danish Green Kidz project further developed their linguistic competences, their plurilingual competences and their intercultural citizenship resolving conflict – in their first foreign language – when necessary and developing values such as mutual understanding and social awareness.

Furthermore, most of the pupils developed what we have called *intercultural environmental citizenship*, challenging taken-for-granted representations of the environment, reflecting on environmental issues and contributing to improve the environment both locally and globally.

In their AIEs and interviews, most pupils emphasized experiencing positive feelings as a result of the project and having positive attitudes towards it. For instance, some Argentinian pupils wrote:

Cuando la profesora aviso de este Nuevo proyecto 'Green Kidz' me senti la chica mas feliz y afortunada del mundo. (Maitena, AIE)

When the teacher told us about the new project 'Green Kidz' I felt the happiest and the luckiest girl in the world.

Me encantó la experiencia me siento afortunada de poder participar de esto ... Yo me sentí entusiasmada, contenta y afortunada. (Andrea, AIE)

I loved the experience I am very lucky to participate in this project ... I felt enthusiastic about it, happy and lucky.

Many Danish pupils said that they had already been studying themes related to the environment in different subjects, but that they appreciated the possibility to investigate this issue in cooperation with another country: 'Emnet har vi haft om før, men det er altid mere spændende når du møder nye mennesker' ('We have worked with the topic before, but it's always more exciting when you meet new people') (interview). The Danish pupils made the point that just talking about the environment in the English class would not have been particularly interesting:

Det har klart gjort projektet meget sjovere, det ville bare have været et kedeligt engelsk projekt, hvis vi ikke havde snakket om Argentina. (Interview)

It has definitely made the project more fun. It would have been a boring English project if we hadn't talked about Argentina.

What made the project enriching was the fact that it was a project in the English language classroom about the environment, which involved pupils from two countries in dialogue and collaboration. Ending with a student quote:

Jeg synes ikke det er sjovt at man... man få bedre indblik hvis man ser det, i stedet for at man læser om det. (Interview)

I don't think it's fun when ... you get a better insight when you see it, instead of just reading about it.

References

Barnett, R. (1997) *Higher Education: A Critical Business*. Buckingham: Open University Press.

Byram, M.S. (2008) *From Foreign Language Education to Education for Intercultural Citizenship: Essays and Reflections*. Clevedon: Multilingual Matters.

Byram, M. (2012) Conceptualizing intercultural (communicative) competence and intercultural citizenship. In J. Jackson (ed.) *Routledge Handbook of Language and Intercultural Communication* (pp. 85–97). Abingdon: Routledge.

Byram, M. (2014) Competence, interaction and action. Developing intercultural citizenship education in the language classroom and beyond. In X. Dai and G. Chen (eds) *Intercultural Communication Competence: Conceptualization and its Development in Cultural Contexts and Interactions* (pp. 190–198). Newcastle-Upon-Tyne: Cambridge.

Byram, M., Gribkova, B. and Starkey, H. (2002) *Developing the Intercultural Dimension in Language Teaching: A Practical Introduction for Teachers*. Strasbourg: Council of Europe.

Byram, M., Barrett, M., Ipgrave, J., Jackson, R. and Méndez García, M.C. (2009a) *Autobiography of Intercultural Encounters: Version for Younger Learners*. Strasbourg: Council of Europe. See http://www.coe.int/t/dg4/autobiography/Source/AIE_en/AIEYL_autobiography_young_en.pdf (accessed 12 July 2016).

Byram, M., Barrett, M., Ipgrave, J., Jackson, R. and Méndez García, M.C. (2009b) *Autobiography of Intercultural Encounters: Context, Concepts and Theories*. Strasbourg: Council of Europe.

Candelier, M., Camilleri-Grima, A., Castellotti, V., de Pietro, J.-F., Lörincz, I., Meißner, F.-J. and Schröder-Sura, A. (2009) *A Framework of Reference for Pluralistic Approaches to Languages and Cultures*. Graz: ECML/Strasbourg: Council of Europe.

Copenhagen Municipality (2014) *Profilskoler i københavn*. See http://subsite.kk.dk/sitecore/content/Subsites/Profilskoler/SubsiteFrontpage/ProfilskolerIKoebenhavn.aspx (accessed 12 July 2016).

Coyle, D., Hood, P. and Marsh, D. (2010) *CLIL. Content and Language Integrated Learning*. Cambridge: Cambridge University Press.

Hagen, L., Knudsen, A. and Peters, T. (2006) *Das Bild der Anderen. Das Kochbuch für E-Mail-Projekte im Deutschunterricht*. Krakau: Goethe-Institut. See http://www.goethe.de/ins/pl/pro/bild/GI_Lehrerhandbuch_09_03_06_150dpi.pdf (accessed 12 July 2016).

Hennessy, E. and Heary, C. (2005) Exploring pupils' views through focus groups. IN: S. Greene and Diane Hogan (eds) *Researching Pupils' Experience: Approaches and Methods* (pp. 236–252). London: Sage.

Muderrisgil, M. and Barrett, M. (2011) *Autobiography of Intercultural Encounters: Results of AIE User Survey. Report to the Language Policy Division*. Strasbourg: Council of Europe.

Punch, K.F. (2009) *Introduction to Research Methods in Education*. London: Sage.

Randersgades Skole (2012) *The Vision for Randersgades Skole/RG International Profile School*. See http://subsite.kk.dk/sitecore/content/Subsites/Profilskoler/SubsiteFrontpage/ProfilskolerIKoebenhavn/RandersgadeSkole.aspx (accessed 12 July 2016).

Stephan, W.G. and Stephan, C.W. (1996) *Intergroup Relations*. Boulder, CO: Westview Press.

7 Understanding Intercultural Citizenship in Korea and the USA

Catherine Peck and Manuela Wagner

After watching the VoiceThread from the Korean student it brought to my attention a cultural difference off the bat – the manners! All of our fellow colleagues said 'Thank you' when signing off from their video or written work and this struck me as a cultural difference right away
(US Student)

At first I was embarrassed because I've never interacted with foreign student from different university(sic) and I was not confident of my English speaking, so I was worried about it so much. However, it made me interested as I shared my opinion and the student asked me some questions
(South Korean Student)

Introduction and Context

The transnational collaboration which forms the basis for this chapter linked participants located in the East Asian nation of South Korea with partners in the northeast of the USA. The two teachers coordinating the project were Catherine, an Australian citizen based in South Korea, who works in language teacher education and academic development, and has worked with undergraduate students and teaching staff from both secondary and higher education contexts, and Manuela, who is an Applied Linguist from Austria and works with graduate students, pre-service and in-service teachers, as well as faculty members on issues related to intercultural competence as well as language teaching methodology.

The teachers' goals in this project were to foster the group goals of intercultural citizenship and critical thinking as described in the Introduction to this book in the context of foreign language teaching. In addition, both considered their specific context and set goals related to it. In South Korea, the participants were undergraduate students in an English as a Foreign Language (EFL) teacher education programme (with an average age of 20). The South

Korean students were undertaking a programme that taught syntax, phonology, discourse analysis and second language acquisition as well as practically oriented teaching methodology courses, and were also concurrently undertaking courses designed to develop their English proficiency. In the USA the participants were graduate students (in their twenties and thirties) in a Literatures, Cultures and Languages programme. The graduate students had some background in foreign language education theory and practice. Their primary focus of research and study however varied from student to student and included areas such as foreign language education, applied linguistics, first language acquisition, and literature in a variety of contexts. Both groups collaborated over the course of a semester to observe and develop concepts of intercultural citizenship through their own transnational and intercultural interactions. The two class groups were selected on the practical basis of their availability, and on the potential to meaningfully explore intercultural citizenship within the courses they were undertaking. The common focus on foreign language education was a major factor in matching the groups as exchange partners. Given the anticipated career paths and majors of the students in both contexts, the potential for formal foreign language education to foster intercultural citizenship was planned to be a central theme of the exchange.

On the surface, the students participating in the project seemed to bring vastly different perspectives to the collaboration. In the Korean context, students of English have extremely limited opportunities to actually use the language in real life (Park, 2009), a generality representative of the experiences of the 25 students, whose average ages were 20–21 years old, participating in this exchange from South Korea. All of the participants were ethnic Korean, South Korean nationals and spoke Korean as a first language. The English proficiency of the group ranged from what the teachers evaluated as proficiency level of 'low' to 'high intermediate' on the American Council on the Teaching of Foreign Language proficiency scale (a comparable level in the Common European Framework (CEFR) of A2 to B1), with the exception of two 'advanced' speakers (CEFR B2). Additionally, less than half of the group had previously travelled abroad or had regular contact with non-Koreans other than foreign language teachers, and thus the exchange represented a rare opportunity to interact with a foreign 'other' positioned outside the teacher–student role relationship – as is reflected in one of the quotes at the beginning of this chapter. As aspiring secondary school teachers undertaking a credit course in intercultural communication for foreign language education, they were also highly conscious of the challenges they foresaw in their future practice owing to lack of such experience, and expressed this in both classroom discussions and written reflections. Their concerns echoed commonly cited issues for Korean EFL teachers, who are frequently reported to feel constrained in their approaches to teaching due to a lack of cultural knowledge and first-hand exposure to the target language culture (e.g. Howard & Millar, 2008; Li, 1998).

Language educators in the USA are also faced with challenges, especially in teaching and assessing intercultural competence in a systematic way (e.g. Schulz & Tschirner, 2008). In contrast to the South Korean group, however, the students in the graduate course in the US context comprised several nationalities (American, German, Egyptian) and were concurrently engaged in teaching Arabic, German or Italian as a foreign language at the university level or preparing to teach Spanish at the secondary school level. They had had diverse intercultural experiences and were highly proficient in English (four were English native speakers and five were fluent non-native speakers of English). Although all students in the graduate course had varied experiences living and studying abroad in a variety of countries, we hoped to provide the opportunity for the graduate students to interact with members from a culture that they were, according to their reports, less familiar with, both in the ethnogeographic/traditional sense of culture and the culture of foreign language education in a markedly different setting ('teaching English in South Korea').

Despite the contrast in profiles between them, both groups were engaged in coursework that entailed analysis and reflection on key intercultural concepts including 'othering', 'essentialism' and 'identity', and this was seen as a good basis to build upon and extend via the exchange, and as a solid foundation for engaging with the concept of intercultural citizenship.

The Project

The web-mediated exchange project undertaken by the partners described above was framed and developed around the following practice-based research question:

> How might the collaboration between undergraduate students in English as a Foreign Language teacher education programme in South Korea and graduate students in a Literatures, Cultures and Languages programme in the USA lead to the development and understanding of Intercultural Citizenship?

This question was explored over the course of a semester long project, and through the students' engagement in a series of purposeful interactions with their international partners, each mediated by a selected web 2.0 platform and implemented through four phases:

(1) The initial phase of self-introductions involved students in the USA producing a short group video, uploaded alongside individual photos and voice-recorded contributions to VoiceThread (voicethread.com), while students in Korea constructed a separate introductory VoiceThread using a combination of text and audio comments.

(2) The second interaction positioned the exchange partners in smaller groupings of three or four in which they attempted to co-construct personal definitions and understandings of the concept of intercultural citizenship, also using VoiceThread.
(3) The third interaction entailed use of Google Docs as a space for exploration; the students in the USA used these to learn more about the social context of foreign language education in South Korea.
(4) The final exchange entailed students in the USA video-recording their tutorial discussion surrounding the action element of the intercultural citizenship construct (Byram, 2008), and sharing this with the South Korean group via Google, where it was viewed in class time and used as a prompt for class discussion and individual written reflections (a stage not included in the initial plan).

In providing students with the opportunity to gain intercultural experiences with an 'other' unfamiliar in several respects – ethnicity, age, language background and educational level – we hoped to bridge gaps between the theory and practice of the development of intercultural competence and citizenship (ICC) (Byram, 2008). Both teachers aimed to facilitate analysis and reflection on the intercultural experience among their students, thereby conceivably bringing about some deeper learning and cognitive, behavioural or attitudinal growth. Further, the teachers aimed to model a means of enabling critical reflection in the learning and teaching of ICC concepts with this project. We hoped that through participating and reflecting on the process of activities and interactions in our project students would be able to try a similar approach in their own (current or future) teaching.

Criticality was seen as an essential precondition for students to create a community of action, as awareness of their vocation in terms of teaching foreign languages as an influential, incisive social and political activity which was needed to understand that ICC does not avoid values/judgements. In the USA, students were also engaged with theories of social justice (e.g. Freire, 1972; Osborn, 2006; Reagan & Osborn, 2002) and reflected upon the meaning of these theories in a variety of contexts, including teaching English in South Korea. Intended learning outcomes for the students engaging in the project thus included the ability to define intercultural citizenship in both personal and theoretical terms, and to articulate ways in which they could act to develop intercultural citizenship among others in the course of their current or future work as foreign language teachers.

Project outcomes were evaluated on the basis of varied data sources; these included student products (videos, VoiceThreads, Google docs, written reflections, action statements and lesson plans, student feedback collected orally and/or in written form during and at the end of the project) and teacher reflections recorded throughout the project. The teacher researchers considered to what extent these sources showed evidence of the principles of education for intercultural citizenship as described in Byram (2008). Space has also been given in this chapter to reflection on unanticipated themes and challenges that arose throughout the exchange.

Significantly, during the project outcomes were formatively evaluated by the teachers as the stages unfolded, leading to some adjustments to plans *while the exchange was in progress.* Wherever possible, these adjustments remained true to the multidimensional objectives of the international project, which had been considered in the initial development of the exchange plan (outlined in Table 7.1).

Adjustments were made to the initial plan represented in Table 7.1 as the project unfolded for a number of reasons. Technical challenges, scheduling issues, a severe storm in the USA that outed power in Connecticut for several days, and feedback from the students themselves were contributing factors to revisions in process. Exchange 1, for example, took considerably longer than planned owing to unexpected technical issues that students encountered accessing the VoiceThread platform, and also because the task of articulating a personal definition of intercultural citizenship was far more challenging for the students than the teachers had anticipated, as reflected in the fairly typical comments from South Korean students below:

> Through this class I thought about the meaning [of intercultural citizenship] by my own schema. But it was difficult for me because this notion is ambiguous.

> I don't have clear concept in Korean. So, expressing my unclear opinion in English is not easy.

For the South Korean students in particular the initial introductions were also in many cases a source of discomfort, as students felt shy presenting themselves to strangers and recording their voices in English. Despite this, students in South Korea did construct VoiceThread presentations that articulated their personal understandings of what being an intercultural citizen might mean – articulating local or 'Korean' notions for a foreign audience. We teachers had thought that would mean considering what this means for them not only at home, but abroad, and in global interaction, and also that key intercultural concepts including 'othering', 'essentialism' and 'identity' which students were encountering in their coursework could be integrated into this initial stage of exploration. However, in general these dimensions were not evident or emphasized in the students' VoiceThreads, which oriented largely around personal experience and domestic policy in Korea concerning migrant worker communities. Reflective notes made by the teacher in South Korea at the time are representative of this:

> The main themes emerging from my students' contributions to the VoiceThreads for me so far are the remoteness and ambiguity of the

Table 7.1 Initial plan of exchanges and objectives

Initial plan	*Objectives*
Exchange 1: Students will introduce themselves to the other class, and then progress to defining intercultural citizenship from their own understanding and perspectives within smaller exchange groups.	• Building a relationship to facilitate collaboration. • Thinking about one's own culture through the eyes of someone else. • reflecting on concepts covered in class. • Articulating a definition of intercultural citizenship and becoming exposed to various perspectives.
Exchange 2: Drawing upon Byram (2008), students will exchange their concepts regarding potential linguistic and conceptual relativism regarding key terms (e.g. identity, nation, citizen, intercultural, community, civic obligation).	• Actively negotiating the meaning of the concepts involved with a foreign 'other'. • Critically reflecting on values underlying their own perceptions.
Exchange 3: Students will investigate, identify and critically evaluate the role of foreign language education, and the implications of foreign language education policy in their own contexts – including the congruence or otherwise of foreign language education and policy with the principles of intercultural citizenship. Outcomes of this process will be summarized for exchange.	• Reflecting on foreign language education policies in one's own and a less familiar context. • Engaging critically with foreign language policies from an intercultural citizenship perspective.
Exchange 4: Students will then articulate their personal motivations and goals in undertaking foreign language education, and contrast these with both those stated in education policy and those implicit in common institutional, social or personal practices in their contexts and with the principles of intercultural citizenship.	• Developing critical cultural awareness. • Establishing a foundation for and undertaking personal action; constituting an action element of the project.
Exchange 5: Students will develop a lesson plan, including its justification for the promotion of intercultural citizenship through foreign language learning appropriate to their own context. Students will exchange the lesson plan they develop for reflection.	• Thinking about applications of theory to individual practice. • Creating a community of practice to reflect on ICC in context. • Undertaking action with a focus and range extended by the process of working with cultural others (as per Byram, this volume, introduction) and constituting an action element of the project.

concept of intercultural citizenship for them, and how much they have struggled to connect this meaningfully to their own experiences and context. It's also been interesting to note that while they are able to engage (if supported linguistically) with the theory & concepts of inter-cultural competence in class time very little of this translates into their contributions on the VoiceThreads. [C. Peck, Project Reflection Notes]

Students in the USA then were asked to respond to these VoiceThreads and thereby add to the presentations; each group consisted of two to three students in South Korea and one student in the USA. Reactions on the part of the students in the USA ranged from sharing personal experiences to trying to steer the conversation to more theoretical explorations of the topic. Students clearly enjoyed engaging with cultural products, perspectives and practices that students from South Korea shared with them. One recurring theme in the US-based students' answers was the need to understand one's own culture before being able to consider becoming an intercultural citizen. Unfortunately, as mentioned before, some students had problems accessing the VoiceThreads their partners had sent them as the following email of a US Students to her teacher shows: 'I received my invitation from my South Korean friend to join, *name of student (original name deleted)*, but I cannot access the VoiceThread at all. It says I do not have permission and there is no contact email to contact her'. Partly because of such issues and partly owing to the generally busy schedules of the graduate students, some potentially interesting questions remained unexplored. In one example, students exchanged comments on the difficulty of defining intercultural citizenship, yet avoided actually attempting the task. In another, students shared per-sonal anecdotes of intercultural experience and discussed the value of mutual respect and positive attitudes, but sidestepped the notion of intercultural citizenship as necessitating *action*. As expected, some groups were more engaged with the project than others, yielding variable outcomes.

Owing to the delays experienced throughout the implementation of the first exchange, we decided to progress directly to exchange 3. This was also adapted somewhat; in this stage, we chose to respond to anxieties expressed by some of the Korean students by repositioning the interactions slightly. A few of the Korean students felt that their efforts had exceeded those of their partners in the USA, who in some cases had been unable to respond to Voice-Threads produced owing to the technical issues mentioned above. Others felt that the task of defining intercultural citizenship had been too ambigu-ous or was beyond their level of knowledge or capability, despite their teach-er's belief that the coursework they had engaged in had supported students' capacity to attempt this. In response, we asked graduate students to initiate exchange via Google docs in which Korean students were positioned as respondents rather than initiators, and moreover as 'expert informants' responding to the questions about foreign language education in South

Korea. US-based students were asked to contextualize their questions. They generally chose to describe the situation of foreign language education in the USA or their country of origin (e.g. Germany) and then asked a few questions related to foreign language education. Examples include questions about how intercultural citizenship can be included in foreign language education, why students choose to study a foreign language, or what policies guide foreign language education and if these policies include aspects of intercultural citizenship. For sample emails see the Appendix.

Exchange 4 from the initial plan was intended to at least have the potential to lead to an action element for the students in the USA. In this stage, students in the USA video-taped a discussion of the action part of Byram's Intercultural Citizenship model. This part of the project was added spontaneously after the teachers shared reflections on the progress in the project so far. It became clear that it was generally difficult to facilitate much synchronous collaboration between the students owing to the time difference and time constraints on all parties involved. On the other hand, the teachers also felt that students in South Korea could benefit from at least observing a discussion in their partners' classroom. Video-taping an authentic discussion situated in the US-based students context and deconstructing it with students in South Korea after viewing it seemed to be a possible way help the South Korean students experience the classroom interaction. The topic of discussion was rather challenging for US-based students. Although they were fairly comfortable by that time with thinking of ways of teaching knowledge and skills related to intercultural competence, they still struggled with the notion that teaching intercultural citizenship and indeed all teaching (of world languages) has a political component (e.g. Osborn, 2006). Students in South Korea then analysed the discussion based on guiding questions provided by their teacher. In addition to responding to the content of comments made by the US students, the Korean exchange partners commented much on the style of interaction and atmosphere observed in the video, as illustrated by the examples below:

> When I watched the video of the students in the US I was so surprised about their fresh expression and creative thoughts. [South Korean Student]

> Most of all, the impressive thing is that they are very active at discussion unlike Korean classroom. Everyone looked comfortable at expressing their opinion. [South Korean student]

The Korean students used the tutorial viewing as a basis for class discussion and written reflection, but undertook the lesson planning task intended to be exchange 5 as their own action, as this was closely tied to the intended learning outcomes of their course. These lesson plans were not exchanged, but tied closely to the project theme as the task was to redevelop a lesson based on materials from the South Korean national curriculum to incorporate the principles and foster development of intercultural competence and intercultural citizenship. Students submitted their lesson plans, including a brief rationale, as part of their course assessment. Overall, students elected to incorporate elements in their plans that were oriented towards development of positive attitudes towards foreign cultures and expanding student awareness of foreign customs, but avoided any explicit focus on the notion of citizenship in their planned teaching. In the USA students wrote a final paper on a topic related to intercultural competence. Specific topics ranged from explorations of how to teach intercultural competence through medieval Italian literature to how to integrate the teaching of intercultural competence in history lessons.

What We Learned

Now we return to our initial question, 'How might the collaboration between undergraduate students in an English as a Foreign Language teacher education programme in South Korea and graduate students in a Literatures, Cultures and Languages programme in the USA lead to the development and understanding of intercultural citizenship?'

Byram (2008) states that:

> Intercultural citizenship education involves causing/facilitating intercultural citizenship experience, and analysis and reflection on it and on the possibility of further social and/or political activity – i.e. activity which involves working with others to achieve an agreed end; creating learning/ change in the individual: cognitive, attitudinal, behavioural change; change in self-perception; change in relationships with Others (i.e. people of a different social group); change that is based in the particular but is related to the universal. (p. 187)

This guiding statement, alongside the *characteristics of education for intercultural citizenship* outlined in the introductory chapter of this volume, inform discussion of the outcomes of this project.

The first characteristic we discuss, and which is typical of intercultural citizenship education as outlined by Byram (this volume) is:

> a comparative (juxtaposition) orientation in activities of teaching and learning, e.g. juxtaposition of political processes (in the classroom, school … country …) and a critical perspective which questions assumptions through the process of juxtaposition. [Project Documentation]

This comparative orientation underpins many of the interactions within the exchange owing to the nature of the tasks and prompts involved (e.g. 'share your personal understanding of what intercultural citizenship means and compare this with your exchange partners' definitions' or 'describe foreign language education in your context and ask your partners questions about theirs'). Physical and temporal juxtapositions of the students' output were enabled by the mediating Web 2.0 technologies, which made contrasts and similarities in students' responses to the tasks highly evident, as the final products integrated the voice-recorded and written comments of partners from each side in one co-authored or dialogically created product. Partners were also able to respond, clarify and negotiate meaning through multiple response moves in the process, and this capability was well utilized in some of the exchanges:

> I feel interested because the American student tried to write a lot of things to think about. I learned her opinion on intercultural citizenship which is similar to our ideas. We posted 2 pictures and opinions to each other, and wrote comments to partner's idea. [South Korean student]

However, not all interactions were easily mediated by the platforms chosen and the asynchronous nature of the communications:

> It was very difficult for me to interacting. We have different view. She wants to ask what I do not intend. I uploaded the photo which symbolized that we should make peace because the world is like one family. However, because of my poor explanation or other mysterious things she wants to discuss the country and the ethnicity ... without facing [each other] the communication is very hard. (South Korean student)

This comment reflects upon an incident in which the South Korean partner's assumption was challenged. The picture the student refers to shows Angelina Jolie and Brad Pitt with their children from various cultures, seemingly with the intention to present an example of different cultures living together in peace and as one family. The US-based student took the opportunity to ask some questions about ethnicity and culture, perhaps in an attempt to start a conversation about topics pertinent to the courses to which the project was linked.

> For me, I look at intercultural communication and competence as a type of mediation. It is the recognition of our social responsibility to others. The picture above that you placed of Angelina Jolie's family is interesting. Two of her children are adopted which represents her social responsibility to others in her creation of a family that is ethnically diverse. But my question is, is this family culturally diverse? If the children are raised in the United States and are more familiar with American culture, what kind of intercultural mediation takes place? Does intercultural communication depend on whether their parents encourage them to engage with

the cultures they were born in? I think this paper makes us think about the differences between ethnicity and culture. (US-based student)

Nonetheless, the Korean student was uncomfortable with the critical stance her partner took in interrogating the concepts of ethnicity and culture, suggesting that her English prevented her from making herself understood. While she may have simply preferred a more harmonious discourse, it is also possible the student was confronted or confused by the unpacking of culture her partner proposed; in contemporary South Korea notions of race, ethnicity, nation, culture and language are still frequently conflated in the public consciousness (Shin, 2006). Even today, speakers of Korean tend to be Korean nationals of Korean descent. 'The correlation between Koreans and the Korean language is almost perfect. That is, (North or South) Korean nationals speak Korean, and most speakers of Korean are (North or South) Korean nationals' (Song, 2011: 10). Regardless of the source, through reflections, the student was at least able to voice her discomfort and thereby begin to examine possible reasons for it. In class discussions, when this topic was likely to be addressed the student would have a clear example of how it feels to be confronted with a different view. This reflects two more characteristics of intercultural citizenship as applied to the current project (see the Introduction to this book):

- Emphasis on becoming conscious of working with Others (of a different group and culture) through (a) processes of comparison/juxtaposition and (b) communication in a language (L1 or L2/3/...) which influences perceptions and which emphasizes the importance of learners becoming conscious of multiple identities. [Project Documentation, for more details see the Introduction to this book]
- Having a focus and range of action which is different from that which is available when not working with Others, where 'Others' refers to all those of whatever social group who are initially perceived as different, members of an out-group. [Project Documentation, for more details see the Introduction to this book]

Identity – in particular self-awareness and the opening of new potential identities – plays an important role in both of these characteristics of intercultural citizenship education. While the initial stage of the project facilitated the participants' self-introductions, the concept of identity and the fledgling existence of a transnational group identity was an undercurrent throughout the various stages of the project. The language mediating identity work was English, which all students spoke with varying degrees of proficiency. As the lingua franca of the group, English was positioned as the sole language for the entire exchange, yet as a subject in itself it was positioned alongside Arabic, German and Italian as only one of several foreign languages taught by the community of participants. For the South Korean participants this aspect of the exchange presented additional dimensions to their evolving sense of professional identity. The students engaged as members of a broader international field of foreign language teachers, as opposed to a typically narrower self-definition as a (future) Korean teacher of English and reflected on their broader global implications. In doing so they were able to rethink issues they had previously only considered in the context of EFL teaching at home.

For the US-based students the context of EFL in South Korea presented a less known context of foreign language teaching. Learning more about that new context provided an additional layer for comparison, for example, when their Korean partners shared with them via Google documents that quite often reading and listening are emphasized more in the teaching of English and that the focus is not necessarily on developing intercultural competence, as per the comments below:

> In my opinion, learning another language is very important because of globalization. However, in our education system, most schools overemphasize only reading and listening skills to receive good grades in Korean SAT rather than conversation. [South Korean Student]

> I think learning language gives us help to think about other cultures and also language includes cultural things. But, Korean education system focusing on English, especially grammar and reading to get good scores. [South Korean Student]

The graduate students – and foreign language teachers – in the USA then had to question whether in the US students do really develop proficiency and intercultural competence or citizenship in all contexts. Similarly, the South Korean students may not have identified so directly the lack of intercultural competence development common within their own foreign language education system had they not needed to consider the nature of the audience the US students provided. These examples of seeing one's own culture through the eyes of the other were further facilitated in classroom discussions. The focus here was on challenging one's own notions and using evidence from a variety of perspectives to make judgements. We believe that this caused critical cultural awareness of the students' own professional and cultural contexts that might have otherwise not happened.

Despite being positioned as teachers-in-training and less advanced in their education than the students in the USA, the Korean students were able to be positioned as expert informants (rather than novices) when responding to queries about education and society in South Korea, which also extended their experience or range of focus beyond what was typical for them outside the dynamics of the exchange. Topics included general questions about foreign language education in South Korea, for example at what age students start learning a foreign language and which foreign languages are learned, to how government policies influence the teaching of foreign language. US-based students also sometimes shared examples of foreign language education in their home countries in addition to the USA. Unfortunately, this interaction occurred at a busy time for both groups of students so that it was limited to one round of question and answer rather than resulting in a prolonged and critical discussion of potentially promising topics. Nonetheless, there were opportunities for students to go beyond the simple acquisition of knowledge. Some students mentioned what they learned in their own reflections of what kinds of action elements they could implement in their teaching. Time constraints, however, prevented the teachers from following up in more detail.

For the students in the USA, aspects of identity were present at several stages of the project. After the introductory VoiceThread sent by her Korean partners a student in the USA admitted thinking 'Oh, we are so American, we didn't say "thank you" or "looking forward to working with you".' She continues:

> But then I thought 'no, don't always pin it on culture before even meeting/interacting with the people. So I tried to find students who didn't say 'thank you' or 'nice to work with you'. Didn't find many. I guess I'll see what happens:-)

At a later point in the semester, another student in the USA described her experience in class and the project as follows 'the one thing I took from the class the most was the idea of a constant dialogue. My social identity, individual identity, and cultural identity are in constant dialogue with each other and with the other various identities of others. From here, I think communication starts to make itself apparent.' In the same email communication and referring to her exchange with her partners in South Korea, she adds, 'I also wanted to add that the Google doc is going very well! Such an interesting conversation!' The last part, in which the student reports on her collaboration with her partners, is an indication of her linking the project, at least to some degree, with her ruminations about identity of the self and others.

All of the activities in the project were planned with the goal of facilitating a 'community of action and communication' as the characteristic below explains.

- creating a community of action and communication which is supranational and/or composed of people of different beliefs values and behaviours which are potentially in conflict – without expecting conformity and easy, harmonious solutions.

Throughout the exchange students were prompted to reflect critically on their own ideas and those that they encountered in their interactions, with no expectation that they would achieve agreement and harmony of perspectives.

Instances where divergent perspectives became clear were considered fertile soil for such reflection, particularly in the Korean context where harmonious dialogue is highly valued – sometimes at the expense of debate. This was evident in the written reflections of the Korean students, some of which have been quoted above, on differences in understanding with their US-based partners and on the apparent freedom with which the US students shared their opinions in tutorial discussions. Certainly, students on both sides made conscious attempts to build community and in doing so appeared cognizant of differences in communication styles that needed to be accommodated. One example of this – an American student noting immediately apparent differences in politeness strategies – has already been outlined in the previous paragraph. Typical examples of this from the reflections of Korean students focused on the apparent ease of the interactions between the multicultural group in the USA:

> Above all they were very cute in the introduction video and it was really new to me because there were some people from different countries. In my class, as you know, there are Korean students only so I can't learn different cultures from native colleagues, but they probably can learn various cultures through their friend so I envied them.

The latter stages of the project explicitly engaged students in action – in the case of the South Korean students this was represented in their approach to modifying or re-designing a lesson from a national curriculum textbook so that the lesson would more actively foster a sense of intercultural citizenship among students. In the USA students engaged in an extended discussion in which they worked towards articulating individual plans for actions they would integrate into their classroom teaching practices. They also planned a final paper in which they reflected on the aspects of ICC that were most challenging and/or interesting to them. In conversations in which Manuela elicited comments from her students about the action element of citizenship, it became apparent that students found it difficult to take that final step. As mentioned above, Manuela and Cathy decided to video-tape one of Manuela's initial classroom conversations with her students about the action component in order to provide students in South Korea with a sample of a discussion in a different context. The fact that US-based students were open to video-taping their conversation can be interpreted as a level of trust that had been established throughout the project, and as such as a sign that the beginnings of an intercultural and transnational community of practice were taking place. Although the students were discussing a topic in which they did not position themselves as experts but rather as novices, they were comfortable enough sharing these conversations with their partners. This beginning sense of community was also apparent in comments made during class conversations about the project. For example, teachers observed a shift in students' use of first person plural pronouns (we and us) instead of 'they and them', clearly indicating beginning group identity. Finally, students in the USA also recorded a 'goodbye video' in order to thank their partners and assure them that they had enjoyed their collaboration.

Perhaps it is the feeling of working with a group of students from different backgrounds that facilitated the implementation of the next characteristic from the document cited earlier: 'paying equal attention to cognition/knowledge, affect/attitude, behaviours/skill'. As is often the case in the teaching and assessment of ICC, it is easy to pay too much attention to aspects related to knowledge or cognition at the expense of affect/attitude, behaviours/skill. This is a challenge both for the teachers and for the students. Students' reflections naturally gravitate towards the 'I did not know that'. However, in interaction with each other, students had to reflect on their and others' feelings, attitudes and behaviours. For example, one student in the USA had initial problems with the technology of VoiceThread. Although her partners had repeatedly invited her to join the VoiceThread, she could not join. When her partners became anxious and disappointed by her lack of response, Cathy mentioned the problem to Manuela, who then shared it with the student. Manuela took this as an opportunity to reflect with her students in class on how these technical issues can be perceived and why. Students had to put themselves in the shoes of their partners. It became clear that the issue was far more complex than they originally assumed. By examining the complexity of this seemingly simple example, students noticed that there might be different interpretations of behaviours and also different expectations.

Despite various challenges encountered, both groups of students were willing to continue their collaboration, yet owing to problems discussed in earlier sections, and the resulting and already existing time constraints, the teachers could not facilitate the planned collaborative action element. A US-based student expressed regret that they did not get to that point. However, students generally admitted that their busy work and study schedules did not allow for a more intense collaboration.

Challenges and Lessons Learned for the Future

Challenges were encountered by the students themselves and the teachers facilitating the exchange. Below we share some of our challenges that we believe could occur in similar projects, followed by lessons learned.

Different requirements of compliance with regulations concerning research with 'human subjects'

In the USA research involving human subjects is strictly regulated by federal, state and institutional requirements. Manuela had to gain approval by her Institutional Review Board by submitting a proposal including a detailed description of the study and especially of what students were expected to do. The main concern in this specific context was to protect the students' privacy and to ensure that their decision to participate did not have any impact on Manuela's evaluation of their performance in the course. Therefore, a third person, who had no prior relationship with the students, came to class to explain the study parameters and ask students if they wanted to participate. Manuela was not allowed to know who had participated in the project until after the grades were due. In other words, all students participated in the interactions with their partners, but Manuela had to wait to analyse data as she only found out who had agreed to be part of the research project after the grades for the semester had been entered. In Cathy's case the university granted permission to conduct the project after simply being informed about the study, and it was up to Cathy to implement procedures of informed consent, preserve students' anonymity, etc., on her own initiative. This resulted in some inhibitions on Manuela's part in sharing data for the purpose of the study during the course. Owing to the time taken in the process of obtaining consent, it was also necessary to start planning early and to be aware of institutional research ethics procedures early on.

Different time zones, academic schedules and unforeseen additional factors

In addition to the known differences in time zones and academic schedules that need to be taken into consideration when planning a transnational project, unforeseen weather emergencies resulting in long power outages and cancelled classes caused scheduling conflicts and required adjustments to the project. A possible way to address this issue in future projects is to be absolutely clear which aspects of a project need to be completed in order to enable the students to achieve the desired outcomes, and to build in ways to adjust the project owing to problems or time constraints that arise in the process in the planning stage. In other words, teachers could identify and mark activities as 'necessary' or 'ancillary' and thereby create alternative project paths. That could facilitate the process of reorganizing the project after unforeseen complications.

Initial problems with technology

Some students in Korea claimed that they did not have access to a webcam or a microphone and others needed to set up a gmail account in order to access VoiceThread. One student in the USA had similar issues with VoiceThread as the program did not accept her email address. Even with thorough preparation (e.g. practicing and trying out the technology used) students can encounter problems with technology. Some practices how teachers can facilitate the use of technology are to (a) show students how the technology used will help them accomplish the project goals, (b) show enthusiasm about the tools themselves and (c) check in with students and ask specifically about technical issues so that the time lost is minimal.

Anxiety owing to different levels of language and age difference

Some students in South Korea seemed to feel intimidated by the fact that they were working with either native speakers or highly proficient speakers of English, who were also graduate students and generally a few years older. In some cases, students were therefore more comfortable interacting in text only, rather than engaging in spontaneous interaction using a webcam and microphone. It became clear that some of the reported technical problems with webcams might have been due to non-native speakers' anxiety about engaging in spontaneous interaction with graduate students in the USA. In their reflections after the first interactions in the individual groups, US-based students commented on their partners' English proficiency in various contexts. One student was reminded of her foreign language learning experience and how she felt when she was not quite able to express everything the way she was used to doing in her native language. Another student shared that she was concerned because she did not understand her partners very well and she did not want to alienate them by saying that to them. Other students were surprised that their Korean partners were quite apologetic about not having set up their microphones. One student mentioned that she was impressed with the Korean students' willingness to 'put themselves out there'. Students were generally aware that it would be beneficial to explain terms that might mostly be used in the USA. In addition to discussing possible strategies with the group of less proficient speakers of the language of interaction, it turned out to be helpful for graduate students to reflect more deeply on what different proficiency levels would mean for their partners as well as for them. Manuela was careful to help students ask questions and put themselves in their partners' position, rather than make assumptions about the language competence of their interlocutors.

Emotion as a flag for intercultural experience touching/impacting in the Korean students' responses

Cathy also observed that sometimes a lack of response by their partners might have been interpreted as rejection rather than miscommunication, as reflected in this comment from her notes at the time:

> While those students like the idea of exchanging very much, and have indicated they want to continue with similar experiences, they have the impression that in this instance their partners were disinterested or have 'ignored' them and their efforts. I have (of course!!) explained to them that their partners may be having technical problems, may be very busy

etc etc, but in some cases to no avail – they are young, and generally much less mature than western students, and so they see it as a 'rejection' and are a bit despondent about it all. As far as they are concerned they made the effort and got no response, and it is quite hard for me to convince some of them otherwise. [C. Peck, Project Reflection Notes]

This realization helped Cathy and Manuela understand that emotion played an important and differential role in the initial interactions of the students.

Owing to time constraints we felt we could not spend much time analysing the situations and using them to explore the affective variables of intercultural communication in more detail. In retrospect, Cathy and Manuela felt that they might have missed a teachable moment as they both believe that a perceived conflict could have been used to gain a deeper understanding of intercultural competence. Through critical thinking activities, students could have investigated their own values and judgements and the role of emotion in this context.

Teachers' assumptions about student autonomy

Because in her context, the participants were all graduate students, Manuela did not want to manage their activities too closely. In addition, Manuela assumed that her students would tell her immediately if there was a technical problem. After Cathy and Manuela touched base during their students' initial interaction and found out that some students had not connected yet, they investigated the reasons and were able to move along the project. Cathy experienced a similar tension between the desire to allow students to take the lead in their interactions and the need provide support and guidance. This led at times to frustration:

Despite forethought and planning, many students were still apprehensive & reticent to upload comments or record their voices – indicating to me that I had underestimated the support they needed. The 'enabling' steps I had taken had been insufficient and I experienced temporary feelings of impatience and frustration which stemmed from my sense that students were expecting to be 'hand-held' and 'spoon-fed'… I recognize that I could have eased this process for students by providing a model self-introduction, or by interacting with & responding to them on the VoiceThread. A conflict was evident, however, between the preference some students may have had for a demonstration of 'what to do' and my strong feeling that I wanted the VoiceThread to be a space for the students' voices, rather than my own, for them have a sense of 'ownership' in which I did not set the tone of the interactions. [C. Peck, Project Reflection Notes]

These experiences caused both Cathy and Manuela to reconsider their notions of when and how to foster autonomy in different learning contexts. In the future, Manuela will specify deadlines for time-sensitive aspects of projects more clearly. She also decided to check in before each deadline to check on her students' progress.

Assumptions about students' prior understanding

Assumptions were made by Cathy about her students' understanding of citizenship in a national sense. Education in South Korea explicitly orients students to patriotic values, and both the national identity and nationalist rhetoric are highly prominent in domestic politics. Nonetheless, the students in her group seemed unsure of the concept of citizenship, and how this notion translated to an intercultural space.

Conclusion

Although Manuela and Cathy were not able to complete all steps of the project, they both felt that they had fulfilled a number of objectives. For the US-based graduate students, the transnational collaboration offered the opportunity to investigate their prior assumptions. While they reportedly felt comfortable interacting with colleagues from different backgrounds, they had to take a closer look at their (inter)actions when their assumptions were challenged. For some this led to the conclusion that one's own development of intercultural competence is an ongoing and presumably lifelong learning process. For the South Korean participants, the exchange represented a transnational focus highly uncommon within national teacher education programmes, where educational theories and approaches are framed within and evaluated from a local context perspective. The project offered a rare and novel opportunity to engage with cultural others, and to do so in a cooperative or collaborative way, as is clear from the student reflections reproduced below:

> I haven't ever had any experience like it … It was so funny to see the pictures and listen to the stories of the students living other side of us. So, if I have one more chance to do it again, of course I just want it.

> I hope I could have more opportunity to take participate in this kind of project really really I hope and want!!!

> It is a great chance to meet other people in other place on the planet! I wish to hear other's opinion and their introduction about their culture.

> …Because having communication with people from another culture rarely happens to me. It will be a great experience.

Notable project outcomes included a recognition of how the challenges our students encountered may also have provided salient opportunities for intercultural learning, and how important tolerance for ambiguity and flexibility (also, and maybe especially) on the part of the teachers are for the success of an international project such as this.

Perhaps the most important lesson learned by Cathy and Manuela was that not all opportunities can be taken up during the project owing to likely time constraints on the part of the students and the teachers. However, with reflection, lessons learned in one project might help their own development of intercultural competence, and thereby assist them in future projects.

References

Byram, M. (2008) *From Foreign Language Education to Education for Intercultural Citizenship. Essays and Reflections.* Clevedon: Multilingual Matters.

Freire, P. (1972) *Pedagogy of the Oppressed.* Harmondsworth: Penguin.

Howard, J. and Millar, S. (2008) Ongoing challenges with language curriculum innovations in Asia: A South Korean case study. *Pacific-Asian Education Journal* 20 (2), 59–75.

Li, D. (1998) 'It's always more difficult than you plan and imagine': Teachers' perceived difficulties in introducing the communicative approach in South Korea. *TESOL Quarterly* 32 (4), 677–708.

Osborn, T. (2006) *Teaching World Languages for Social Justice.* Mahwah, NJ: Lawrence Erlbaum.

Park, J.S.Y. (2009) *The Local Construction of a Global Language: Ideologies of English in South Korea.* Berlin, Mouton De Gruyter.

Reagan, T.G. and Osborn, T.A. (2002) *The Foreign Language Educator in Society: Toward a Critical Pedagogy.* Mahwah, NJ: Laurence Erlbaum.

Schulz, R. and Tschirner, E. (eds) (2008) *Communicating across Borders: Developing Intercultural Competence in German as a Foreign Language.* Munich: Iudicium.

Shin, G. (2006) *Ethnic Nationalism in Korea: Genealogy, Politics and Legacy.* Stanford, CA: Stanford University Press.

Song, J.J. (2011) English as an official language in South Korea: Global English or social malady? *Language Problems and Language Planning* 35 (1), 35–55.

Appendix

Sample email 1 from graduate student in USA to partners in South Korea

Hello _____, _____, _____!

I hope you are doing well and that your semester at your university is going well. Our semester is about to finish and the weather is starting to get very cold! Right now it's about 35 F (1.6 Celsius), and this morning I saw the frost on the grass – a sign that winter is very near.

I would like to ask you some questions regarding language education and perhaps we can have a discussion about it through email. It would be great to hear your ideas and thoughts! Here are some of the questions I had regarding language education:

(1) Here in the USA, we offer a programme called English as a Second Language. This is a programme in which English is taught to those who don't speak English as their first language. For example, if someone from Ecuador comes to the USA and only speaks Spanish, he or she will be placed in an English as a Second Language classroom in order to learn English. Is there something similar in Korean that encourages those who do not speak Korean to learn the language? If this programme exists, is it obligatory? What do you think about it?

(2) When you learn a foreign language in elementary school, high school, and at the university, is culture also taught? If so, how is it taught?

(3) What kind of methods are you interested in using when you teach English that help in creating intercultural citizenship and intercultural competence? I would love to share with you some of the methods or activities I like to use when teaching Italian as well!

I look forward to hearing your responses!
Kindest regards,

Sample email 2 from graduate student in USA to partners in South Korea

Hello _____ and _____,
I hope you are doing well! Here, the end of the semester is coming very soon, and we are all busy writing and reading for our final papers. 2 weeks ago, we celebrated Halloween in the USA, and I was having a big party with over 20 people at my place. During Halloween, everyone is wearing costumes … I was a creepy clown. One of my friends was dressed up as Psy, and we also danced to Gangnam Style. I had to think about you guys! I did not know about the song before you introduced it in the VoiceThread when we started our conversation, and now it is on the radio quite often. I have pictures of the party in the attachment.
I have some questions for you about foreign language policy:
In the USA, most students are required to take 1–2 years of a foreign language in high school in order to graduate and depending on the discipline 2–4 semesters in college. In Germany, however, 5–10 years of a second language are required based on the region and school (this can start as early as the 2nd year and continues throughout middle and high school). Most schools require 2 foreign languages while some high schools require 3 foreign languages to graduate. In college, there is no language requirement. Is there a foreign language requirement in South Korea? What age do you start

learning? Are you required to learn more than 1 language? What is your personal experience with learning foreign languages in school?

In America, the most common foreign language is Spanish (French, German, and Italian are close runner- ups.) The main reason for this is the influx of Spanish speakers into the country. In Germany, the most common foreign language is English (this is mandatory); the most common second languages are French, Spanish, and Latin. What languages are offered at your schools? What language did you choose? Why did you choose it?

In Germany, the language of the immigrant is Turkish and Russian. However, this language is not common in schools. However, in America, the immigrant language is also the most widely studied: Spanish. What are the immigrant languages in South Korea? Are they taught in the schools? Would you personally take this language if it was offered?

In America, the majority of students take a language because it is (a) required or (b) they hope to maintain a higher economic status (better jobs; more money). By the time the students reach college and take it past the required amount, there is usually a cultural interest in the language, but the underlying factor is still the ability to find a job and be competitive in the job market. The consensus among the Germans in our group is, students in Germany take a language because it is (a) required or (b) they have an interest in the language and culture. How is the learning of a foreign language valued in your society? Is this view different depending on a social status? Why do students take a foreign language? Why did you choose a profession that teaches a foreign language?

I am looking forward to your answers,

Greetings from America.

8 Mural Art and Graffiti: Developing Intercultural Citizenship in Higher Education Classes in English as a Foreign Language in Argentina and Italy

Melina Porto

Description of the Project

The La Plata–Padova project was an online intercultural citizenship project carried out in 2013 between second-year undergraduate students of English at Universidad Nacional de La Plata in Argentina and second-year bachelor's degree students in English at Università degli Studi di Padova in Italy. About 100 students participated in Argentina and 75 in Italy. The project addressed the topic of mural art and graffiti and challenged the students to research, analyse and reflect on these forms of expression. The Argentinean students also worked on the citizenship component of the project with secondary school students in La Plata. In Argentina the project was led by Melina Porto and in Italy by Marta Guarda. This chapter is written by the former, but in all other respects this was a joint project. The joint activity is therefore described for both groups and their teachers, but in the second part of this chapter the emphasis will be on the data analysed from the Argentinean group.

The two project leaders met with the help of the UNI-collaboration platform (www.uni-collaboration.eu) rather than through the wiki that was used by others in this book. One month was available for planning, which involved Skype meetings and email conversations. The project had linguistic, intercultural and citizenship aims, developed from the theoretical framework described in the Introduction to this book.

Linguistic and intercultural aims

By the end of the project, the students would be able to:

*   appreciate linguistic diversity in the English, Spanish and Italian languages;
*   engage in research skills;
*   engage in intercultural dialogue with others;
*   analyse critically (audio) visual media images, texts, practices, etc.; and
*   become familiar with online platforms and programmes such as Prezi and Mural.ly.

Citizenship aims

In this dimension, the students would be able to:

*   demonstrate willingness and ability to engage in dialogue with others;
*   allow others to express their viewpoints, avoiding hostility and confrontation and resolving conflict when necessary;
*   develop values such as respect, mutual understanding, social awareness and openness; and
*   transfer knowledge to others by engaging in civic participation locally.

The project began with the Argentinean and Italian participants researching mural art and graffiti (their meaning, history, some specific cases, etc.) in their own foreign language classes. In Argentina, brainstorming began with pictures and photographs of murals and graffiti to continue to explore different existing definitions taken from different sources. The students were encouraged to find information from different sources and bring them to class for discussion.

In addition, the students in each country left their classrooms to explore their communities by strolling around their towns in order to photograph existing murals and graffiti. With the material gathered they built a corpus of street art in their towns and uploaded their discoveries to a wiki that we created especially for this project and that we called the Padova–La Plata wiki.

The online communication stage began in April 2013 and went on for two months. In weekly Skype sessions, which were recorded and uploaded to the wiki, the students started by getting to know each other. The teachers provided prompts but ultimately they were free to talk about what they wished. English, a foreign language for all the students, worked as a lingua franca here.

In the following step, the students described the social and historical meanings they associated with the murals and graffiti they had photographed in their communities and shared their views online with their project partners. The aim of the task was to reach an agreed concept of mural art and graffiti, by discussing whether these are a form of art or a form of vandalism. Students also explored the possibility that there might exist a transnational culture of graffiti, with common features across countries. To this end, they shared their corpora of murals and graffiti in their own towns and looked for differences and common ground.

The final stage in the online communication phase involved students in a collaborative task where they designed their own mural or graffiti. Working in small groups of mixed nationalities, they cooperated in the creation of a piece of work that reflected their own representation of youth identity through the use of a tool called Mural.ly. In this way, students developed their understanding of how identity can be enacted through these forms of expression. As the students engaged in this task, an international identification emerged, as we shall see later.

In a post-cooperation stage, and in order to encourage yet further reflection, each Argentinean student completed the Autobiography of Intercultural Encounters (AIE) (Byram et al., 2009) in English.

Intercultural Citizenship

As explained in the Introduction to this book, each project was to attempt to develop a citizenship dimension of students' engagement in their own community which would be informed by the collaboration they had engaged in, and the insights from this which might not have appeared if they had been working only within their own group and their own national perspective.

In this case, the citizenship dimension was realized in the Argentinean branch of the project through the development of bonds with others beyond the university level. This had been planned in advance with a colleague from a public secondary school in La Plata, Verónica Di Bin. The university students were instructed to engage in online communication with her group of secondary school pupils from Colegio Nacional Rafael Hernández, who had also addressed the topic of mural art and graffiti in their English classroom at the beginning of 2013, in anticipation of the cooperation with the university students. They had photographed murals and graffiti locally too. In addition, they had chosen one mural or graffiti in a local school, and had interviewed the head teacher or principal about it, focusing on aspects of regional and international youth culture present in these artistic expressions. They had also interviewed the house owners in the neighbourhood where this school is located to ask about their opinions, feelings and reactions towards the mural or graffiti in question.

The communication online, using Skype, between the university students and the secondary school pupils took place in October and November 2013 and was to lead to the design of some civic action that would have an impact on their community. The pupils and students together actively engaged with their communities in a number of ways. For example, they created a documentary on teenage muralism and other forms of expression in La Plata and they wrote a letter to the principal of the school and rector of the university requesting a strategy to allow for artistic expression in the school and the university.

Some university students experienced difficulties in their attempts to work with the secondary school pupils and eventually formed small groups among themselves. Different groups engaged in various activities: some taught a lesson on mural art and graffiti in a shelter home for poor women who are victims of domestic violence; others drew reverse graffiti in a local square (an environmentally friendly way of creating temporary or semi-permanent images on walls or other surfaces by removing dirt from a surface); a third group published an article in the university newspaper; and a fourth group drew a mural in collaboration with children from a primary state school in La Plata.

Evaluation

In this part of the chapter, the focus shifts from explaining and describing the teaching and learning activities to evaluation using the data that were collected as part of the project.

There were several types of data. Some data were conversational, such as the chats in the wiki and the recorded Skype sessions between the Argentinean and Italian students, and the Skype conversations between the Argentinean university students and secondary school pupils. Other data were documentary and involved photographs, written reflection logs, videos and the AIE. Students had agreed beforehand that their data could be anonymized and used for research purposes.

The data were analysed for evidence of:

(1) an international identification between the Argentinean and Italian students;
(2) criticality involving new ways of seeing things and taking action locally.

International identification, we hoped, would emerge as university students in the two countries worked on collaborative tasks, identifying with the mixed-nationality groups as newly created transnational groups without a national allegiance. We also sought evidence for this as students reflected on their experience in logs and the AIEs.

Criticality was analysed in terms of the framework provided for project participants from Barnett (1997), as explained in the Introduction. It was observed clearly in the civic actions that the Argentinean students engaged in, and it also traversed the project as the students observed, analysed and discovered aspects related to the Italian peers, their background and communication with them, and as they reflected upon their experience with the project.

An international identification

Collaboration as a basis for change in identification
The design of murals was a collaborative activity amongst the Argentinean and Italian students and it was during the undertaking of this task that an international identification developed. This means that the students temporarily suspended their national or regional identifications and developed a new bond as an international group.

Figure 8.1 shows one of the murals that the students created, where some representative pictures and quotes by famous people were selected. While the quotes appear between inverted commas, the centre is occupied by a message that embodies this group's voice: 'Party is **our** key word! Having fun is **our** best hobby!' The pronouns **our** and **we** (emphasis added) are evidence of an international identification and the aim of their mural is 'to put many posts with a word or phrases that **we** have in common, to demonstrate **our** relationship or the project ... **we** write **our** names' (Skype conversation).

This international identification pervades the Skype conversations as can be observed in the following extract where the emphasis in bold shows that the group truly appropriated the project as their own:

ITAL1:   I have also, I have an idea!
ARG2:   Ok!
ITAL1:   For our project! (Skype conversation)

Figure 8.1 Collaborative mural

The group then continues to describe how they conceptualized their mural:

ITAL1: Unify both **our** ideas, what **we** like about this graffiti, why **we** choose this graffiti, and also a sort of tribute about, for the artist. For example, Blue is an inspirator for the artist, the street artist all over the world because ... He can create works, but always with a very deep meaning. And then can insert also **our** source and what **we** learnt about ... from this experience, of course.

ARG3: **We** have to look for something that represents the project.
(Skype conversation)

In the Skype conversations this group discussed the various meanings they associated with the pictures they had selected for the mural (our emphasis in italics) in this way:

ARG1: I found a graffiti of four girls, I think they are prostitutes.
...

ITAL1: Because the style is the same, there're balloons that are rising, so we can unify the, the concept of graffiti as work art, and graffiti as write, writings.
...

ITAL1: Stencil, black and white, with the red balloon that is the, *the symbol of the friendship and love,* so ...

ARG1: Yeah

ITAL1: The balloon that ...

ARG2: Yes!

ARG1: There is the ... the concept of *the distance between Italy and Argentina.*

ARG3: Yeah.

ARG1: And in the other hand, there is *the concept of the relationship.*
(Skype conversation)

Evidence of an international identification is again in bold. The four group members discuss the meaning of the graffiti they chose to include in their mural in detail and introduce the theme of the distance between Argentina and Italy, but also their own groups' closeness in terms of bonding and relationship. This leads to a discussion of the role of imagination in people's lives in the following extract ('with imagination we can be wherever we want') and how with imagination 'distances are not so far'. The international identification emerges again: '**we** still have a good relationship, **we** enjoy the project'.

ARG2: It's like the girl will, will, will fly away with that balloons, meaning that in that journey, in that trip, she'll find something that she'll get along, that she'll feel comfortable with, that day is not her home enough, let's say, but highest, higher.

ITAL1: Yeah.

ARG1:   Yeah. I like it.
ARG2:   Mmm but, but **we still have a good relationship, we enjoy the project**.
ITAL1:   Yeah.
ARG1:   Yeah.
ARG2:   That's what I mean …
ITAL1:   And the … it would, would be, represent also the fact that *with imagination we can be wherever we want.*
ARG3:   Yeah.
ITAL1:   And also that the *distances are no so* …
ARG2:   *Far.* (Skype conversation)

In the excerpt below, the group continues to reflect on the tension between distance and friendship. Distance is here understood not only in a geographical perspective but also in terms of conflict, otherness and stereotyping ('the stereotypes, the words, the words and the differences'). Interestingly, the message the students want to convey is a key theoretical tenet of an intercultural citizenship project of this kind, which is that conflict can be resolved peacefully and cooperatively: 'imagination in your graffiti, and friendship destroy the other, the other, the world and conflicts between nations that are useless in the relationship of the human being'. The emphasis is on what brings human beings together ('friendship and the love are above everything').

ITAL1:   Yeah, yeah. Because *maybe distances are just a concept that something, that someone that makes bigger than what is … in reality.*
ARG3:   Yeah.
ITAL1:   I don't know if I explained ok (laughter).
ARG1:   Yeah.
ARG2:   Yes, yes, yes (laughter).
ITAL1:   And the other one I put it is a concept that [is] a little bit difficult but I'll try to explain.
ARG2:   (laughter)
ITAL1:   I think it's two people…, maybe you and us.
ARG2:   Ah ok.
ITAL1:   From two different countries, ok? That goes on *the stereotypes, the words, the words and the differences because friendship and the love are above everything* so also *imagination in your graffiti, and friendship destroy the other, the other, the world and conflicts between nations that are useless in the relationship of the human being.*
ARG3:   Ok.
ARG2:   Yeah.
ARG3:   It's good.
ARG2:   I like it too.
ARG3:   Yes. (Skype conversation)

Laughter in this previous extract appears to bring the Argentinean and Italian students together and occurs at points when they express a common understanding of the notions of friendship and distance. Laughter could then be interpreted as another way in which the international identification was revealed in this group.

Furthermore, the Argentinean students all reflected on this international identification in their AIEs (emphasis added in italics). For instance, Amalia reflected on the strong bond that she had created with the Italian peers (emphasized by bold as above):

> *I strongly believe that during the Intercultural Project, both Italian and Argentinean students became one single group working collaboratively* ... While talking, the hour passed very quickly and, by the end of the communication *it was almost like being in contact with very good friends!*
>
> At first **we** got to know each other. **We** talk about ourselves, our lives, hobbies and family. Then **we** mentioned the differences between Italy and Argentina, especially differences between the culture and university. *At this point, I felt really identified with them* as they were about to sit for a final exam and we were in the same situation. *I think **we** were able to share our fears and anxieties via Skype.*
>
> Moreover, **we** shared information about **our** countries ... Sara, one of my Italian peers was from Cracow, Poland. While talking with her, she explained to us what had happened in her country in the past, when War World II took place. In this way, we got to know that, during that time, Poles and Jews were classified as subhumans and were targeted for eventual extermination. I was shocked while listening to her, as she told us about something which had been extremely important for her family and her lovely country. *I think that, thanks to this project, **we** were able to discuss ideas that wouldn't have emerged in the national context. Although Sara was very far away, **we** could feel her emotions as if she were next to us.* ...
>
> Finally, I have to say that *my peers and I felt really sorry when the project was near to the end as we truly enjoyed talking every week! Even today, **we** get in touch via Facebook to keep sharing **our** lives.* (Amalia, AIE)

As Amalia mentions in the last paragraph, the bonding continued after the project had finished. Through the confrontation with different perspectives, students were able to place themselves in their partners' shoes, and it is important to note that Amalia does not speak just for herself here: '*we could feel her emotions as if she were next to us*'.

The collaborative task thus engaged students in adopting a comparative perspective in terms of:

(1) knowledge – for instance, the research about the topic that the students undertook at the beginning of the project; the descriptions of murals and graffiti after they photographed murals and graffiti in their cities; and the characterization of this type of art in each country;
(2) actions – for instance, researching; interviewing experts to gain knowledge; building a portfolio of murals and graffiti;
(3) attitudes – exploring diverse attitudes and preconceptions towards this type of art.

The following AIE extract by Patricia shows these three dimensions in the comparative perspective (emphasis added in italics):

> Before meeting the girls, *I was doing some research* and found out the following … *What I liked the most about it was* that the fact that the topic in discussion was related to art. *By definition, art is the use of the imagination to express ideas or feelings, particularly in painting, drawing,* etc., so that means that everything is acceptable and appropriate and therefore nothing can be wrong; there is no unique interpretation of whatever you can analyse. *It was really interesting and exciting* to see how each of us had different visions and interpretations of a certain object. (Patricia, AIE).

The relational aspect and working with others is central in this comparative perspective (*'I never tried to impose on the girls* or say that what they were saying was wrong or unacceptable. In fact, *I accepted their opinions as valid,* and *I tried to see their points so as* to make my knowledge of the world become richer.', Karina, AIE) and the students all acted as 'intercultural mediators'.

The online communication stage in particular fostered processes of comparing and contrasting (emphasis added italics) leading to self-awareness as well as awareness of otherness as the following reflection log written after the project was completed shows:

> One of the first things that called our attention was the similarities we encountered between our Italian peers and us, *as the Skype sessions went along.* We had expected to face differences other than common aspects, considering the distance that separate us, together with the well-known but still important factor of living in a community which is, in many ways (culturally, politically and socially) distinct from theirs. (Final reflection log)

Worth noting too is that after this transnational project, the students were conscious of change and in some cases used the term themselves. For example, students experienced a modification in their appreciation of art, in their attitudes and in their worldviews:

> I think there was *a radical change* in the way I consider art, and this project has had a strong influence on me. (Patricia, AIE)

Honestly, I didn't want to do the project at first. Sometimes I didn't want to speak or I just wanted to do something else. But throughout the project, *I realised that I was enjoying* the things we talked. (Aldana, AIE)

It also changed me because now I have another vision of some things, such as culture and interaction with people that have other customs. (Karina, AIE; emphasis added)

Finally, the collaborative murals turned out to be a form of political action as described in the Introduction to this book. This is important because this collaborative stage was not intended to bring about citizenship activity. As the students developed an international identification, the collaboration led to the first two levels of engagement named 'pre-political': students worked with others and reflected critically on their own assumptions and those of others (level 1); and they worked with others, reflected critically and proposed possible alternatives and changes (level 2). In the next section we turn to the issues of criticality and action.

Criticality and Action in the World

Together with reflection, comparative perspectives and consciousness-raising, criticality is essential in intercultural citizenship (Byram, 2008, 2012, 2014; Gainer, 2012). Students' work and conversations cited above provide evidence of the level of criticality involved in the project. The students consciously reflected upon the fact that the project involved people and perspectives from another country and realized that this experience helped them question and challenge their own preconceptions and biases and learn new things. In her AIE, Karina said: '[The project] made me be more open minded. Now I can see others' point of view, ideas or beliefs. The awareness of cultural otherness serve me to re-evaluate my own everyday thoughts, feelings and behaviour.'

As explained in the Introduction, Barnett (1997) distinguishes three 'domains' in which criticality can appear: propositions, ideas, theories – the subject matter of university study; the internal world of the individual; and the external world. There was evidence of engagement with all three domains.

Propositions, ideas and theories

Essentially, this domain refers to what the students learn. In this project, they learned about Italy and life there, about youth identity as expressed in mural art and graffiti in Argentina and Italy, and about communicating with members of another cultural group, among other aspects. In her AIE, Karina wrote:

I found this encounter very interesting. *I have learned not only more about the Italian culture and art but I also learned more about my own country.* And that is wonderful. I had to make research about street art in Argentina, and I also had to find a way to explain my Italian peers about our customs. It was difficult to explain what MATE is! … By talking to them [the Italian peers], *I've realized how important it is to* meet new people. You can always find someone interesting. In a very practical sense, meeting new people is our doorway to new possibilities, experiences, and knowledge. *You can find new insights and ways of looking at the world.* (Karina, AIE; emphasis added)

Patricia, also in her AIE, said:

At first, I was not aware of the history of graffiti and of how much effort artists put into their works. *Besides, I did not know that* in every piece of art, the artists reflect what they have on their minds, so it is not something that they paint just because. *Instead,* it is something that they do with a purpose in mind and it has a certain meaning, usually connected with some aspect of the society where they live … *Now, I can say that I am much more aware of all those facts.* In fact, when I find myself walking across the streets, and I see a graffiti painted in a wall, I stop and think of the possible meaning that the artist who painted want[s] to convey and I also try to provide my own interpretation of the artwork. (Patricia, AIE)

The internal world of the individual

The students reflected upon their own beliefs, biases and preconceptions and gained conscious awareness of them. This happened in the de-centring and perspective-taking described above with respect to their ideas and concepts. For instance, Pamela wrote: '*At first I didn't like the topic much.* Before sharing our opinions and searching information about this topic, *I neither felt interested in graffiti nor knew that there are different kinds of graffiti.*' She then went on to analyse her pre-existing prejudices, as she now thinks positively about graffiti: '*This experience made me think positive* about graffiti artists and their works of art' and she became aware of her own learning process: '*The project taught me how* artists can express themselves through graffiti *and how* people appreciate the effort and creativity of those artists' (Pamela, AIE).

Reflection on language is also present and Karina mentioned that in order to take her Italian peers into account, she had to make adjustments to the way she was accustomed to using language: 'I also learned to introduce myself to other people in a different way. I am a person who needs body language a lot and this time I was unable to use it. *That obliged me to make use of my second language differently.* Longer sentences, more vocabulary, paraphrasing, etc.' (Karina, AIE). This was in part as a consequence of the AIE itself which deliberately asks users to think about their use of language – in this case a lingua franca – and is intended to develop the user's 'communicative awareness'. Critical thinking about language use leads to change in sociolinguistic competence.

The external world

This domain involves going beyond critical thinking, criticality and reflexivity towards critical action. It requires, as a first step, a re-conceptualization of one's ideas and perspectives but also some form of critical action. The civic actions in the local community that the Argentinean students engaged in are an example. Pamela for instance said: 'My classmates and I decided to give a talk on graffiti and Mural art to women in need, who were students of one of my classmates. It was a really touching and enjoyable experience' (Pamela, AIE).

It is this focus on the external world which makes the link between Barnett's framework and the aims of citizenship education and in the following section we consider how participants began to combine their critical insights with action in the external world.

Citizenship and civic and political ethos

As mentioned above, this project was undertaken as part of a language course. The students were easily able to see the benefits of the project from a linguistic perspective as we have seen already and Estefanía (AIE) said: 'During the Skype sessions we had to paraphrase ourselves most of the time. *When I listen to the recordings, I realize I made silly mistakes* as regards my use of the language. It is a really difficult task to express yourself and be fully understood by others – especially if they belong to a different culture. However, we could always fix the misunderstandings' (emphasis added).

The intercultural dimension of online communication with the Italian group was also easily acknowledged and welcomed by the students, as Patricia shows in her AIE:

> For this kind of encounters, it is important to be open minded and to be ready to learn from the others, being ready and able to agree or disagree in a respectful and polite way. It is also crucial to bear in mind that we all have different ideas and that cultures are not the same, so we should be able to accept the opinions of the others as well as their behaviour, habits and their local customs.

Likewise, Estefanía expressed enthusiastically:

> I have to admit that at first I felt pretty anxious and nervous. I had never met people via Skype so I didn't know what to expect. However, the girls

were so friendly and kind that, by the second Skype session, it was like talking to one of my best friends! (Estefanía, AIE).

The citizenship dimension, however, was difficult for the students to appreciate as they struggled to see its relevance to the course they were undertaking. For instance, in her AIE, Aldana said: *'At first I didn't want to do it* [the project], I thought that it was useless and even a waste of time. *I'd rather doing other things such as compositions or reading* but as soon as I started with the sessions I completely changed my mind. I started thinking that it was necessary and helpful as we started using our language differently... And I really liked it. It was quite an experience. *What I just needed was patience and interest on it'* (emphasis added).

As Aldana said, the students needed patience and time to appreciate the value of becoming involved in action in their local community. Once they took part in the project, they themselves came up with insightful and engaging activities.

The civic actions in the community were varied. For instance, one group travelled to Berazategui, a town near La Plata, and taught a lesson about mural art and graffiti to a group of 'women in need' who were enrolled in a governmental social relief plan that encourages them to go back to education.

Another group of students created leaflets in Spanish and in English describing both types of expression (murals and graffiti) for distribution around the university and the city centre. Photographs of the experience were taken and uploaded onto the wiki. Others interviewed people in three different cities to investigate the ways in which graffiti is conceptualized and they compiled a document with their main conclusions.

A third group produced reverse graffiti, which is an environmentally friendly way of creating temporary or semi-permanent images on walls or other surfaces by removing dirt from a surface. They created several prototypes of a swallow in different transparencies, stuck them on walls in a neighbourhood of La Plata, and using brushes with a mixture of water and soap, cleaned the walls to create their reverse graffiti. Figure 8.2 shows the students 'in action'.

Another group also created graffiti themselves and drew on a wall in one street in Alejandro Korn, a city 55 km away from La Plata (Figure 8.3). They named it 'Graffito' and wrote an reflection log narrating their thinking behind the idea, and about the development of their civic action and the message that they wished to convey, which is that language and art bring people together despite cultural differences. This message illustrates the first two levels of pre-political engagement referred to before, and the fact that the students actually went to the city and painted their graffiti illustrates higher levels of engagement.

Figure 8.2 Students create reverse graffiti in La Plata

Figure 8.3 Graffito by the local students in La Plata

In their log, they wrote:

As regards the Action in the Community which had to be based on all the work and talks we have had with our Italians partners, we came up with a great variety of ideas but we finally decided to do a graffito as our final project. *What we wanted to transmit to the community with our graffito is that it does not matter how different we are, from where we are or the language we talk, what it is important is that art, for instance graffiti, can be shared and enjoyed by anyone because art does not impose limitations.*

Our graffito has different globes and inside each globe the word 'hello' is written in different languages but that does not mean that language limits us, *we must greet people with our hearts, with our souls, without thinking how different we are. We are all the same, and language is the way we communicate and our personality and soul is the way how we understand each other.*

We consider that doing a graffito referring to language was an outstanding idea as we included the most significant thoughts we have been working throughout the year: language and graffiti. In this project we want to transmit to people how important language is for us and, besides, how we can communicate with anybody without sharing the same cultures or customs. *We need to know how to greet others with our souls and from now on: 'Saludemos con el alma' [Let's say hello with our souls].*

Fortunately, doing the graffito was not difficult. We were lucky to come across 'Acción Poética' whose members gave us all the help we needed and all the tools required. We chose Alejandro Korn as the place we wanted to start our graffito and 'Sociedad de Fomento del Barrio Santa Ana' as our building. We painted the whole wall white and once it was dried we started our meaningful black lines upon it. Every now and then a group of students or different people from the neighbourhood went pass looking at us with astonishment. It took two hours to be finished but we finally managed it. We are very grateful to 'Acción Poética' who helped us enormously and guided us through the painting. We hope we can transmit to the others how important language is and that there are no limits when communicating with others. (Final reflection log)

Another group of students went to a local square in La Plata called *Plaza Malvinas* and, after explaining the project to passers-by, they asked them to draw or paint something based on a video they had prepared. Children joined in, and the students used the resulting drawings to build a mural on one of the university's walls, uploading photos of the experience: www.dropbox.com/sh/xiqk1fkzxsqvsii/Wv5ujhI9M6

These actions in the community illustrate the concept of 'critical cultural awareness' or *savoir s'engager* in Byram's (1997) model of intercultural communicative competence. The levels of political engagement explained in the Introduction to this book were attained by some students, in particular level 3, whereby learners engaged with others and seek to understand their perspective; they reflected critically, proposed change and took action to bring about change in their own society. Level 4 of political engagement, which involves learners working in a transnational community to bring about change in their respective societies, is illustrated here in the actions in the community described above.

Difficulties and Challenges Ahead

There are sometimes constraints set by expectations of students and teachers – and those responsible for curricula in general – that prevent a full realization of all the levels of criticality and action in the community. This was the case in the Padua branch of the project. The Paduans did not attain the stage of civic action because of the constraints of their language course. There is a challenge for the future here, about how to make linguistic competence-oriented courses not only intercultural but also citizenship-oriented. In this respect, other research has shown that, even when full implementation is not possible, there is still an important development taking place (Yamada, 2010), and students can attain certain levels but not always the highest (and therefore not the action level, for instance). There is value in one group attaining lower levels of criticality while another group reaches higher levels as in this project.

The collaborative civic action stage between the Argentinean university students and secondary school pupils also brought about unexpected difficulties which are an issue for the future. The former were extremely reluctant to work with the secondary school pupils from Colegio Nacional Rafael Hernández as they perceived a lack of commitment on their part and expressed concerns regarding their lower proficiency in English. One student described the problem as follows:

> Habíamos quedado para hacer la última Skype session el miércoles pasado, la chica del Nacional no apareció, llegué corriendo a mi casa para estar a las 19hs en punto y estuve una hora sin hacer nada esperando para ver que hacíamos y al final terminamos cancelando todo. Ayer a la noche recién apareció la chica, nos pidió disculpas .... una semana después!!! lo cual me parece una falta de responsabilidad total, si sabía que nos íbamos a juntar, nos podría haber avisado antes o por lo menos disculparse al día siguiente, no a la semana ... la verdad que para andar haciendo cosas que nadie tiene ganas ni voluntad de hacer.... no funciona para nadie. (Carlina, university student, email to teacher, 10 May 2013)

> [We had arranged our last Skype session for last Wednesday, but the girl from the Colegio Nacional (National School) never turned up. I hurried home as fast as I could to make it on time at 7 p.m. and I spent an hour doing nothing as I was waiting to see what she would do. In the end we had to cancel everything. The girl didn't turn up until last night, when she apologized ... one week later! which I consider to be a complete lack of responsibility. She knew we were going to meet, so she could have told

us before or at least apologize the next day instead of doing it the week after.... Really, doing things that nobody is willing to do wouldn't work for anybody.

Carlina was not alone in having difficulty in seeing this stage as an opportunity to improve their language skills, and in underestimating their younger peers in terms of engagement and commitment. Eventually, with the help of the teachers in the school, some groups overcame the difficulties and preconceptions and finished with the agreed steps, namely the online communication stage and the civic actions in the community.

This shows that adopting an intercultural citizenship pedagogy in the foreign language classroom requires dialogue, experimentation and reflection for a slow and gradual change of thinking among researchers, teachers and students. The students in La Plata needed time to appreciate the overall value of the project, being at first unable to perceive the educational value of engaging in collaborative tasks with the Italian partners, and would have been satisfied just with the online communication stage, for example: 'It was a bit annoying that they made us do so many tasks, some of which did not had anything to do with our encounters with the girls' (María, AIE). It was necessary to engage in dialogue with the students to address this issue, by sharing a document with them that made explicit not only the linguistic aims of the project but also those related to the intercultural and citizenship dimensions. It was also explained to them that they were enrolled in state and free graduate education and that this project was an opportunity to give back to the community something of what they were receiving through their education.

These actions reaped benefits as by the end of the project; in her AIE María referred to the project as a 'unique opportunity' and expressed that 'I really enjoyed it'. Other students were even more enthusiastic:

I don't actually know which my thoughts were [at the time of the Skype sessions]. I believe that at that time I thought I was doing it just because I needed to fulfill the task for the project. *Then, I noticed that* I was meeting interesting people, that I was practicing and improving my English, that I was enlarging my art knowledge and most importantly, that *I was pleased with the experience. ... It's fantastic how* technology can connect two different countries separated by the ocean ... *It really pleased me and I am very happy about it! ...* As a conclusion, *I can say that I felt superb during this experience!* (Karina, AIE)

Clearly teachers need to be prepared to face similar difficulties as they implement an intercultural citizenship project of this kind. There are also difficulties related to the online component and in this respect O'Dowd (2007, 2015) and O'Dowd and Waire (2009) offer practical advice. Despite these complexities, the students' final AIEs were positive in spirit and their civic actions in the community were creative, committed and moving beyond what we had initially expected.

References

Barnett, R. (1997) *Higher Education: A Critical Business*. Buckingham: Open University Press.

Byram, M. (1997) *Teaching and Assessing Intercultural Communicative Competence*. Clevedon: Multilingual Matters.

Byram, M. (2008) *From Foreign Language Education to Education for Intercultural Citizenship*. Clevedon: Multilingual Matters.

Byram, M. (2010) Linguistic and cultural education for *Bildung* and citizenship. *Modern Language Journal* 94, 318–321.

Byram, M. (2012) Conceptualizing intercultural (communicative) competence and intercultural citizenship. In J. Jackson (ed.) *Routledge Handbook of Language and Intercultural Communication* (pp. 85–97). Abingdon: Routledge.

Byram, M. (2014) Competence, interaction and action. Developing intercultural citizenship education in the language classroom and beyond. In X. Dai and G. Chen (eds) *Intercultural Communication Competence: Conceptualization and Its Development in Cultural Contexts and Interactions* (pp. 190–198). Newcastle-Upon-Tyne: Cambridge Scholars.

Byram, M., Barrett, M., Ipgrave, J., Jackson, R., Méndez García, M.C. (2009) *Autobiography of Intercultural Encounters. Context, Concepts and Theories*. Council of Europe, Language Policy Division. See http://www.coe.int/t/dg4/autobiography/Source/AIE_en/AIE_context_concepts_and_theories_en.pdf (accessed 23 August 2013).

Gainer, J. (2012) Critical thinking: Foundational for digital literacies and democracy. *Journal of Adolescent and Adult Literacy* 56 (1), 14–17.

O'Dowd, R. (2007) *Online Intercultural Exchange. An Introduction for Foreign Language Teachers*. Clevedon: Multilingual Matters.

O'Dowd, R. (2015) The competences of the telecollaborative teacher. *The Language Learning Journal* 43 (2), 194–207, doi: 10.1080/09571736.2013.853374

O'Dowd, R. and Waire, P. (2009) Critical issues in telecollaborative task design. *Computer Assisted Language Learning* 22, 173–188.

Yamada, E. (2010) Reflection to the development of criticality: An empirical study of beginners' Japanese language courses at a British university. *Intercultural Communication Studies* XIX (2), 253–264.

9 Language and Intercultural Citizenship Education for a Culture of Peace: The Malvinas/Falklands Project

Melina Porto and Leticia Yulita

Planning the Project

The Malvinas/Falklands project aimed to create a culture of peace amongst undergraduate students learning foreign languages in higher education institutions in Argentina and the UK. As defined by the United Nations, a culture of peace is 'a set of values, attitudes, modes of behaviour and ways of life that reject violence and prevent conflicts by tackling their root causes to solve problems through dialogue and negotiation among individuals, groups and nations' (UNESCO, n.d.). The idea for this project grew and developed between June and December 2012 as part of a call by Michael Byram to create a network of projects on intercultural citizenship. A partnership was quickly formed between Melina Porto in Argentina and Leticia Yulita in the UK. Two reasons motivated us to choose the topic of the Malvinas/Falklands war. Firstly, this war is seen in strongly nationalist terms both in Argentina and the UK and, because of this, intercultural and citizenship issues are clearly involved. Secondly, the year 2012 saw the commemoration of the 30th anniversary of the war and in this sense the topic was timely and significant in the political agendas of both countries.

It was relatively easy to plan this project, not because it was simple but because we understood each other well and we had similar work styles and shared the same interest in this research area. In addition, both of us were Argentinean and Leticia had lived in the country until 2004 when she emigrated to the UK. This gave us a unique perspective from where to explore intercultural citizenship in connection with the conflict. The three-month planning stage was intensive, comprising email conversations and Skype meetings, and resulted in a detailed week-by-week plan of shared tasks as well as tasks that would be specific for each country. Each of us had specific course requirements that we had to respect, and which we needed to build into the project. In addition, it was hard to accommodate the different academic schedules to fit the project. The academic year finishes by the end of November in Argentina while in the UK it starts at the end of September. We were aware that this gave us little time for the online communication phase, and that the students would have to work against these time constraints too. During this phase, we opened a wiki, which we used as a shared virtual classroom.

The Socio-historical Context

Any choice of topic has social and historical significance, but in this case we knew we were dealing with a very sensitive issue and it is important to explain the context before we move to the detail. The following two subsections provide a brief overview of the dominant governmental messages in Argentina and the UK in relation to the Malvinas/Falklands conflict.

The Malvinas/Falklands conflict from an Argentinean perspective

The Malvinas/Falklands war was fought in April 1982 between Argentina and the UK over the Malvinas/Falkland Islands and South Georgia and the South Sandwich Islands. The islands are known as the *Islas Malvinas* in Argentina, formed by Gran Malvina, Soledad and several other smaller islands. The history of the war is part of *Efemérides*, an official document that outlines national historical facts to be taught in primary schools nationwide. In the secondary education sector the Malvinas/Falklands conflict is taught as part of a subject called 'citizenship education'. The overarching aim of primary and secondary education in Argentina as in many countries is to create and develop an Argentinean identity. The Ministries of Education at provincial and national levels include *Efemérides* related to the conflict (for instance, Portal Educativo del Estado Argentino, n.d. and Ministry of Culture and Education of the Province of Buenos Aires, n.d.).

Argentina has claimed the ownership of the Malvinas islands since the nineteenth century and, more emphatically, since the beginning of democracy in 1983, and although it was defeated in the 1982 war, the *Efemérides* present the islands as Argentinean. What is interesting here is that the dispute over sovereignty is generally not addressed at schools. The motto *Las Malvinas son argentinas* [The Malvinas islands are Argentinean] can be frequently seen or heard, and has become a feature of noticeboards in schools and in the media. There is a strong patriotic sentiment in the country, which is often revealed in discourses of territorial ownership and nationalism that focus on the conflict, and 2 April, which represents the day that the Argentinean troops disembarked on the islands to reclaim them, has become a national bank holiday in memory of the veterans of the war.

The war and its consequences are multifaceted and involve military, political, economic, diplomatic, cultural and ideological dimensions. The war is usually associated with colonialism and imperialism on the part of the UK (Borón, 2005; Borón & Vlahusic, 2009). Furthermore, Cristina Fernández de Kirchner, the President of Argentina, and David Cameron, Prime Minister of the UK, have engaged in verbal confrontations in local and international media. For instance, Kirchner accused Cameron of running a 'crude colonial power in decline' and has dismissed Britain's position as 'mediocrity bordering on stupidity' (http://www.guardian.co.uk/world/2011/jun/17/kirchner-cameron-falklands-british-row). Different newspapers in each country reflect different attitudes and positionings towards Kirchner and Cameron, and towards the Argentinean and British perspectives on the conflict.

The Malvinas/Falklands conflict from a British perspective

The islands are known as the Falkland Islands in the UK, and in April of 1982, most British people would only have had a vague idea of where the Falkland Islands were; somewhere close to the South American continent, nearest to Argentina, would have been the best guess of many British citizens. That was to change very suddenly when news broke of an invasion by Argentinean troops, taking everybody by surprise – including most of the UK Government. Historical arguments over the sovereignty of the Falklands were thrust into sharp focus as Prime Minister Margaret Thatcher mobilized the Armed Forces in an eventually successful attempt to 'win back' the islands.

Previously, the Falklands were another of those far distant outposts (such as Hong Kong and Gibraltar) that had once belonged to the British Empire and had occasionally been the subject of national interest when other countries made claims upon them. Now they had become a focus of renewed national pride as the supposed Argentinean 'imposters' were duly removed by British troops; hundreds died on both sides but the 'natural order' was restored. It would have been very unlikely for any British Prime Minister not to have responded militarily to the invasion, but Thatcher took political advantage of the war to increase her standing in the opinion polls to remain in Office until 1990 when election defeat in 1983 seemed more likely. This is evidenced by the MORI Polls (n.d.): February 1982 showed Conservative 30%, Labour 33% compared with June 1982 – Conservative 48%, Labour 28%. Today, despite a costly military presence maintained on the islands, the 'ownership' issue does not remotely affect British people in their day-to-day lives. This does not mean that they would 'give them away', especially after the financial and human costs in reclaiming them, but they prefer to let the islanders themselves choose their own future. This attitude is, naturally, antagonistic to Argentina's desire to own the islands.

The Project

About 80 language undergraduates in two Argentinean and British higher education institutions participated in our project. In Argentina there were 50 future teachers and translators learning English as a foreign language in their second year of undergraduate studies, while in the UK there were 30 first- and second-year undergraduates (some of whom were international students) learning Spanish as a foreign language at BA (Hons) level. All of the students were aged 18–22 and had a B2/C1 language level, as per the Common European Framework of Reference. This project, also described in Porto (2014), was planned as a case study research with elements of action research and had linguistic, intercultural and citizenship learning objectives. On successful completion of the project, we aimed for the Argentinean and British students to be able:

- To analyse and understand the power of the media in constructing stereotypical images of otherness, and its impact on one's thinking and behaviour towards 'others'. Media here refers to any 'text' that can be 'read' and 'interpreted', in a variety of sign systems and mediums, including print, non-print, visual, digital, multimodal or others (Hagood & Skinner, 2012; Handsfield et al., 2009). The students should explore a historical event using varied texts, mediums and resources.
- To read critically media of all kinds (involving processes of analysis, synthesis and evaluation (Waters, 2006)). In particular the students should challenge taken-for-granted representations of others constructed by the media in each country.
- To produce 'text' critically (Handsfield et al., 2009), for instance PowerPoint presentations, posters, advertisements, leaflets, videos, etc.
- To use contemporary media to engage in intercultural dialogue with others.
- To interact with others on the basis of values of respect and mutual understanding, allowing others to express their viewpoints, avoiding hostility and confrontation and resolving conflict cooperatively when necessary.
- To engage in civic participation in their local communities.

The first stage: Introductions and attitudes towards the war

The project began by encouraging students in each country to reflect in writing, in their foreign language, on the preconceptions they had of each other, and on their perspectives on the war. This initial writing task revealed that, at the start of the project, the Argentinean students' prior knowledge of the Malvinas/Falklands conflict was considerably higher than that of the UK-based students. Evidence of this can be demonstrated by the fact that six out of 30 students in the UK stated that they 'knew nothing about it', while the remaining 24 made comments such as follows:

No sé mucho sobre la Guerra de las Malvinas. Pienso que fue entre los británicos y la gente de Argentina. Es todo. [I don't know much about the Malvinas War. I think that it was between the British and the Argentineans. That is all.]

Sé que fue un conflicto entre países. Creo que los ingleses querían tener las islas. No sé nada más. [I know that there was a conflict between countries. I think that the British wanted to have the islands. I don't know any more.]

Hubo una guerra en las islas Malvinas. Eran parte de Argentina, pero ahora son parte del Reino Unido. [There was a war on the Malvinas Islands. They were part of Argentina, but they are now part of Great Britain.] (Initial written reflective task, UK-based students)

On the other hand, the Argentinean students had previous knowledge from school and considered the project as an opportunity to learn more about the conflict, in particular about different positions and viewpoints, as can be gleaned from the following data:

Este fue un tema en el que siempre estuve involucrado y siempre me interesó. [This is a topic I have always been involved in and interested in.]

El proyecto me sirvió para volver a repasar los temas sobre Malvinas vistos en el secundario. [The project helped me revise the issues relating to Malvinas that I had learnt at secondary school.]

In class discussions, the students speculated about the possible attitudes that the English and the Argentineans might have towards each other today, whilst reflecting on the role of the media in shaping those attitudes. Students considered how those media representations and images would affect communication with each other during the online communication exchange.

After this, a research phase followed where students learnt about the conflict using a wide range of texts (magazines, documentaries, interviews, videos, newspapers, etc.). Guided by their teachers' questions, students analysed not only the current media coverage of the conflict in both countries, but also the historical media coverage at the time the war took place, with a specific focus on viewpoints from the younger generations, including those of the islanders. All of these tasks were done in the students' foreign languages – English and Spanish. To prepare for their class discussions, the students watched the film *Iluminados por el fuego [Blessed by Fire]* (2005) by Tristán Bauer as well as BBC documentaries, and worked with the song *Brothers in Arms* by Dire Straits, the *Time* magazine cover of 31 May 1982 and a variety of media resources.

This stage aimed to familiarize the students with the Malvinas/Falklands conflict given that it had taken place before they had been born and they knew little about it, particularly the UK-based students. On the basis of this research and discussion stage, the students designed PowerPoint presentations about the war and posters using Glogster, Prezi and Mural.ly and uploaded the outcomes to the wiki. The Argentinean students completed the Autobiography of Intercultural Encounters through Visual Media (AIEVM; Council of Europe, 2013), which encourages reflection on intercultural encounters experienced through visual media such as television, magazines, films, the internet, etc.

This stage reflects the first level of pre-political engagement, defined in the Introduction to this book as learners engaging with others, and reflecting critically on their own assumptions, and those of the other. Here, the students engaged with others using the resources, documents and artefacts mentioned above. During the dialogic and cooperative work online, described in the next section, this first pre-political level of engagement was achieved by the online exchange between the Argentine and UK-based students (virtual engagement with others) and also by interviews with war veterans (engagement with others in person).

The second stage: Dialogic and cooperative work online

The second stage was the exchange, whereby the Argentinean and UK-based students communicated online, following written guidelines, using Facebook and the chat option in the wiki but mainly using Skype and Elluminate live! (a web conferencing program that works as a virtual classroom, made available for the project by the University of East Anglia). After an initial period in which they got to know each other, groups of mixed nationalities, of between four and six participants, were formed. The groups explored the influence that the mass media have in forming and perpetuating stereotypes and their impact on intercultural communication. The main task for each group during this dialogue phase was to collaboratively create an advertisement for peace aimed at bringing a point of contact between the Argentinean and the English positions over the conflict. All of the advertisements were uploaded to the wiki.

Initially we decided that the Spanish and English languages would be used on alternate days but we discovered that this was beyond our control as the students chose the language they wanted to use on each occasion and generally used both languages during each Skype session. Each Skype/Elluminate live! session was recorded and uploaded to the wiki.

Furthermore, the Argentinean students interviewed an Argentinean war veteran in Spanish, who visited their classroom. The interview was recorded and uploaded to the wiki. Similarly, the UK-based students interviewed an English war veteran in person and used Elluminate live!, which allowed the Argentinean students to participate virtually and ask questions. This interview was also made available in the wiki.

After this stage, the Argentinean students completed the Autobiography of Intercultural Encounters (Byram *et al.*, 2009) individually – a resource designed to encourage people to think about and learn from intercultural encounters. As noted before, this dialogic and cooperative stage of the project is a realization of level 1 of pre-political engagement, which means that learners engage with others to reflect critically and propose/imagine possible alternatives and changes. The collaborative leaflets for reconciliation provide evidence of their imagined alternatives, and some of these leaflets can be found at the following websites:

- http://www.youtube.com/watch?v=c0twtAmpTno&feature=youtu.be (accessed over 380 times at the time of writing);
- http://www.glogster.com/sofigeido/malvinas-ad/g-6l5ivb3voi3c1ssvleap 1a0;
- http://youtu.be/clWCcXHMUsw;
- http://thefalklandsmalvinasproject.blogspot.com.ar/search/label/Home.

The final stage: Intercultural and citizenship dimensions

The final stage of the project was the citizenship phase, during which the students became involved in civic action in their local communities. It is important to note that none of the students who participated in this project had prior experience of intercultural citizenship in their language study. The experience reported here is a first attempt at embedding these dimensions in the English language course in Argentina and in the Spanish language modules in England. Although the students were made aware of the intercultural and citizenship dimensions implicated, they were not required to become familiar with the theoretical framework underpinning the project.

The UK-based students as one whole group planned an event showcasing the Malvinas/Falklands project as part of the celebrations of the 50th anniversary of the University of East Anglia in 2013, but for reasons beyond their control it was cancelled. As a result of this, the UK-based project partners were unable to develop the citizenship dimension of the project, and there are no examples of civic action from them to report. On the other hand, the

Argentinean students participated in a variety of civic actions, such as uploading materials to the wiki (e.g. videos and photographs) describing their experiences, examples of which can be found online (http://thewarwasalie.blogspot.com.ar/; http://www.facebook.com/TheWarWasALie). The impact of these students' community engagement activities can be gleaned from the Facebook comment made by an Argentinean war veteran shown in Figure 9.1.

Other students planned and taught lessons about the war in diverse educational settings. For instance, one group taught a class in a local English language school (http://www.youtube.com/watch?v=UvXTV5ZwQiY&feature=youtu.be), whilst others engaged the academic community through lectures or delivered talks in a poor neighbourhood in cooperation with '*Un techo para mi país*' [A roof for my country], an NGO that teaches adults to read and write (http://www.youtube.com/watch?v=Wx3z6FTknyY). Another group created awareness-raising leaflets about the war, which they distributed in their city (Figures 9.2 and 9.3), and uploaded photographs of their civic action to the wiki as testimony of their experience.

Other students engaged in civic action by raising awareness of the war in a radio programme called *Alerta Cotorra*, broadcast online every Thursday evening from 7 to 9 pm using a video as a trigger for the discussion. Others developed teaching materials about the conflict, which were later used by a primary school teacher.

We will present further details later as we analyse the nature of these actions. However, for the moment it should be noted that these civic actions are a realization of levels 3 and 4 of political engagement, defined in the Introduction to this book as 'learners engage with others seeking their perspective/advice, reflect critically, propose change and take action to instigate change in their own society' (level 3) and 'learners create with others a

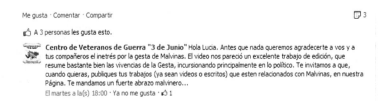

Me gusta · Comentar · Compartir   ☐ 3

👍 A 3 personas les gusta esto.

Centro de Veteranos de Guerra "3 de Junio" Hola Lucia. Antes que nada queremos agradecerte a vos y a tus compañeros el inetrés por la gesta de Malvinas. El video nos pareció un excelente trabajo de edición, que resume bastante bien las vivencias de la Gesta, incursionando principalmente en lo político. Te invitamos a que, cuando quieras, publiques tus trabajos (ya sean videos o escritos) que esten relacionados con Malvinas, en nuestra Página. Te mandamos un fuerte abrazo malvinero...
El martes a la(s) 18:00 · Ya no me gusta · 👍 1

English translation
War veterans centre 'June 3ʳᵈ'. Above all, we would like to thank you and your classmates for your interest in Malvinas. We thought your video was an excellent piece of edited work, which summarises the experiences of the war quite well, touching upon the political aspect mainly. You are cordially invited to publish your work (whether videos or written) related to Malvinas on our webpage, as and when you wish. Please accept our strong Malvinas-like hug …

Figure 9.1 Facebook comment made by an Argentinean war veteran

Figure 9.2 Awareness-raising leaflet about the war created with Glogster

transnational community, reflect together, propose and instigate change in their respective societies' (level 4).

Analysing Intercultural Citizenship in this Project

Given that 80 students participated in the project, large amounts of conversational and documentary data were produced. Conversational data comprised the chats in the wiki and on Facebook as well as the conversations in Skype and Elluminate live!, whilst documentary data comprised posters, PowerPoint presentations, written reflection logs, videos, advertisements, the Autobiography of Intercultural Encounters (AIE) and the Autobiography of Intercultural Encounters through Visual Media (AIEVM). We looked at these data focusing on the questions important to the topic of this book as laid out in the Introduction, although we are aware that there are other ways to analyse the data, such as looking for changes in language competence, analysing changes in attitudes or analysing the nature of the cooperation. In particular, our analysis involved finding evidence for the key components of

Figure 9.3 A student distributes a poster resulting from the project in Plaza Rocha, a centrally located square in La Plata

intercultural citizenship in foreign language education as described in the Introduction, namely:

(1) an international identification among the Argentinean and UK-based students, different from their national or regional identifications;
(2) challenging of the 'common sense' of each national group within the international project, through the skills involved in intercultural competence such as observing, discovering, describing, analysing, comparing and contrasting, relating, interpreting, perspective taking and de-centring; and
(3) criticality involving not only new ideas gained through the project but also substantial changes reflected in concrete actions as per the domains and levels in Barnett (1997), described in the introduction to this book.

We obtained permission and ethical approval to reproduce student material and to illustrate the findings with data excerpts from various sources through the use of pseudonyms in order to ensure confidentiality and non-traceability.

International identification

As part of the online communication stage, the Argentinean and UK-based students had to design an 'advertisement for peace' collaboratively. As they created their adverts in small groups of mixed nationalities, they considered its purpose and intended audience, its topic and main structure, the content (the message, using both English and Spanish) and para-textual information (e.g. the visual or audio-visual components of their advert). For instance, one group (comprising three Argentinean and two British students) began the discussion of some of these aspects during a Skype conversation in this way:

ARG1:   About the advert I think **we** _should stand for something very clearly,_ _because it is for peace-making._ _It should be very visual_ because **we** want it to be striking. I think that **we** _should stand for the end of the conflict._

ENG1:   **We** _could make a video?_ **We** _could create a script all together, and then each record our own section, and put it all together at the end._ (Skype conversation, October 2012; emphasis added)

The international identification among group members emerged from the beginning of this collaborative work and is reflected here, for instance, in the use of first person plural pronouns (in bold). At the same time, there is evidence of the students' critical evaluation and reflection (underlined in the extract), a component of intercultural competence, in the use of modals like should. The use of <u>should</u> in the underlined expressions simultaneously reflects the first level of criticality in Barnett's terms, 'critical skills', in the first domain of criticality, 'knowledge'. The group was evaluating critically their position towards the conflict. In addition, the group may have unwittingly intended to de-centre the audience of the advert, in other words, encourage them to distance themselves from their own perspectives, and this is reflected in the use of the adjective _striking_. The students appeared to wish to 'strike' their audience.

In the continuation of this conversation, the group made several decisions related to the content and structure of their advert. The international identification is pervasive and we highlight it in bold. The students decided to include quotes from the Argentinean and English veterans that they interviewed during the project (in italics), and at this point the extract reveals the true collaborative spirit of the task as, for instance, one of the students wished to include some words by a veteran but had not realized that they could draw from the existing interviews:

ENG1:   So how much speaking are **we** having? I would have thought the 'less is more' thing would be better in an advert?

ENG2:   Not a lot, I think. A bit of background in English.

ARG2:   Ok.

ENG2:   Reasons why the war was a bad thing ... And then **what we need to do now to change the prejudices**.

ENG1:   Ok, sounds good.

ARG2:   _Maybe_ **we** _could put something an English veteran said in English ... and something an Argentine veteran said in Spanish ... related to peace, of course._

ENG2: *Do **we** have those quotes?*
ENG1: *How do **we** get hold of an English veteran?*
ARG2: *I remember the English veteran you have to interview, he said something like 'there are no winners in war'. That's short and effective.*
ENG1: I like it. *What are **we** going to get from an Argentinean veteran?*
ENG2: Could **we** have that as text over the pictures?
ENG1: Yes, that's a good idea.
ENG2:   Ok. Awesome. (Skype conversation, October 2012; emphasis added)

   The group planned the focus of their advert to be on 'reasons why the war was a bad thing ... and then what we need to do now to change the prejudices'. The idea of 'change' is significant because the aim of any inter-cultural citizenship project is not only to facilitate intercultural citizenship experience but also to foster analysis and reflection upon it. These compe-tences in turn encourage changes of different kinds on the individual as well as changes in the relationships that each individual has with others. The students themselves underwent different types of changes, as we will illus-trate later, and in their advert they aimed to instil change in others, in this case by proposing the need to overcome people's prejudices about the war.

   In another Skype conversation, the same group identified the main idea they wanted to convey, namely that despite differences, people have a lot in common (in italics). This focus on what brings human beings together, and on commonalities, is again a key tenet of intercultural citizenship. Evidence of the international identification is highlighted in bold and evidence of criti-cality and reflexivity in Barnett's sense as mentioned before is seen again in the use of the modals <u>should</u> and <u>must</u>.

ENG1: It would be more effective if **we** have a few statements that make an impact, rather than lots of smaller ones.
   ...
ENG2: Are **we** still going to record **our** voices or will it just be text over pictures with the music?
ARG3: What are **we** going to communicate? I mean are **we** going to talk as Marisa [ARG2] said about prejudices? I think that is a great idea.
ENG2: Yes the prejudices bit will come into the '**what we need to do**' section. Like, 'in order to change the preconception **we** hold of each other'... etc.
ARG2: Ok, do you want to record **ourselves** or do you think that the texts and the song are enough?
ENG1: I think the texts and song might be enough. I'm not sure you would be able to put the speech in over the song, and still be able to hear both.
ENG2: I agree. White text on the black and white photos with John Lennon over the top will be perfect.

ENG1: Yes, that sounds good.
ARG3: *I think* **we** <u>*should*</u> *try to say that, after all, we are all the same.*
ENG2: If the picture fades really slowly into one another...
ARG3: Yes, I like that.
ENG1: Yes, and that's a good idea, Pía [ARG3].
ENG2: **We** could kind of end on that ... like: '*the war has created this boundary between* **our nations** *due to prejudice.* **We** <u>*must*</u> *end this because we are all the same.*'
ENG1: Yes. (Skype conversation, October 2012; emphasis added)

Evidence of an international identification can also be observed in advertisement for peace shown in Figure 9.4, revealed once more through the use of first person plural pronouns, such as 'nuestra generación' [*our generation*], 'entre nosotros' [*between us*], 'we', 'us', 'for all of us', words like 'generación' [*generation*] and 'together', and first person plural verb forms in Spanish 'naciéramos' [*we were born*], 'tenemos' [*we have*], etc.

This advertisement also challenges the 'common sense' of each national group, which together with the international identification is another characteristic of an intercultural citizenship project as outlined in the Introduction. This occurs in this case through the skills of comparing and contrasting, done visually by colouring the Malvinas/Falkland islands with the flags of both nations and by combining both languages, English and Spanish. It is also done by juxtaposing quotes from the two veterans of the war, as well as quotes by John Lennon (English) and José Luis Perales (Argentinean). This juxtaposition shows that, despite the confrontation represented by the location of both

Figure 9.4 Collaborative advertisement for peace

flags in the advert, there is a message of peace and harmony stressing that the Argentinean and British peoples can live together harmoniously. A distinction is also pointed out between governments on the one hand, and people on the other ('*The governments* can do whatever they want *but* don't let them determine what you think'; emphasis added). At this point, the advert adopts a general and impersonal tone – 'Si ellos pueden, todos pueden' [If they can, everyone can] – and speaks to a general audience.

The advert simultaneously speaks directly to its reader: 'don't let them [the media] determine what you think'. The words of the students, in the initial fragments in Spanish and in English, reflect their views as an international group (in bold):

Para **nuestra generación** ésto es algo que pasó antes de que **naciéramos**, y, por lo tanto, no **tenemos** razones para tener malos sentimientos entre **nosotros.** [For people of **our generation** this is something that happened before **we were born**; therefore there's no reason for **us** not to get on **with each other.**]

We shouldn't let the media tell **us** what to think, what to say, what to do, **we** shouldn't continue arguing. It makes no sense at all. The governments can do whatever they want but don't let them determine what you think. **We** can be together and create a better future for all of **us**.

These extracts also show evidence of other skills of intercultural competence, necessary in intercultural citizenship, such as observing, describing and analysing ('Para nuestra generación *ésto es algo que pasó antes de que naciéramos*') as well as criticality and reflexivity ('*por lo tanto, no tenemos razones para …*'; '*We shouldn't* let …'; '*we shouldn't* continue arguing'; '*It makes no sense at all*'; '*We can* be together and create *a better future* for all of us'). The use of *should* in the sense illustrated earlier in the Skype conservations is to be noted again. These skills of observing, describing, analysing and reflecting critically simultaneously reflect the first level of criticality in Barnett's terms ('critical skills') in the first domain of criticality ('knowledge'). There is also a very critical attitude towards the media ('We shouldn't let the media tell us what to think, what to say, what to do') that shows that this group of students were able to analyse and understand the power of the media in constructing stereotypical images of otherness and their influence on people's thinking and behaviour towards others, which was one of the aims of the project.

In short, the collaborative work involved in the creation of the advertisements resulted in an international identification, where the students from both countries, in groups of mixed nationalities, became a 'transnational community'. Through processes of comparing and contrasting, the groups engaged in initial forms of political engagement, in particular the first two levels called 'pre-political'.

Challenging 'common sense' and national perspectives as a path to intercultural citizenship

Through processes of comparing and contrasting, the students challenged their own presuppositions and beliefs, and the national basis of many of these, a characteristic of intercultural citizenship outlined in the Introduction to this book. The next data sample is part of Camilo's AIEVM. He chose a cartoon, which was published in *The Sun* on 18 June 1982, four days after the war had finished, and entitled it 'The political grief the Falklands left'. The cartoon shows Leopoldo Galtieri and Michael Foot sobbing for being so unpopular in their countries. Camilo added the caption 'I know your feelings, Leopoldo, no one loves me either!' and remarked that 'They resemble the stereotype of the military leader and a politician, especially by their clothes'. When reflecting upon the image, the processes of comparing and contrasting clearly emerged (in italics):

> They are male, both politicians. *One of them* is British, *the other* Argentinean. The fact that they are together, drowning their sorrows in the 'Lonely heart's club' is an ironic way of expressing that *they are in the same position*, or at least that *now they have the same reputation. For Galtieri,* the fact the Argentina lost the war was like touch paper to a wave of hatred towards him. *For Foot, on the other hand,* winning the war meant the victory of M. Thatcher and, by extension, the Conservative party, which reduced the Labour party's hard-won popularity. (Camilo, AIEVM, November 2012; emphasis added)

The word 'striking' in the next extract shows evidence of de-centring, which begins when something attracts our attention and we realize that other positions exist apart from our own. As Camilo expressed:

> *It was a striking image.* Although one reads about the British views regarding Argentinean politicians, I think the effect of a cartoon like this is stronger. At a glance, the image gives you lots of information. I have seen this kind of image before, but *this one really caught my attention.* The comparison between a British and an Argentinean politician, both suffering for the political effects the war had left, is brilliant. (Camilo, AIEVM, November 2012; emphasis added)

This extract simultaneously shows the processes of comparing and contrasting previously mentioned and underlined in the extract. Additionally, the de-centring observed here began with the discovery of the stereotype of the military leader and the politician: 'They *resemble the stereotype of the military leader and a politician, especially by their clothes.*' Later in his AIEVM, Camilo talked about feeling *'astonished'* by his own discovery as he engaged in the intellectual exercise of comparing the two politicians, whose countries had just been at war, now together grieving over the effects of it, as again evidence of de-centring.

De-centring leads to perspective-taking, which is essential in intercultural citizenship as students move away from their own positions and place themselves in 'somebody else's shoes' in an effort to see things from new points of view. In the following example, Camilo says how he thinks other Argentineans would feel towards Leopoldo Galtieri and how some British people might feel towards him, whilst he considers English attitudes towards Michael Foot. It is interesting to see that Camilo devotes a few lines to focusing on 'young people' like him, bringing in an intergenerational dimension.

> At the time, *I think most Argentinean people would agree that* Galtieri is object to mockery for being such a bad national leader have led the country to a state of general backwardness: economic recession, political uncertainty, a sense of dilapidated patriotism and social distrust of the national leaders.

> *Some British people would adhere to this feeling. As for M. Foot, I believe that those who supported him might have felt sorry for him and angry towards the conservatives, who, in turn, must have enjoyed it very much.*

> ...

> *I guess a lot of Argentinean people would have the same opinions as me. British opinions, on the contrary, may be more diverse. I suppose, anyway, that young people may find the need to* look for some information about Galtieri, M. Foot, the war, and the history of both countries during the 1980s to fully understand the image. (Camilo, AIEVM, November 2012; emphasis added)

This extract shows the central role of one's views and prejudices within these processes of de-centring and perspective-taking. Camilo cannot leave aside his personal opinions and evaluative comments about Galtieri and his government: 'Galtieri is object to mockery *for being such a bad national leader ... a sense of dilapidated patriotism and social distrust of the national leaders*'. At the same time, and at another point in this task, Camilo is able to question the national basis of his own views, an essential skill in intercultural citizenship: 'Because the opinions are generally shared, especially if those people belong to the same age group. *The role of the media and the way the topic is dealt with at school shape our ideas towards the issue.*'

Finally, as previously noted, the project encouraged students to research the conflict, on not only the basis of the initially described planned tasks but also out of their own curiosity. As part of writing his AIEVM, Camilo looked for information about Foot and the cartoonist, as we show below. Not only did he search for information, but he also explored the dictionary and other internet sources to provide a detailed analysis and interpretation of three elements that appear in the cartoon: a bird holding an umbrella to protect itself from Galtieri's and Foot's tears, a dog and a creature (a female figure with a huge nose and frog's legs) mopping the floor.

I didn't know who M. Foot was, so I had to research a little on the Internet.

[Information about Foot and the cartoonist follows]

Firstly, I think that thing mopping the floor is a supporter of the Tories, *because of her (it looks rather like* a woman) expression, *which is somewhat* triumphant and self-satisfied.

As for the dog, I believe it may be connected with the English term 'dogfight', *which means (Oxford, 2010):*

(1) a fight between aircraft in which they fly around close to each other
(2) a struggle between two people or groups in order to win something
(3) a fight between dogs, especially one that is arranged illegally, for entertainment

Therefore, the dog could be an allusion to the air conflict during the war. However, in my opinion, the dog represents the task force, all those people who went to the war in order to 'win the islands' (similar to the 2nd meaning). *If this is the case, the fact that the dog is crying implies that he* also has suffered as a result of the conflict, *although such suffering is different from that of Galtieri or Foot. Funnily enough,* the cartoonist has decided to present these two as the main characters of the scene, going back to the importance of the political effects the war had had.

Finally, the bird (carrying an umbrella) is a frequent image in Franklin's work. (You can check it out here: http://www.original-political-cartoon.com/gal lery/artist/franklin-stanley-1930-2004_30.html)

I think that it epitomizes the members of the Conservative Party. *In a more general perspective, birds represent:*

• endless freedom
• leadership
• strength in numbers
• hope

These are the features we could relate to the Tories at the time. After the war had ended, they were immensely popular and *a symbol of* firm leadership and strength. (Camilo, AIEVM, November 2012; emphasis added)

The project thus fostered research skills. Camilo, in his free time and moved by his own initiative, investigated two historical figures, in addition to the cartoonist. He used the dictionary, searched internet sites, provided alternative and simultaneous interpretations for the three elements in the cartoon ('the dog could be an allusion to … However, in my opinion the dog represents …'), hypothesized ('If this is the case, the fact that … implies that …'), evaluated those interpretations ('although … is different from …'), projected his own views ('I think that it epitomizes') and reflected and exercised his critical thinking ('These are the features we could relate to the Tories at the time'). Simultaneously these examples show that Camilo reached at this point the first two levels of criticality following Barnett (1997), i.e. 'critical skills' and 'reflexivity', but this time beyond the first domain of 'knowledge' (i.e. different understandings of the war) towards the second and third domains, namely 'self' and 'world', respectively. 'Self' is manifested here in Camilo's self-reflection processes and 'world' is revealed in his reflective research about historical events and figures.

Camilo did all of this using English, his foreign language, in a number of sophisticated ways, and it is feasible to speculate that he may have experienced some language development as a result of this project. However, we cannot ascertain this with confidence since students were not administered a pre and post language test.

Criticality, reflexivity and critical cultural awareness

The conversational and documentary data revealed the criticality and reflexivity that the project stimulated in the students. The juxtaposition of the Argentinean and British perspectives on the war, on which all classroom tasks were based, brought to the fore diverse perspectives and attitudes and encouraged participants to question and challenge their own preconceptions, biases and prejudices. We have just illustrated how Camilo acknowledged the influence of the media and the school in the formation of the opinions that he and his Argentinean classmates held about the conflict. Another student, Marcia, in her final reflection log from December 2012, said: 'Aprendí que no tengo que quedarme con un solo lado de la historia ya que las versiones no siempre encajan' [I learned that I don't have to stick to one side of the story because versions don't always match'].

More specifically, criticality in this project was achieved at three of Barnett's levels. The first level involves propositions, ideas and theories, and refers to what the students learned. This occurred in the first domain of criticality, 'knowledge', and within the first two levels, 'critical skills' and 'reflexivity'. For instance, the students learned about the war from a historical perspective, gained first-hand insights about it through the testimonies of the two war veterans, and also experienced communication with members of another cultural group (in many cases, for the first time in their lives, especially among the Argentinean students). According to the students' own testimony in logs and feedback evaluation forms, their learning in the domain of 'knowledge' was broad and can be categorized in terms of (1) *Content*, (2) *Technology*, (3) *Language*, (4) *Intercultural communication*, (5) *Critical self-reflection* and (6) *Critical action in the world*, as follows:

(1) *Content* – gaining knowledge about the war from the Argentinean and English perspectives and first-hand experience about the conflict. This is revealed in comments such as 'fue una gran oportunidad para *experimentar una representación más viva* sobre Malvinas' ['it was a great opportunity to *experience a more vivid representation* about Malvinas'] (Carlos, reflection log).

(2) *Technology* – gaining knowledge and experience in using research and technological tools. For instance, one student said: 'Participar de este proyecto me dio la posibilidad de aprender a utilizar mejor la computadora y obtener otras herramientas para hacer más sencillo algunos trabajos. Es decir, por ejemplo aprendí a usar Skype y Elluminate live!, aprendí a utilizar algunas herramientas de PowerPoint o movie maker, etc.' ['This project gave me the opportunity to improve my computer skills and to use new IT tools, such as Skype, Elluminate live!, PowerPoint, movie maker, etc.'] (Lucía, reflection log).

(3) *Language* – developing confidence in Spanish and English language skills, with a specific focus on gains in language use. Marta (reflection log) wrote: 'Respecto al lenguaje, logré un poco más de fluidez y seguridad a la hora de hablar y a la hora de escribir aprendí bastante vocabulario y a su vez, comencé a utilizar algunas estructuras que antes no utilizaba, por ej. inversiones, con el fin de hacer mis textos un poco más complejos y con un mejor manejo del lenguaje' ['As far as language is concerned, I gained fluency and confidence in speaking. As for writing, I acquired more vocabulary and started using structures that I had not used before, for example, inverted sentences, with a view to making my writing more linguistically sophisticated'].

(4) *Intercultural communication* – gaining knowledge about and experience in intercultural communication. This is demonstrated in comments such as 'El proyecto me ayudó a ampliar mi contexto cultural. Me parece que ponerse en contacto con gente de otros ambientes, países o culturas siempre tiene un resultado positivo' ['*The project helped me broaden my cultural context. I think that getting in contact with people from other contexts, countries or cultures is always positive*'] (Luciana, reflection log).

(5) *Critical self-reflection* – developing (self) awareness, de-centring from their own positions and being able to consider alternative perspectives. In addition to Barnett's first domain called 'knowledge', within which this type of learning can be framed, critical self-reflection in this category

also illustrates Barnett's second domain of 'Self', involving the students' internal world. The students reflected on their own values, prejudices and preconceptions and became increasingly aware of them. Evidence of this can be gleaned from Carolina's observations in her AIE: 'We were raised in very different cultures and we were taught very differently … It helped me see the facts from a different point of view … At the beginning all I had was a very partial view of things and now I can understand the opposite point of view.'

(6) *Critical action in the world* – reflecting on the civic actions in their local communities that the students engaged in. This involved Barnett's third domain of criticality, 'the external world', at the two higher levels of critically called 'refashioning of traditions' and 'transformatory critique in action'. We dwell upon this dimension in greater detail in the next section.

Civic and political engagement

As noted earlier, the actions in the community that the students carried out are forms of civic and political engagement that can be understood within the notion of 'critical cultural awareness' or *'savoir s'engager'* (Byram, 1997, 2008; Byram & Guilherme, 2000). They illustrate the citizenship dimension of the project and involved the students acting collaboratively in their local communities in a variety of civic actions. Although time-consuming, the students welcomed this phase of the project and suggested some activities that reflect level 3 of political engagement as explained in the Introduction to this book: students working collaboratively with others, becoming familiar with their views and perspectives, and on the basis of critical reflection, proposing change and taking action in their own community. The lessons about the war that the students planned and delivered in diverse settings, such as language schools, universities and community centres, exemplify this. At the same time, these lessons illustrate Barnett's third domain of criticality, 'the external world', in the first two levels of criticality, i.e. problem-solving (how can we teach others about the conflict?) and reflexive practice (can we adapt what we learned to make it accessible to others?).

Level 3 of political engagement had unanticipated ramifications and the civic actions that the students planned illustrate again Barnett's third domain of criticality, 'the external world', but at the highest levels of criticality, namely refashioning of traditions (new and shared understandings of the war) and transformatory critique in action (transferring the knowledge and reflection gained to others). For instance, one group of students contacted and interviewed a primary school teacher who had also been working on the Malvinas/Falklands conflict with her pupils and they shared information and details about each other's projects. This is an example of Barnett's level of criticality called 'transformatory critique in action' within the domain 'world', i.e. the students proposed and carried out a civic action that implied a collective reconstruction of the war. In a reflection log, one of the students described the experience in the following way, showing that they were able not only to take action (do something with an impact in their society) but also to gain reflexive understandings about the war (the level of criticality called 'refashioning of traditions' in Barnett's terms):

> I was told that there was another Malvinas project taking place at my city Daireaux and I decided to have a talk via telephone with the project leader. … The project is called 'Ellos lo dieron todo por la patria' [They give it all for their country]. Here, students during free hours at school, made some cardboard flowers and a big rosary to send to Darwin's cemetery at Malvinas. They also met a number of veterans that are part of 'Asociación de Veteranos de la Guerra de Malvinas' (AVEGUEMA) in Buenos Aires. The objective of this conversation was to exchange our projects with those students involved in the project in order for them to be known by as many people as possible. They really like our Project; they thought it was a great idea to have information about British people, how they lived the war and which were their points of view in relation to it not only a few years ago but also nowadays. (Estefanía, written reflection about the action in the community stage, December 2012)

All the civic actions that the Argentinean students carried out in their community (sharing the project with social media, teaching lessons, distributing leaflets in public places, talking on the radio, etc.) are evidence not only of level 3 of political engagement as we showed earlier but also of levels 4 and 5 of engagement. In the Introduction, the editors define these levels as 'learners create with others a transnational community, reflect together, propose and instigate change in their respective societies' (level 4) and 'learners from two or more societies identify an issue which they act upon as a transnational group' (level 5). The key at these levels is learners from different social groups acting as a transnational group and while these actions were designed and carried out by the Argentinean students on their own, they would not have engaged in these actions without the previous work with the British students in the different stages of the project, which led them both, Argentinean and British, to develop a bond as a transnational group, evidenced in the Skype conversations and collaborative leaflets through the use of first-person plural pronouns.

The students were aware of their political activity and this means that they not only acted in the real world (i.e. carried out their civic actions) but also reflected on the political role they were undertaking. The following reflection log shows that they took action (i.e. they did something with an impact in their society such as sharing a video about the war in Facebook and

YouTube). This is evidence that they reached the third domain of criticality in Barnett's terms, 'the external world' ('we propose to ...'), whilst at the same time they gained reflexive understandings about the need for them to engage in this form of political action ('Furthermore, we want to encourage its knowledge and its discussion through this short interactive video'). This illustrates the level of criticality called 'critique-in-action' in Barnett's terms (again within the third domain), or in other words, they engaged in a collective reconstruction of the world through the transnational work involved in the project and the transnational/international identification that they developed as a group.

> We propose to show the global community a video which entails different points of view in relation to Malvinas/Falklands conflict. It shows different testimonies from veterans, ordinary people and the government.
>
> The purpose of our proposal is to find out what ordinary people thinks about the considered topic. Furthermore, we want to encourage its knowledge and its discussion through this short interactive video.
>
> This work is addressed to people who use social networks not only to socialize but also to inform themselves about historical matters.
>
> The video has been uploaded in You Tube and then shared on our personal Facebook accounts to promote people to express their opinions about such an important event in the history of Argentina and UK. (Written description of the action in the community stage, December 2012)

Conclusion

We feel that our first experience in implementing this type of project was a success but this achievement was not without its difficulties. Leticia Yulita's identity as an Argentinean national in the British context can be considered as both an advantage and a limitation that may have impacted on her students. Firstly, her Argentinean identity revealed itself in the choice of topic, for it reverberated with her personal life. The evidence in student feedback forms indicates that students highly valued the opportunity to have access to an insider perspective of the issue as provided by an Argentinean national. However, this same aspect of her identity can also be considered a limitation to the project. Since Leticia experienced the anguish of having a friend involved in the Malvinas war when she was a teenager, it is highly likely that her personal history may have affected class discussions as a way to deal with feelings and thoughts that had greatly disturbed her as a young woman. This might possibly have led the students' thinking and discourses, and therefore there was a greater need on her part to become self-aware of her ideologies and honest about what she was avoiding and what she was foregrounding, what she was limiting and what she was broadening in her questions and comments in the classroom. This awareness that, potentially, she could have influenced students' thinking and discourses, made her careful about overcoming a potential limitation of the project as much as she could. However, it should be noted that, no matter how hard she tried to avoid bias in the classroom, she could not deny her Argentinean nationality, but tried to monitor it more closely and systematically, rather than intuitively, by carefully thinking and writing questions for class discussions prior to her teaching. This was seen as a way to allow for more control of her bias. However, now with the benefit of hindsight, we believe that keeping a journal and reflecting on it on an ongoing basis would have greatly assisted in making her national positionality less loaded.

On a pragmatic level, there were also a few difficulties relating to the logistics of the project. We were faced with the initial difficulty of accommodating two different academic schedules, which left us with little time for the online communication stage. In addition, given that there were only two months for this stage of the project, we overcame difficulties as they arose. For example, some students needed extra facilitation from us to carry out specific tasks, whilst others experienced delays or lack of replies from their project partners, which prompted our intervention by talking to individual students to ensure participation. Our teaching plans needed readjustment and required an amount of flexibility and versatility on our part. Furthermore, the civic actions in the community stage were time-consuming and required a lot of effort and hard work from the students. As a result of this, we, as their teachers, responded to these actions in equal measure by providing feedback. This involved long hours of reading, downloading project-related materials from the wiki, following internet links and writing our comments and words of appreciation on the shared wiki.

The Malvinas/Falklands project touched upon a topic that is inherently political in nature and in the last stage of the project we discovered that many of the students, in particular the Argentinean students, were themselves already politically active and committed to civic action in their communities. For instance, the action in the community that involved a group of Argentinean students teaching a lesson about the war in a local NGO was the initiative of one student who worked regularly as a volunteer in this NGO. This dimension was not anticipated, and with the advantage of hindsight, we now believe that we could have benefited from gathering data about the students' past experiences in political and civic forms of involvement as Barrett (2012) suggests (for instance through initial surveys and questionnaires). Furthermore, we are currently refining this citizenship component in our planning of future projects along the theoretical framework of citizenship and human rights education described in Osler (2012a, 2012b, 2013), Osler and Starkey (2003, 2004, 2006) and Starkey (2002, 2005, 2008). One step in this direction, as Osler (Porto, personal communication, 2014) suggests, is to include an explicit citizenship and human rights framework within the project through prior specific consciousness-raising activities. The students' critical deconstruction of the notion of citizenship that we described earlier echoes Osler's notion of 'critical patriotism', which requires a critical stance towards the patriotic and the national within one's nation. Their analysis of this notion in the Skype conversations shows that they were ready for this explicit citizenship and human rights framework.

We are aware that the sensitive and political nature of the topic addressed in this project can make language teachers uncomfortable and wonder why this is their business after all. In this respect, we can bring in the editors' words from the Introduction when they argue that foreign language education can contribute to education by developing criticality and encouraging civic action in the community, or in other words, by combining foreign language teaching with the principles and practices of citizenship education. At the same time, it should be noted that the topic in an intercultural citizenship project of this kind does not necessarily need to be as obviously sensitive and political as here and this book illustrates other options.

Finally, this partnership between Universidad Nacional de La Plata in Argentina and the University of East Anglia in the UK, which grew and developed initially thanks to our personal and professional bonds, was formally acknowledged by our institutions. This formal support has contributed to the strengthening of this bond. After this first project, we also worked collaboratively in another one about the 1978 Football World Cup and Dictatorship in Argentina (reported in the following chapter) and we are currently designing a new project for the future. This is unique to our partnership and indicates that we have moved from an isolated implementation towards a broader approach in which we have adopted intercultural citizenship as a continuous *practice* in our foreign language higher education contexts.

Acknowledgements

We are extremely grateful to John Manders for his perceptive observations and initial editing of this chapter, in addition to his contribution to the section about the British perspective on the Malvinas/Falklands conflict. We are also greatly indebted to Gabriela Iacoboni who provided vital support with the wiki. Finally, our heartfelt gratitude goes to all the students from Universidad Nacional de La Plata, Argentina and University of East Anglia, UK who participated in this project.

References

Barnett, R. (1997) *Higher Education: A Critical Business.* Buckingham: Open University Press.

Barrett, M. (2012) The PIDOP project: An overview. Unpublished report, University of Surrey, UK. See http://www.fahs.surrey.ac.uk/pidop/ (accessed 16 July 2016).

Borón, A. (2005) Un imperio en llamas [An empire on fire]. *Observatorio social de América Latina* VI (18), 271–287.

Borón, A. and Vlahusic, A. (2009) *El lado oscuro del imperio. La violación de los derechos humanos por los Estados Unidos.* [The Dark Side of the Empire. The Violation of Human Rights by the United States.] Buenos Aires: Ediciones L.

Byram, M. (1997) *Teaching and Assessing Intercultural Communicative Competence.* Clevedon: Multilingual Matters.

Byram, M. (2008) *From Foreign Language Education to Education for Intercultural Citizenship.* Clevedon: Multilingual Matters.

Byram, M. and Guilherme, M. (2000) Human rights, cultures and language teaching. In A. Osler (ed.) *Citizenship and Democracy in Schools: Diversity, Identity, Equality* (pp. 63–78). Staffordshire: Trentham Books.

Byram, M., Barrett, M., Ipgrave, J., Jackson, R., Méndez García, M.C. (2009) *Autobiography of Intercultural Encounters. Context, Concepts and Theories.* Council of Europe, Language Policy Division. See http://www.coe.int/t/dg4/autobiography/Source/AIE_en/AIE_context_concepts_and_theories_en.pdf (accessed 1 September 2014).

Council of Europe (2013) *Images of Others. An Autobiography of Intercultural Encounters through Visual Media.* Strasbourg: Council of Europe. See http://www.coe.int/t/dg4/autobiography/AEIVM_Tool_en.asp (accessed 16 July 2016).

Hagood, M. and Skinner, E. (2012) Appreciating plurality through conversations among literacy stakeholders. *Journal of Adolescent and Adult Literacy* 56 (1), 4–6.

Handsfield, L., Dean, T. and Cielocha, K. (2009) Becoming critical consumers and producers of text: Teaching literacy with Web 1.0 and Web 2.0. *The Reading Teacher* 63 (1), 40–50.

Ministry of Culture and Education of the Province of Buenos Aires (n.d.) See http://abc.gov.ar/docentes/efemerides/2deabril/index.html (accessed 30 April 2015).

MORI Polls (n.d.) See https://www.ipsos-mori.com/researchpublications.aspx (accessed 30 April 2015).

Osler, A. (2012a) Higher education, human rights and inclusive citizenship. In T. Basit and S. Tomlinson (eds) *Higher Education and Social Inclusion* (pp. 293–312). Bristol: Policy Press.

Osler, A. (2012b) Teaching for inclusive citizenship, peace and human rights. In P. Cowan and H. Maitles (eds) *Teaching Controversial Issues in the Classroom: Key Issues and Debates* (pp. 71–83). London: Continuum.

Osler, A. (2013) Bringing human rights back home: Learning from 'superman' and addressing political issues at school. *The Social Studies* 104 (2), 67–76.

Osler, A. and Starkey, H. (2003) Learning for cosmopolitan citizenship: Theoretical debates and young people's experiences. *Educational Review* 55, 243–254.

Osler, A. and Starkey, H. (2004) *Study on the Advances in Civic Education in Education Systems: Good Practices in Industrialized Countries.* UK: Centre for Citizenship and Human Rights Education, University of Leeds and Institute of Education, University of London.

Osler, A. and Starkey, H. (2006) Education for democratic citizenship: A review of research, policy and practice 1995–2005. *Research Papers in Education* 24, 433–466.

Portal Educativo del Estado Argentino (n.d.) See http://portal.educ.ar/noticias/educacion-y-sociedad/efemerides-2010-los-derechos-h.php (accessed 30 April 2015).

Porto, M. (2014) Intercultural citizenship education in an EFL on-line project in Argentina. *Language and Intercultural Communication* 14 (2), 245–261.

Starkey, H. (2002) *Democratic Citizenship, Languages, Diversity and Human Rights: Guide for the Development of Language Education Policies in Europe from Linguistic Diversity to Plurilingual Education.* Strasbourg: Council of Europe.

Starkey, H. (2005) Democratic education and learning. *British Journal of Sociology of Education* 26, 299–308.

Starkey, H. (2008) Diversity and citizenship in the curriculum. *London Review of Education* 6, 3–8.

UNESCO (n.d.) Culture of Peace. What is it? See http://www3.unesco.org/iycp/uk/uk_sum_cp.htm (accessed 30 April 2015).

Waters, A. (2006) Thinking and language learning. *ELT Journal* 60, 319–327.

10 Human Rights Education in Language Teaching

Leticia Yulita and Melina Porto

Project Description

Our intercultural citizenship project was an approach to human rights education in language teaching and involved the study of the 1978 Football World Cup held in Argentina at the time of a military dictatorship. It was aimed at addressing human rights violations and enhancing awareness of democratic participation by empowering students to become 'transformative intellectuals', i.e. citizens engaged in self and social change through knowledge and action (Giroux, 1999; McLaren & Farahmandpur, 2005). Students were invited to research the 1978 World Cup during the 'Dirty War' (1976–1983), a period that was euphemistically referred to by the government of the time as the 'Proceso de reorganización nacional' ('Process of National Reorganization'). During this time, anyone suspected of being a subversive or an anarchist was abducted, often tortured, or made to 'disappear'. The kidnapped people became known as 'desaparecidos' (the 'disappeared'). During this period of extreme military repression, totalitarianism and censorship, anyone who expressed their dissent put their life at risk. Despite this, the mothers of the disappeared gathered in Plaza de Mayo, a square in front of the site of Argentina's government, in non-violent demonstrations, calling for their children. They carried pictures of their missing children and wore white scarves on their heads that symbolized their children's nappies. This soon drew international attention to the brutalities and abuse of power that permeated the most basic aspects of existence in Argentina's society.

The project involved Spanish and English language students at Bachelor level from the University of East Anglia in the UK and Universidad Nacional de La Plata in Argentina. As we shall see in more detail below, students shared information, developed ideas and engaged in discussions about the collaborative design of a leaflet to raise awareness of media manipulation and censorship during international sporting events. During the life of the project, a Uruguayan sports journalist and writer based in France acted as an observer and editor and provided useful insights for the UK-based students' essays. The project outcomes included oral presentations, reflective essays, Skype conversation transcripts and leaflets, all of which were the sources of data for our research. The Argentinean students also completed the Council of Europe's Autobiography of Intercultural Encounters (http://www.coe.int/t/dg4/autobiography/default_en.asp).

There were 76 students of English in Argentina and 23 students of Spanish in the UK, organized in smaller groups, generally consisting of one UK-based student per three to four Argentinean students. Discussions took place through an academic networking site, known as a 'wiki'. There, the students were able to introduce themselves to their groups and invite them to converse further through Skype. During the weeks that followed, the students held group Skype conversations where they were able to speak to each other from across the globe. The students were also instructed as to which days they were able to speak Spanish or English; through this, both UK-based and Argentinean students were able to practise their speaking and listening skills and further boost their confidence when speaking a foreign language. The wiki space and Skype were considered as interactive grounds with the potential for shortening distances (geographical, linguistic, cultural, ideological, etc.) through dialogue, with the aim of raising awareness of media manipulation.

There were several stages to the project:

- Stage 1 – Introduction (students researching the topic);
- Stage 2 – Intercultural Communication (students interacting in the wiki and Skype);
- Stage 3 – Citizenship (students engaging in 'action in the community');
- Stage 4 – Reflection (students reflecting on the process).

Stage 1: Introduction

The students, in their respective foreign language classes and without interacting online yet, were encouraged to gain knowledge about the 1978 World Cup and the dictatorship period through a variety of resources provided to them as the starting point for their research. In addition, students were required to search for other materials of their choice, such as newspaper articles, films, documentaries, photos and books to bring to class and share with their classmates. The students were informed that the audience of their research was their project partners across the globe and the task carried out in the classroom focused on gaining awareness of the power of the media in creating stereotyped images of people and events by reflecting on the questions in Table 10.1.

This task served as the starting point in terms of knowledge of media manipulation during sporting events and provided the basis for the cooperative task set in stage 2 of the project. During this introductory stage, students also got to know each other virtually through the 'wiki'; participants

Table 10.1 Questions to prompt reflection and criticality on the research undertaken by the students

English	Spanish
What is the image of the 1978 World Cup that your chosen materials construct?	¿Qué imagen del Mundial 1978 construyen estos materiales?
How would you describe the media representation of the 1978 World Cup in the materials you have selected?	¿Cómo lo representa cada uno de los medios de comunicación escogidos?
If you had to tell someone of your age about what you found in these materials, what would you tell them?	Si tuvieras que contarle a alguien de tu edad sobre estos materiales, ¿qué le dirías?
How would you describe the image constructed of Argentineans in these materials?	¿Qué imagen de los argentinos construyen estos materiales? Descríbela en detalle.
How would you describe the media representation of the Argentine Military Junta (1976–1983)?	¿Qué representaciones construyen los medios de comunicación de la Junta Militar (1976–1982) en Argentina?
What is the impact of these media representations on the ways you would relate to a military officer in Argentina or to a family member of a disappeared?	¿Cómo influyen estas representaciones en la manera en la que te acercarías a un militar o a un pariente de un desaparecido en Argentina?
What is your personal opinion of this sporting event within the social–political context of repression in an authoritarian regime?	¿Cuál es tu opinión personal acerca de este evento deportivo dentro del contexto sociopolítico de dictadura de la época?

introduced themselves through a brief description and a photograph of themselves. After this interaction phase, students were instructed to form mixed-nationality groups in preparation for the next stage.

Stage 2: Intercultural Communication

In this stage students Skyped with each other in their groups and shared the information they had gathered in stage 1. This task was followed by a comparison of the socio-political circumstances of the 1978 World Cup with another sporting event that had taken place under similar circumstances. Students recorded their conversations using their phones, tablets and iPods, and uploaded them onto the wiki. They then created a bilingual leaflet, where they stated their position about the manipulation of the media in their selected sporting events from both the Argentinean and British perspectives. It was up to the groups themselves to find and choose a suitable comparison for the 1978 World Cup, and this led to a wide variety of leaflets being produced by the end of the project. Comparisons to the 1978 World Cup included the 1934 World Cup in Italy, the 1936 Olympics in Berlin, the 2008 Olympic

Games in Beijing, the 2012 Olympics in London and the 2014 Winter Olympics in Sochi, which had not actually taken place when the project was being completed. As students created their leaflets, they considered the following:

- the main topic of the leaflet;
- textual information (the message, both in English and Spanish);
- paratextual information (the visual and audio-visual components);
- the specific purpose of their leaflet;
- their intended audience;
- their artefact's circulation.

Students had 10 days to plan and design their leaflet using Skype and the wiki. Upon completion, they uploaded their leaflets onto the wiki under the banner of 'bi-cultural projects'. All of the students involved in the project were able to see each other's productions, which became objects of reflection and opinion.

Stage 3: Citizenship

The students were encouraged to take 'action in the world', thus bringing the principles of citizenship education into the foreign language classroom. Students were requested to undertake the 'action in the community' stage outside class time and to upload at least two pieces of evidence onto the wiki as testimony of their experience, in the form of a video, photographs, a sample of the webpage or a report. Unfortunately, owing to institutional constraints, the UK-based students were not involved in this phase of the project but they were able to learn about and comment on the Argentine students' actions in the community using the wiki. Examples of the Argentine students' community engagement activities involved creating posters and drawings, which were later showcased on the Facebook pages of the project, and interviewing the relative of a 'desaparecido'. Students also delivered a number of talks in diverse educational settings, such as a primary school, a teacher education institution and La Plata School of Medicine. Finally, the students conducted a survey to find out about how much the youth in La Plata knew about this period in Argentine history.

Stage 4: Reflection

An essential aspect of the project involved a reflection stage once the project was completed, involving students thinking about the following issues by providing clear examples to illustrate and justify their points and arguments:

- whether their assumptions and beliefs about the 1978 World Cup and socio-political climate in Argentina were confirmed or challenged by the project;

- how the project contributed to their understanding of a different cultural group (the 'disappeared', the relatives of the 'disappeared', the Military Junta, university students from another part of the world, etc.); and
- the educational dimension of the project through the analysis of Skype conversation transcripts.

On completion of the project, the students were able to:

- explore and reflect on a historical cultural event of contemporary relevance;
- satisfy their curiosity through engagement in research skills;
- appreciate linguistic diversity in the English and Spanish languages;
- critically analyse (audio)visual media images;
- critically analyse representations of the historical event constructed by the media;
- raise awareness among other people of the power of the media in manipulating thinking and behaviours;
- demonstrate a willingness to engage in dialogue with others;
- engage in intercultural online dialogue with others;
- develop the ability to listen to, respect and work together with individuals from diverse cultures;
- allow others to express their viewpoints, avoiding hostility and confrontation and resolving conflict when necessary;
- create a temporary transnational community;
- develop values such as respect, mutual understanding, social justice, human rights and openness;
- transfer knowledge to others by engaging in civic participation locally;
- be better prepared to face the challenges of working in multilingual and multicultural environments.

Critical Pedagogy as the Driving Theory

Critical Pedagogy was the over-arching theoretical framework of this project. Critical Pedagogy is ideologically founded in the Eurocentric philosophical and educational schools of thought of Critical Theory and Postmodernism, influenced by French Post-structuralism. Early Critical Pedagogy was greatly influenced and shaped by the Frankfurt School and owes much of its current thinking to the works of Henry Giroux. However, Critical Pedagogy is given a non-Eurocentric stance through the thinking of Brazilian Paulo Freire, whose work was conducted in a Latin American context (Guilherme, 2002). Freire draws his thinking from Dewey's educational theory and is recognized as the founder of current conceptualizations of Critical Pedagogy. However, Critical Pedagogy does not end with Freire, although his influence as a Brazilian working in a Latin American context, as opposed to Western European, cannot be denied. His perspective is important as he gave voice to people in local and peripheral contexts.

Critical Pedagogy is difficult to define because of its flexibility and eclecticism and multiple applications in diverse social and historical contexts. However, there are major principles underpinning its philosophy. It is a pedagogy of 'reflection, dissent, difference, dialogue, empowerment, action and hope' (Guilherme, 2002: 17). It involves addressing questions of power, social injustice and inequality. It also involves interrogating taken-for-granted assumptions and hegemonic discourses. Critical Pedagogy is concerned with democratic education and social and individual improvement (Giroux, 1992), social solidarity and public responsibility. Critical Pedagogy is an established field, whereas Intercultural Citizenship Education in foreign language teaching is a developing field. The key figures in the application of a critical pedagogical model to the field of intercultural education are Manuela Guilherme and Alison Phipps. Both scholars centre their discussions on citizenship through Critical Pedagogical approaches.

The ideology underpinning our project centred on rejecting education as an act of 'depositing content', i.e. rejecting our roles as 'depositors of information' with the students memorizing it and regurgitating it mechanically. Freire (2009) encapsulates this ideological standpoint in binary terms, with the teacher as knowledgeable and the students as ignorant in direct opposition. He refers to it as *the banking approach*, whereby students are domesticated and overwhelmingly controlled by the power of the teacher. Banking education, as an exercise of domination, is sometimes not perceived by teachers themselves, who are unaware of the need to abandon such practices and feel that the students need to be taught, talked to and indoctrinated. Freire (2009: 53) encapsulates this concept as follows:

> The teacher talks about *reality* as if it were *motionless, static, compartmentalized*, and *predictable*. Or else he (*sic*) expounds on a topic completely *alien to the existential experience of the students*. His task is to 'fill' the students with the contents of his narration – contents which are *detached from reality*, disconnected from the totality that engendered them and could give them significance. Words are emptied of their concreteness and become a hollow, alienated, and *alienating verbosity*. (Emphasis added)

Freire's point here is that the students are seen as passive recipients of a fragmented 'motionless', 'static', 'compartmentalized' and 'predictable' view of reality, who accept the curricular choices imposed on them by the teacher. These curricular choices are for Freire topics far removed from the students' experiences, 'alien' to them, and therefore students' creativity is annulled and criticality suppressed in the best interests of the oppressors. In opposition to this, our ideological standpoint in our project centred on regarding students as critical intellectuals in dialogue with us in a process whereby we presented the material to the students for their deliberations and we re-considered our earlier preconceptions as the students expressed their own thoughts (Freire, 2009: 57).

Implementing a Democratic Pedagogy

During the life of the project, we felt that the more we applied the principles of Critical Pedagogy to our project, the more we developed our democratic competences as educators. Following a Freirean perspective, we rejected the view of domesticating the students into believing our views and instead we took the responsibility of liberating and emancipating them by providing them with opportunities for transformation. Shor (2009: 291) asserts that:

> By inviting students to develop critical thought and action on various subject matters, the teacher herself develops as a *critical-democratic educator who becomes more informed of the needs, conditions, speech habits, and perceptions of the students, from which knowledge she designs activities and into which she integrates her special expertise.* Besides learning in-process how to design a course *for* the students, the critical teacher also learns how to design the course *with* the students (co-governance). A *mutual learning process develops the teacher's democratic competence in negotiating the curriculum and in sharing power.* (Emphasis added)

For this project, we took Shor's point here by providing an enabling environment for the students to bring the knowledge, the content and the themes, from which we, as their teachers, designed tasks and activities, thus developing our democratic competences. Pavlenko (2005: 55) advocates Freire's pedagogy of organizing instruction around students' 'daily experiences' rather than around a 'fully predetermined curriculum', a pedagogy that focuses on 'generative themes based on student life, not on didactic lectures based on teacherly discourse' (Shor, 2009: 298). Freire saw 'generative themes' taken from students' immediate experiences and everyday life as the starting points for problem-posing, and as central resources for critical learning in the curriculum. His critical pedagogical approach involves teaching learners how to read the world and employs students' language and experiences as the basis of instruction:

> Themes may come from an incident in a particular student's life, a problem in the community, or an idea that a student latched into from the media, the news, or a classroom activity. Writing, reading, talking, acting, and reflecting are the key ways through which generative themes develop. (Peterson, 2009: 307)

Thus, we employed a 'generative theme' approach in this project by allowing an organic development of issues introduced by the students themselves, which, as Peterson states, were incidents, problems, ideas and narratives that emerged during Skype discussions. As teachers, it was necessary for us to engage in a process of de-centring from the dominant view that only our teaching causes learning. As a result of this, in the creation of this project we focused on *facilitating* the learning rather than on *doing* the teaching, and to this end, we ensured that there were many other resources for learning (not just us), such as students' peers, personal experiences, research, creativity and interviews. In this process, students became *subjects*, rather than *objects*, of the world, a major tenet of Critical Pedagogy, which places students as *subjects*, at the centre of the curriculum.

Students as Transformative Intellectuals

We chose Critical Pedagogy as the framework for our project because it provided us with the tools to encourage students to become 'transformative intellectuals', i.e. learners who transcend time and space in their own personal experiences and engage in a process of reflection that looks at 'past experiences' and relates them to 'future action' (Díaz-Greenberg & Nevin, 2004: 51). This critical pedagogical notion of 'transformative intellectuals' is closely linked to Barnett's highest level of criticality (1997), which recognizes the transformatory potential of knowledge to change the self and the world as valued citizenship skills, as explained in the Introduction to this book. Thus, in this project, a historical sporting event in times of repression and dictatorship was reflected upon to increase knowledge and raise awareness of human rights. The aim was to develop learners as global citizens compelled to promote and protect fundamental freedoms worldwide. The students, as 'transformative intellectuals', started with the 'here and now', with present situations and circumstances, in order to move on into the future. 'Transformation' is a key concept in Critical Pedagogy, which in Wink's words means:

> Freire and Marx provide deep roots for critical pedagogy that are reflected in *learners turning their beliefs into behaviours for self- and social transformation*. The ideas we grapple with are not just for the safe confines of the four walls of the classroom. The whole idea is *to improve the quality of life for ourselves and for others in our community.* (Wink, 2010: 114; emphasis added)

Based on the understanding that the 'future is something we build in the present' (Wink, 2010: 111), students in this project were encouraged to develop their awareness of human rights activism, of barbaric tortures and abductions, of secret executions and despicable acts of stealing babies in the hope of future collective struggle and transformation for a more democratic society. The ultimate goal was, as Wink observes, to improve their own lives (*self-transformation*) and the lives of others in their community (*social transformation*). This is the view of 'transformative intellectual' that we took in this project: the students as individuals who move forward and look ahead, but also look at the past in order to understand who and what they are, so that they can build their future more wisely. However, it should be noted that, as their teachers, we were aware that we could only create agendas of possibility for we believed that not every student might have wanted to engage actively in the project as 'critical pedagogy does not guarantee that resistance will not take place' (McLaren, 2009: 80).

The pedagogical decision to encourage students to research the 1978 World Cup within the context of the military dictatorship in Argentina (stage 1 of the project) was based on the tenets of Critical Pedagogy, particularly on Freire's concept of 'humanization' and McLaren's notion of 'praxis'. Freire (2010) proposes a process of 'humanization', whereby individuals attempt to be more human by using their knowledge for self and social transformation by eliminating 'pain, oppression, and inequality' (McLaren, 2009: 74). The newly gained knowledge in stage 1 raised awareness of the impact of the military dictatorship during the 1978 World Cup on the present so that students would feel 'obliged' to critically intervene in the future and transform reality (Freire, 2009). Stage 1 thus served a dual function. On the one hand, it provided opportunities to learn about the infringements of human rights and abuse of power during a major international sporting event in the hope that this newly gained knowledge would lead to humanization for, as Freire (2009: 59) would put it, the future is 'hopeful' and 'prophetic'. On the other hand, it created the basis which allowed students to take action in the world in stage 3 of the project, or in critical pedagogical terms, to engage in 'praxis'. McLaren refers to this phase as an 'informed actions' stage, i.e. actions based on our learning, which involves students using their learning to promote 'justice and freedom'.

As noted earlier, during stage 3, the Argentine students interviewed a relative of a 'disappeared' and described the experience in a report. They delivered presentations in schools, community centres and other universities. Students also contributed to the collection of art and artefacts of the Argentine museum *Museo de Arte y Memoria* with their interview and media extracts and they designed a webpage, blogs and Facebook pages to showcase their project to the community. Although the UK-based students were unable to develop the citizenship dimension of the project, they served as a preliminary audience for the Argentinean students as a means of clarification before they engaged with the community in Argentina. All these critical pedagogical interventions had a clear purpose – to use students' newly gained knowledge for self and social transformation, or in McLaren's terms, to empower learners to develop the 'kind of courage needed to change the social order where necessary'. Shor (2009: 293) argues that 'theory' alone is just empty words – 'theory' in the context of our project was the learning gained through research. To us, Shor's idea was of particular relevance in the creation of a project that not only involved gaining new information through research, but also action promoted by this new learning. During the life of the project, we ensured that there was an explicit link between the newly acquired information and the world, for as Freire would put it, theory without experience is 'words without the world', hence abstract discourse.

Data Analysis

This section presents the analysis of conversational data (Skype conversation transcripts) and documentary data (leaflets, reports, reflection logs) as sources of evidence for the effectiveness of the project.

Content analysis, defined as 'the process of summarizing and reporting written data – the main contents of data and their messages' (Cohen *et al.*, 2007: 475), was the method employed for data analysis. This was in research methodology terms a case study, with some elements of action research, since the findings informed, and were informed by, classroom practice and ongoing data analysis. The number of participants totalled 99, of which 23 students were UK-based (20 British, one Italian, one German and one Belgian) and 76 were Argentinean. Most of the research participants were female (10 male and 89 female) in their late teens and early twenties. The cohorts consisted of groups of first and second year undergraduates in each of the two universities learning English and Spanish as foreign languages. Informed consent was obtained from all the participants who were given sufficient information describing the goals and procedures and the method employed and an assurance that confidentiality and anonymity would be maintained. All participants were informed that, although quotes from the data collected would be used for analysis, in an attempt to reduce the possibility of being recognizable, names would be avoided. What follows is an account of the main findings presented under four dominant discourses: (a) Discomfort and De-centring; (b) Empathy and Solidarity; (c) Comparing and Contrasting; and (d) Naming the World.

Discomfort and De-centring

The Council of Europe *Charter on Education for Democratic Citizenship and Human Rights Education* (2014) is an important reference point for language educators interested in developing projects with a focus on the prevention of human rights violations. However, it should be noted that teaching for democratic citizenship may involve a 'pedagogy of discomfort' (Boler &

Zembylas, 2003), whereby students are 'challenged to move beyond their comfort zone into new and unfamiliar territory, and into states of dissonance and discomfort' (Santoro & Major, 2012: 309). Particularly in cases where the purpose of the teaching is 'to unsettle taken-for-granted views and emotions', 'some discomfort is not only unavoidable but may also be necessary' (Zembylas & McGlynn, 2010: 3). Fleming (2006: 131) notes that 'controversial issues' in intercultural citizenship education are 'unavoidable' when trying to resolve 'tensions and ambiguities between competing concepts', a view shared by Guilherme (2007), Byram (2008) and Holliday (2011), who regard citizenship education as preparing learners to live together in an increasingly diverse world. For these scholars, teaching should deal with issues like human rights and social injustice for a more democratic engagement in a globalized world. 'Questions of value' (Fleming, 2006) and attitudes like equality and social justice based on personal experiences should be the focus, even if this means teaching through 'conflict' or through 'cultural faultlines' and 'ruptures' (Kramsch, 2000).

Skype conversational data provide evidence of discomfort experienced in students' discussions of the dictatorship years during the 1978 World Cup, as follows:

ARG: Everything about this period usually really **moves** me and **gives me goose bumps**.

ARG: What gives me goose bumps is the fact that one of the main **centres of detention was a few meters away from de major stadium where the entertainment of the moment was happening**.

ARG: I don't know what **evil** mind can even think about that, it is so **perverse**.

UK: Yeah …

ARG: That's beyond being **violent**.

ARG: Yes! It's **psychological evilness**. You have to be **cynical** about it, I mean you're **kidnapping** people and **torturing** them. [emphasis added]

Here the UK-based student appears to act as a catalyst for the Argentineans. As the students described their views on the kidnappings and tortures in terms of strong words, such as 'evil', 'perverse', 'violent' and 'cynical', they physically experienced these strong emotions through 'goose bumps'. We hoped that this discomfort would lead to self-transformation that would challenge them to critically intervene in reality (Freire, 2009) for the development of social responsibility and transformation. In addition, here the students were also developing two important intercultural citizenship skills – critical evaluation and reflection.

Evidence of 'discomfort' can also be observed in the following piece of data:

ARG: Just **imagine** how you'd feel like, if you'd been in that place ... because it was for quite a long time, it ended in 1983, just imagine **if you and your people couldn't say anything and couldn't express the way they feel and think**.

UK: **It's impossible to think**...it's impossible to think not being able to talk without freedom.

ARG: And also **imagine** that your life was at risk. Just **imagine**, if you spoke you could be killed, so if you'd been in that situation, what would you have done? How would you have felt? Just put yourself in these people's shoes.

ARG: Like, what would you feel and what would you have done if you'd been in that situation.

UK: It really is so **hard to try to imagine**, which is the problem, I think because nothing like that is happening here at all. It's really **hard**. It's **hard** to think for anyone in this country ...

ARG: It's **difficult** for me also ...

ARG: I have to say this, I'm sorry, but you cannot ask people that, this way

ARG: I'm not asking like that!

ARG: Yeah but it's hard to ... ponerse ... how can you say this? ponerse en el lugar del otro [put in somebody else's shoes]

ARG: Put ...

ARG: **Put yourself into somebody else's shoes**... I mean, it's not an easy question to ask.

ARG: Está bien ... perdón si te incomodé, Abi [OK, I'm sorry if I've **upset** you, Abi]

UK: Mm?

ARG: Perdón si te sentiste incómoda, like uncomfortable [Sorry if I've upset you ... if I've made you feel **uncomfortable**] (Emphasis added)

As can be gleaned from this piece of data, one of the Argentine students encourages the UK-based student to de-centre, or in other words, to view the world from another perspective by placing themselves in the 'shoes of the other'. There is acknowledgement of the intellectual challenge posed by de-centring as evidenced in the use of 'hard', 'difficult' and 'impossible' to explain the demanding task of adopting a new positioning to view the world from the perspective of the other. De-centring is a desirable intercultural citizenship skill, and the fact that it is the students themselves who promote its development is important and supports our view that not all learning comes from teaching. Fundamentally, it is the students themselves who employ a 'pedagogy of discomfort' that disentangles strong emotions by stepping outside their comfort zones – an emotional investment and dialogue that we, as educators, believe is a necessary step for self-transformation in intercultural citizenship education.

In the case of the Argentinean students, the project engendered a more 'bodily' experience with varying levels of emotional investment, whilst in the case of the UK-based students, the project stimulated more of an 'intellectual' experience. This does not mean that those who engaged emotionally did not engage intellectually or vice-versa, but that the Argentinean students tended to display a stronger affective investment, as would naturally be expected since the project dealt with an issue of contemporary impact in their society. The following piece of data is also evidence of this:

ARG: The thing is, when I was little, **my parents told me** about the dictatorship and everything. **I actually found it difficult to understand**, because I was **born and raised during democracy**, so I could never imagine how a group of people can just take the power. And also, this is kind of funny, when I was little, these spots of **Abuelas de Plaza de Mayo** [Grandmothers of Plaza de Mayo] started, because they were **looking for their grand-kids**. So **I had this crazy secret hope of being an adopted child, to have this secret life, then having two families and lots of gifts for my birthday**.

UK: Yes, but that's not usually how it works. Unfortunately, and **I'm speaking out of complete ignorance**, I apologise, but I think it's probably the opposite, you find out that it's something that is not so cool and on the contrary, it's **something painful: your mother couldn't raise you or she died or something**.

ARG: No, I know, **I totally agree**, but **I was like five years old** and I remember there was a show about some twins that were adopted separately and they eventually found each other and then both families ended up together. Well, I don't know, **I had this completely wrong idea that being adopted was the best thing ever because you had two families and so double the gifts in your birthday**. The thing is that I was watching **TV** and every time I saw these spots of Abuelas de Plaza de Mayo that were looking for their grand-kids, and the slogan was '**if you have any doubts about your identity, come with us, we're looking for you**'. I never heard the part of 'if you were born between 1976 and 1983' so I was like 'oh they are talking about being an adopted child' and once I went straight to my mom and said **'hey mum, am I adopted**? Can I go to these ladies' and ask them?' And mum was like 'no, little, they're talking about a different thing; and **you're not adopted at all**, you saw pictures of me being pregnant and many others of you as a little baby' and I was like 'oh bummer!' I wanted to be an adopted child. **And so that was the first approach I had to this topic. My parents told me** they were looking for teenagers and young adults because there was a time where 'bad guys' stole little babies from their mothers. (Emphasis added)

This particular memory, triggered by the project itself, can be taken as a contribution to the creation of an international collective memory. As can be gleaned from the data, this student's identity as an Argentinean citizen is constructed with a personal story told to her by her parents of him having had a 'secret crazy hope' of being an adopted child. When she was five years old, the student constructed a narrative in her imagination, possibly as a result of being exposed to the predicament of the families of the disappeared as portrayed in the media. In the project, her individual memory forms part of a collective memory, passed from one generation to the next and shared by other Argentineans in a network of links and ties that bind them together. However, what is important here is the fact that this intergenerational infantile, dream-like version of the severe pain and ordeal experienced by the victims of the military regime now forms part of the international collective memory that the project has created.

One of the purposes of the project network, articulated in the documents which were shared on the pbworks wiki referred to in the Introduction to this volume, was to create an international/transnational community during the life of each individual project. In Skype conversations, students constructed an international/transnational identity, which united their members temporarily, through stories such as this one. The way past events were remembered and interpreted by Argentinean students and the fact that they were shared with the UK-based students can be taken as evidence of the construction of an international community through the formation of an international collective memory.

Empathy and Solidarity

It is the mission of intercultural citizenship education to inculcate empathy skills and a sense of solidarity. The following piece of data reveals how empathy and solidarity are built during the course of the conversation:

ARG: Do … Did … Do you find it **interesting** what you have done with the **project**? I mean the **information** you have to search.

UK: Yes! I think it's really **interesting**. Emm, I also think that, emm, it's **interesting** to know how the Junta Militar, they ... because it was such a big thing to be able to hide.

ARG: Uh huh.

UK: Yeah, no, it's really **interesting**. There was something in England that happened in **Liverpool**. Do you know where Liverpool is?

ARG: Yes!

UK: Have you heard about the **Hillsborough disaster**?

ARG: Emm, no. Haha.

UK: Emm, it's something that happened in **England, about 20 years** ago, and **a stadium of football**. And **it's kind of the same as the World Cup but a little bit less**.

ARG: Aaah, okey.

UK: So, yeah. In Liverpool the **football match the stands collapsed and lots of people died**. And the police, **the police hid all the evidence because it was their fault**, so they hid all the evidence and they ...

ARG: Oh, such a bastard.

UK: Yeah! Haha. **I found that's quite similar to the Copa** [World Cup].

ARG: Yeah. Maybe the difference is that the Junta was emm, how I can say that? Many people during many years.

UK: Yeah, ... But, **I think that the <u>pain</u> or <u>what you feel is the same as what we feel</u>**.

ARG: Yeah, yeah. **But it wasn't as bad as the World Cup but it was still quite bad**. (Emphasis added)

The 1989 Hillsborough disaster the UK-based student refers to here was an incident that occurred on 15 April 1989 at the Hillsborough Stadium in Sheffield, UK. During the FA Cup semi-final match between Liverpool and Nottingham Forest, a human crush resulted in the deaths of 96 people and injuries to 766 others. The incident has since been blamed by some on the police for letting too many people enter the stadium, and remains the worst stadium-related disaster in British history, and one of the world's worst football disasters. In September 2012, the Hillsborough Independent Panel concluded that up to 41 of the 96 fatalities might have been avoided had they received prompt medical treatment. The report revealed multiple failures by other emergency services and public bodies that contributed to the death toll. On 19 December 2012, a new inquest was granted in the High Court, to the relief of the families and friends of those who died at Hillsborough.

As is illustrated in this piece of data, in an attempt to find commonality between the different experiences lived in their respective countries, both students engage in a discussion of two sports-related events that have caused 'pain'. As the Argentine student talks about the atrocities committed by the government during the 1978 World Cup, the UK-based student talks about the human crush that caused deaths and injuries in the Hillsborough disaster. Both students display a feeling of unity as they showed common concerns, reciprocal understanding and identification with each other.

With the benefit of hindsight, it could be argued that some people in Argentina may have suspected they were being lied to, but found themselves unable to react owing to the repressive nature of the dictatorship. In sharp contrast to this, given the apparent free and democratic society of the 1980s UK, it was highly probable that most people believed the authorities' version of events at the time and only discovered the truth much later. Therefore, it is tempting to conclude that it may be easier to manipulate public opinion if individuals are made to believe they live in a free society. As the students compared these two sports-related events during their Skype discussion, they talked about the time of repression in Argentina being overshadowed by the 1978 World Cup and the UK government deflecting blame on the supporters by calling them hooligans in order to avoid public authority figures appearing to have been the cause of the Hillsborough disaster. We take this piece of data as evidence of the students developing a relationship of solidarity and empathy in their collective struggle for a more democratic world.

Comparing and Contrasting

Figure 10.1 shows a leaflet which compares the 1978 World Cup in Argentina with the 1934 World Cup in Italy and provides evidence of the development of the intercultural skills of comparing and contrasting.

The 1934 World Cup, hosted and won by Italy, was the second world championship for football teams. As can be gleaned from this piece of data, the students highlight the fact that the 1934 World Cup was a high-profile instance of a sporting event being used for political purposes. This is evidenced in the message the students write in their leaflet 'The fascist regime had always regarded sport (football in particular) as an easy way to have pretext for national pride and also, as the perfect way to convey political propaganda'. Benito Mussolini was keen to use the tournament as a means of promoting fascism and exploited the popular culture of football for the benefit of his regime. Mussolini used Italy's triumph at the World Cup as an opportunity to gain international prestige, or as the students put it, 'Mussolini wanted Italy to be considered a powerful and mighty nation by other countries'. In addition, the students' willingness to convey the message that Mussolini used the World Cup as a way to mould a national identity for

Figure 10.1 A leaflet comparing the 1978 World Cup in Argentina with the 1934 World Cup in Italy

Fascist Italy is revealed in the choice of Mussolini's quote in the leaflet that reads 'no matter how much you consider and observe the future and human development, whatever the passing political circumstances might be, fascism does not believe in the possibility nor in the usefulness of peace'. Finally, this leaflet provides a good example of the skills of comparing and contrasting as demonstrated in the students' own words, 'another country, another regime, new abominations to conceal, but always with the same mechanism'.

The following Skype conversation extract shows how the students developed the skills of comparing and contrasting as they discussed the curricular choices in their respective countries:

ARG: There in **England or in Europe** in general, do teachers talk about this? In school?

UK: **No, they don't talk about it**, I've **never heard about it** but I don't really do history, but it's **not really spoken**, I think.

ARG: Oh, I see, oh well … As it is the main … the most important event here in **Argentina**. We **talk about this a lot, we are told about this.**

ARG: Since high school … Since we are children

…

UK: I know it is not nice. It didn't seem nice.

ARG: It's pretty similar to what happened in Aleman … Germany but with the Nazis. Of course there are many differences, but …

UK: Yeah
ARG: It was a dictatorship
UK: Yes

   …

ARG: they were **kidnapped** and **disappeared**. You may not know …
UK: I know about **babies disappearing** and **being adopted**
ARG: Yes! It's kind of a **hard issue** here. There are many organizations where erm … they kind of look for these people that they do not know that they may have been adopted at that time.
UK: Yeah
ARG: and there's these cases of children, I mean they are like grown-ups, they are like thirty something and now, they know they had been kidnapped by these people but they consider them their parents … (Emphasis added)

In this piece of data the UK-based student states that human rights violations during the Argentinean military dictatorship are not studied in the British educational system, whilst, understandably, in Argentina it appears to be a main subject area that permeates primary and secondary education. As a result of these curricular choices in different cultural contexts and the fact that the project was about an Argentinean issue, our project led to two different student experiences.

Naming the World

This section analyses conversational and documentary data related to the design of the leaflet, where evidence of the students' search for words, symbols, quotes, photos, texts and images to 'name' the world is pervasive. For Freire, learners become more human by taking responsibility for transformation in their society, which is only possible through a process of 'conscientização' and 'naming the world'. 'Conscientização' is often equated to consciousness-raising and refers to the process whereby students raise awareness of the social realities that shape their lives and make sense of their own experiences as a response to a dialogic 'problem-posing' method of education. In 'problem-posing' education, teachers and students figure out the world dialogically. From a Freirean perspective, it is only after a process of awareness-raising that certain elements, which have always existed, start to be perceived, reflected and acted upon. Action, therefore, begins after consciousness is developed, and only after students 'name' and 'read' the world. The data that follow provide examples of students' 'naming the world' and demonstrate the process of transformation that the students embark on as they create their leaflets for a more just and humane world.

UK: So we decided to … We selected an image and we decided to select **a photograph with a scarf** on it which was what Madres and Abuelas de Plaza de Mayo used to protest because of the disappearance of their grandchildren and sons and daughters. And we decided to write a title which is **'Deportes, desaparecidos y dictadura'**. Well, you saw it because I sent it to you.

UK: Yeah, yeah.

ARG: What do you think about it?

UK: Yeah, it's really nice, it really goes. I didn't realise that your part of the leaflet was facing the picture, though. That's good.

UK: Ok. And … I mean, on the picture we decided to write **an extract from the prologue of *Never Again* which was written by Ernesto Sábato** and, well… it talks about how these events sometimes showed society that they don't have to happen again, to occur again, this type of tragedy.

ARG: un folleto, tiene tres caras, como el de la pizza, miren … [a leaflet has three sides, like a pizza leaflet … look]

ARG: bueno en la portada poner como si … ponerle de título… ehh, algo como bueno, **'la verdad oculta'** o no, no sé, **'la verdad disfrazada'** o algo … un título así … [on the front cover, we could put a title like the 'hidden truth' or the 'disguised truth', or something like that].

The leaflet the students created after this discussion is illustrated in Figure 10.2.

In the previous conversation extract and in this leaflet, through dialogue the students find ways of 'naming' the human rights violations during the 1978 World Cup. These include a photo of the Mothers of Plaza de Mayo and a few slogans written by the students themselves such as 'Deportes, desaparecidos y dictadura' ['Sports, Disappeared and Dictatorship'] and 'la verdad oculta'/'la verdad disfrazada' ['hidden truth/disguised truth']. The students also incorporate the voice of a well-known Argentinean writer called Ernesto Sábato, of immense seriousness and brilliance, who wrote a detailed report of the deaths and disappearances during the 'Dirty War' in 1984. This report entitled *Nunca Más* ['Never Again'], a bestseller in Argentina, discloses narratives of those who were tortured and descriptions of those who were killed. The students chose to include an extract from the prologue of *Nunca Más* in their leaflet. By integrating a voice of moral authority into their leaflet, students joined forces with Ernesto Sábato to 'name' the atrocities committed

Figure 10.2 Leaflet created by the students for a more just and humane world

during the last military regime in Argentina, thus adding weight to their collective struggle for social justice.

In their leaflet, the students used the picture shown in Figure 10.3 of a white headscarf, which represents the living legacy of courage, hope, solidarity, pain and fight for freedom of the Mothers of Plaza de Mayo. The headscarf, a symbol for the nappies worn by their disappeared children has the slogan *Nunca Más* written on it from Ernesto Sábato's report.

In another leaflet (Figure 10.4) the students created a distorted version of the 1978 World Cup official logo to commemorate the event and to 'name' social injustice. The image manipulates sound and meaning in the Spanish language with the intent of creating an impact on the reader. On the one hand, it replaces 'Argentina 78' with 'Asesina 78' ['asesina' means *murderer*] and on the other hand, it plays on the use of the word 'copa' (the literal meaning is *cup*, in this context alluding to the World Cup) in the slogan 'No me copa' (Argentinean slang for *I don't like it*). The alliteration of the words 'Argentina' and 'Asesina' together with the word play in the slogan and the alteration of the 1978 World Cup official logo bleeding provide an effective way of exposing media manipulation and human rights violations that were overshadowed while hosting this international football event.

Figure 10.3 Leaflet designed by the students, showing a white headscarf, which represents the living legacy of courage, hope, solidarity, pain and fight for freedom of the Mothers of Plaza de Mayo

In the following Skype conversation extract, students make reference to the government media manipulation to create arguments that favoured their interests. Students talk to each other about quotes, phrases and headlines taken mainly from magazines that 'name' the lies made by the leaders

Figure 10.4 Leaflet created by the students showing a distorted version of the 1978 World Cup official logo to commemorate the event and to 'name' social injustice

of the Military Junta. As a way of publicly condemning and denouncing the deceitful underhand messages, students chose to incorporate the following quoted lies in their leaflet – 'we are an organised country', 'this country is changing', 'Argentineans are right and human' and 'we show the world what Argentineans are like' – as examples of the government dishonesty.

ARG: En las revistas incluso … en las revistas por ejemplo, salían titulares … como … 'somos un país organizado' o … cómo decían otros? [in the **magazines** for example there were a few **headlines** like **'we are an organised country'** … and what do the other ones say?]

ARG: 'este país está cambiando', ehh … había un … o sea … eran frases o citas de gente que decían cosas buenas sobre el país, cuando en realidad estaban pasando muchas cosas malas y entonces no se decía … no se hablaba de la realidad. Sólo se contaba una parte. ['**This country is changing**' … these are some of **phrases** or **quotes** … things that they were saying when in fact the reality was quite different]

ARG: … con diferentes frases. Y por ejemplo, lo que estábamos hablando hoy de cómo los medios desvirtuaban la información, por ejemplo, esta es una frase que dice: 'los argentinos somos derechos y humanos'. Eso era una ehhh … una propaganda del gobierno. [These **phrases** … for example, today we were talking about how they distorted the information, for example, there's a **quote** here that says **'Argentineans are right and human'.**]

UK: So what was that for?

ARG: Eso era propaganda que hacía el gobierno, ehhh … y bueno, podes ver cómo era una mentira, porque se contradecía con lo que en realidad estaba pasando … this one is significant, because it says … 'mostramos al mundo cómo somos los argentinos'. [This is government propaganda …. but as you can see it was all **lies**, because the reality was very different … this one is significant because it says **'we show the world what Argentineans are like'.**]

In another leaflet (Figure 10.5), students used this wall of photos of some of the 30,000 people that vanished without a trace during the Dirty War so that they can be remembered as individual human beings. Each of these faces represents a different life with a unique story, dreams and hopes, but all with the same end – elimination. The faces of the women on this wall represent those who were abducted; some of them were pregnant, whilst others were made pregnant during detention, usually through rape by their torturers.

Figure 10.5 Leaflet created by the students showing a wall of photos of some of the 30,000 people that vanished without a trace during the Dirty War

Their faces also act as a reminder of those newborns who were handed over to childless military and police couples. Importantly, this wall of photos in the leaflet raises awareness of one of the most brutal crimes against humanity.

In another leaflet (Figure 10.6), students 'name' the world by clearly stating their contribution to humanity. This piece of data can be taken as evidence of self-transformation and an invitation for others to engage in civic responsibility for social transformation. As can be gleaned from the blurb, students acknowledge that crimes against humanity are still a feature of contemporary societies around the world and use human and organ trafficking as examples of grave violations of human rights. The message in this leaflet is a call for justice and action in the real world.

Conclusion

An important aspect of this project was the focus on human rights education in language teaching for the development of students as 'transformative intellectuals' engaged in self and social change for a more democratic world. The project aimed to demonstrate how the study of the 1978 World Cup within the socio-political context of a military dictatorship can address issues relating to basic human rights, such as freedom of speech, thought and belief. As evidenced in the findings presented earlier, the educational value of the project also lies in the development of intercultural citizenship competences, such as de-centring, comparing and contrasting, empathy and solidarity, while creating an international community and 'naming' the world through photos, quotes, images, symbols and slogans.

Grandmothers of Plaza de Mayo

The grandmothers of Plaza the Mayo is a human rights organization with the goal of finding the children stolen during the dictatorship. It was founded in 1977 and its president is Estela de Carlotto. There were more than 500 children stolen and illegally adopted.

Only the 10 percent were located., 107 grandchildren. Since 2008, The grandother of Plaza de Mayo have been nominated to five Novel Prize.

2013

Actualmente, si bien vivimos con una política democrática, siguen faltando desaparecidos de la época. Pero lo que es más lamentable aún, es que más personas siguen desapareciendo a consecuencia de la trata de personas y el tráfico de órganos.

Como parte de nuestro granito de arena para que esto deje de ocurrir, deberíamos concientizarnos a cerca de lo sucedido, no olvidar, pero si avanzar para que realmente exista una democratización justa y respetable.

Translation of the Spanish text in the leaflet
Despite living in a democracy nowadays, many of the disappeared have not yet appeared. Unfortunately, more and more people keep disappearing owing to human and organ trafficking. Our small contribution to stop this from happening is to help raise awareness of these issues. Do not forget any of this and keep working hard for a respectable and just democratic society.

Figure 10.6 Leaflet created by the students in which they 'name' the world by clearly stating their contribution to humanity

Our project can also provide a springboard on which to base further projects in the future with the intent of raising awareness of barbarous acts in the world. The students in this project discussed crimes against humanity like torture, cruelty, inhumanity and degrading treatment that resulted in strong emotional responses, mainly rage and discomfort. This outrage empowered students to take the responsibility to use their knowledge for awareness-raising of human rights violations through the creation of leaflets, a webpage and talks in order to foster justice, peace and freedom from fear in the community, both at local and global levels.

Acknowledgements

We are extremely grateful to John Manders for providing us with the idea for the topic of this project and for contributing with his knowledge of world sporting events, in addition to his perceptive observations and meticulous editing of this chapter. Also our deepest appreciation goes to Adolfo Guidali for his contribution in this project, especially for his insightful comments on the students' essays. We are also indebted to Gabriela Iacoboni for managing the wiki and welcoming the project in her classroom. We also wish to express our heartfelt gratitude to all the students from Universidad Nacional de La Plata, Argentina and University of East Anglia, UK who participated in this project. Special thanks to those students who contributed with the transcriptions of the Skype conversations, and our wholehearted appreciation to Dan Siddorn for his careful organization of the data.

References

Barnett, R. (1997) *Higher Education: A Critical Business*. Buckingham: Society for Research into Higher Education and Open University Press.

Boler, M. and Zembylas, M. (2003) Discomforting truths: The emotional terrain of understanding difference. In P. Trifonas (ed.) *Pedagogies of Difference. Rethinking Education for Social Change* (pp. 110–136). New York: Routledge Falmer.

Byram, M. (2008) *From Foreign Language Education to Education for Intercultural Citizenship: Essays and Reflections*. Clevedon: Multilingual Matters.

Cohen, L., Manion, L. and Morrison, K. (2007) *Research Methods in Education* (6th edn). Abingdon: Routledge.

Council of Europe (2014) *Charter on Education for Democratic Citizenship and Human Rights Education: Democracy and Human Rights Start with Us – Charter for All*. See http://www.coe.int/t/dg4/education/edc/Source/Resources/Charterforall_EN.pdf (accessed 9 April 2014).

Díaz-Greenberg, R. and Nevin, A. (2004) Listen to the voices of foreign language student teachers: Implications for foreign language educators. In A. Phipps and M. Guilherme (eds) *Critical Pedagogy: Political Approaches to Language and Intercultural Communication* (pp. 48–61). Clevedon: Multilingual Matters.

Fleming, M. (2006) The concept of intercultural citizenship: Lessons from fiction and art. In G. Alred, M. Byram and M. Fleming (eds) *Education for Intercultural Citizenship: Concepts and Comparisons* (pp. 130–143). Clevedon: Multilingual Matters.

Freire, P. (2009) From *Pedagogy of the Oppressed*. In A. Darder, M. Batonado and R.D. Torres (eds) *The Critical Pedagogy Reader* (2nd edn) (pp. 52–60). New York: Routledge.

Freire, P. (2010) *Education for Critical Consciousness*. London: Continuum.

Giroux, H. (1992) *Border Crossings: Cultural Workers and the Politics of Schooling*. New York: Routledge.

Giroux, H. (1999) Rethinking cultural politics and radical pedagogy in the work of Antonio Gramsci. *Educational Theory* 49 (1), 1–19.

Guilherme, M. (2002) *Critical Citizens for an Intercultural World: Foreign Language Education as Cultural Politics*. Clevedon: Multilingual Matters.

Guilherme, M. (2007) English as a global language and education for cosmopolitan citizenship. *Language and Intercultural Communication* 7 (1), 72–90.

Holliday, A. (2011) *Intercultural Communication and Ideology*. London: SAGE.

Kramsch, C. (2000) Teaching language along the cultural faultline. In D.L. Lange, C.A. Klee, R.M. Paige and Y.A. Yershova (eds) *Culture as the Core: Interdisciplinary Perspectives on Culture Learning in the Language Curriculum* (pp. 15–31). Minneapolis, MN: Center for Advanced Research on Language Acquisition.

McLaren, P. (2009) Critical pedagogy: A look at the major concepts. In A. Darder, M. Batonado and R.D. Torres (eds) *The Critical Pedagogy Reader* (2nd edn) (pp. 61–83). New York: Routledge.

McLaren, P. and Farahmandpur, R. (2005) *Teaching Against Global Capitalism and the New Imperialism, a Critical Pedagogy.* Oxford: Rowman and Littlefield.

Pavlenko, A. (2005) Gender and sexuality in foreign and second language education: Critical and feminist approaches. In B. Norton and K. Toohey (eds) *Critical Pedagogies and Language Learning* (pp. 53–71). Cambridge: Cambridge University Press.

Peterson, R. (2009) Teaching how to read the world and change it. In Darder, A., Batonado, M. and Torres, R.D. (eds) *The Critical Pedagogy Reader* (2nd edn) (pp. 305–323). New York: Routledge.

Santoro, N. and Major, J. (2012) Learning to be a culturally responsive teacher through international study trips: Transformation or tourism? *Teaching Education* 23 (3), 309–322.

Shor, I. (2009) What is critical literacy? In A. Darder, M. Batonado and R.D. Torres (eds) *The Critical Pedagogy Reader* (2nd edn) (pp. 282–304). New York: Routledge.

Wink, J. (2010) *Critical Pedagogy: Notes from the Real World* (4th edn). NewYork: Merrill.

Zembylas, M. and McGlynn, C. (2010) Discomforting pedagogies: Emotional tensions, ethical dilemmas and transformative possibilities. *British Educational Research Journal* 38 (1), 41–59.

Reflections: Learning from the Challenges and Seeking Ways Forward

Michael Byram, Irina Golubeva, Han Hui and Manuela Wagner

In this book we have reported on the outcomes of a project in which a group of volunteer members of a network of teachers in schools and universities set out to teach and investigate intercultural citizenship and criticality in a variety of collaborative and transnational settings. This involved learners and teachers in 11 countries in the Americas, East Asia and Europe. We intend these reports to be examples of the kinds of projects that readers could implement, in suitably modified forms, in their own contexts. It is for this reason that we asked authors to give a rather detailed account of the planning, implementation and analyses of outcomes and to share the challenges encountered in the various contexts in order to offer possible ways to address them but also to openly acknowledge the fact that collaborative projects very rarely happen without 'bumps in the road'.

As explained in more detail in the Introduction to this book, the immediate stimulus for the project came from publications at the University of Durham on education for citizenship (Alred *et al.*, 2006) and the relationship between foreign language education and education for citizenship (Byram, 2008). The project aims were to establish, with the help of action research projects, if and how citizenship education could become the teaching content of foreign language teaching and learning, and in particular how it might lead to the development of criticality in learners. Here we drew above all on the work of Barnett (1997) and also introduced the notion that international work should be underpinned by internationalism, i.e. a sense of identification beyond national identification and a willingness to work together with people of other countries.

We hope that, after reading the past 10 chapters, the reader will be convinced that the resounding answer to our question whether intercultural citizenship education can become the focus of language education is: 'Yes it can – and should'. There are many compelling reasons for this view, which we can give from academic and educational literature and from current world events. One other reason, however, is based on the results in the study in the first two chapters. In Chapter 1, Golubeva, Yakimowski and Wagner investigated students' perceptions related to global citizenship in Hungary and the USA and Han, Song, Jing and Zhao in Chapter 2 conducted a survey study to ask their students at two Chinese universities about their knowledge of and attitudes related to intercultural and/or global citizenship. One important conclusion was that undergraduate students in the USA and Hungary tended to emphasize aspects of global citizenship that were unrelated to education. They defined global citizenship as something they achieve through living in other countries and through travelling. If this is an indication of what learners generally might believe, then we need to start sharing with them what they can learn in our classrooms, and how education can help them. This means that we also need well-developed plans to teach them intercultural citizenship competence, and we hope that the projects presented in Chapters 4–10 are examples that will help to develop a more systematic approach.

As we have seen in the previous chapters, learners can make big strides towards becoming intercultural citizens and critical thinkers in our classrooms. In our projects we learned that fifth, sixth and seventh graders (Chapter 6), as well as high school learners (Chapter 8) and undergraduate and graduate students in universities and colleges (Chapters 7, 9 and 10) can develop intercultural citizenship and criticality in their foreign language classroom. We also learned that pre-service teachers can develop important skills in order to teach culturally diverse classrooms (Chapter 3).

The topics covered in the projects range from foreign language education in teacher education in South Korea and the USA (Chapter 7) and Sweden (Chapter 3), to issues of sustainability in Denmark and Argentina (Chapter 6) and in Japan (Chapter 5), mural art and graffiti (Chapter 8), historical conflicts between countries (Chapter 9), sport and human rights (Chapter 10).

Most projects encouraged learners to look at critical issues related to social justice or human rights, for example conflict and peace (Chapters 9 and 10), laws, rights and preconceptions related to language education (Chapters 2 and 7) and sustainability (Chapters 5, 6 and 8). Such topics lend themselves for a number of reasons:

- they constitute an important part of intercultural citizenship education;
- they help learners take a critical look at complex topics; and
- they motivate learners to take action in their own intercultural and transnational intercultural communities.

While projects shared the goal of implementing an agreed theoretical framework, suitably amended to circumstances, as well as further developing their learners' linguistic skills in their foreign language, learning objectives in each project varied owing to the context in which it was conducted. In Chapter 3, Lundgren, and in Chapter 7, Peck and Wagner, set out to model activities that future teachers in the class could potentially emulate in their classrooms if they found the experience valuable. Yamada and Hsieh in Chapter 4 explored teaching approaches that allowed them to integrate inter-cultural citizenship education into courses for beginner-level language learners/users while also addressing important questions of ownership of language for foreign language learners. In Chapter 5 Houghton and Huang and in Chapter 6 Porto, Daryai-Hansen, Arcuri and Schifler planned a number of environmental citizenship outcomes. While in Chapter 8, Porto and partners used mural art to help learners express their views on important issues, in Chapters 9 and 10 Porto and Yulita integrated human rights issues more directly into their curriculum.

Several levels of collaboration were involved in the implementation of the different phases of the project. All the teachers were part of the initial group that committed to implementing the action projects within the agreed theoretical framework. Smaller groups (mostly pairs, sometimes groups of three or four) then worked on their specific projects together. In most of the projects, learners were then also asked to collaborate in their tasks, sometimes in pairs or small national or transnational groups and sometimes within their big 'national' group or the big 'transnational group'. The goal was to form a bonded, international group of learners in each project as well as in the collaborative work of the smaller groups. Predictably, that goal was realized to a higher degree in some projects than in others. For example, projects that planned and completed an action component – 'action in the community' – in which the learners worked towards a common goal, seemed to facilitate aspects of international identification more than those that did not complete such a component. Analyses of student reflections and comments in the various projects show that generally learners suspended their identification with the national way of thinking and acting in order to find new 'international' ways of acting because the teachers designed the activities so that they addressed the different elements of intercultural citizenship. In Chapter 6, for example, there is clear evidence that fifth- to seventh-grade learners can develop an international identification, and the skills involved in intercultural citizenship, to deconstruct stereotypes and to develop criticality and critical cultural awareness. Additionally, most of the learners developed what the authors of Chapter 6 called 'intercultural environmental citizenship', challenging taken-for-granted representations of the environment, reflecting on environmental issues and contributing to improvement of the environment both locally and globally.

It may be of importance to mention here that some groups in the projects were already quite international because of their setting (e.g. the graduate students in the USA in Chapter 7 came from different countries and had different linguistic backgrounds, and the international undergraduate students at a university in Japan in Chapter 4 came from different backgrounds and were studying Japanese in Japan), while others came from more homogeneous cultural and linguistic backgrounds. This issue will be taken up again under the heading 'Challenges and Possible Solutions' below, but it is worth keeping in mind when re-visiting the different projects and their outcomes here. By asking learners to complete tasks in collaboration with their partners from another country and often also by asking them to reflect on how they felt about their collaboration, the participants were urged to question their belief systems. In some cases this led to the learners' development of a new way of thinking and acting, one that was influenced by their international collaboration. In some cases learners were asked to apply that new way to 'knowledge', to 'self' and to 'the world' right away, as for example in learners in Argentina and Denmark in Chapter 6, in Japan, in Chapter 5, and in Italy, Argentina and the UK in Chapter 8. In other projects, learners were unable to implement an immediate action component but teachers instead made it clear to their learners that they should at least have the skills to do so in the future (e.g. Chapters 4 and 7).

The projects utilized a variety of instructional tasks and resources. For example, learners were asked to conduct research on the internet, design online and hard copy posters, prepare and give presentations in various formats and often in transnational collaborative groups (e.g. PowerPoint, Prezi, VoiceThread), interview members of the community or in the transnational group, collaborate to create a page on Facebook or on class wikis, create brochures and leaflets and distribute them, write blogs, teach a class on the researched topic in the community, develop lesson plans that implement intercultural competence, co-author a Google document, write reflections about their collaboration and their development of intercultural citizenship, conduct surveys among their family members and friends, analyse documents such as reports on the Falklands/Malvinas War or foreign language education policy documents, create songs, publish their work in local newspapers, have a conversation with transnational partners on Skype or Google Hangout, or meet the partners on Elluminate live! to design a banner. Many of the tasks were also used to assess student learning. Additional assessment tools included the Council of Europe's *Autobiography of Intercultural Encounters*, involving self-assessments of skills and attitudes related to intercultural citizenship.

In terms of linguistic outcomes, most projects were successful in combining intercultural citizenship education and criticality objectives with the goal of developing communication skills in the target language. In Chapter 4, Yamada and Hsieh address the important issue of how to achieve these goals with students of beginning to intermediate proficiency and find that, with careful planning and an approach that asks important questions about the relationship of language and power and language and inclusion, it is indeed possible to be successful. We will revisit the topic of proficiency as a challenge later, but it is important to emphasize here that certain challenges for learners, when they are put in situations in which they want to communicate and feel that they might not yet have all the necessary tools, can also contribute to their learning if the teachers are able to balance the learners' frustrations and motivations and provide enough scaffolding for them to be successful. Although undergraduate students in South Korea, for example, first felt that they had a disadvantage when they communicated with graduate students in the USA, they also saw that their collaborations and interactions offered tremendous opportunity for their development of communicative skills in English. In Chapter 6, Porto and colleagues reported that most of the learners in the Green Kidz project further developed not only their linguistic competences but also their plurilingual competences, by becoming aware of their partners' respective native languages.

However, predictably and understandably, most colleagues also found that not all their goals were realistic owing to time constraints and other unforeseen challenges.

Challenges and Possible Solutions

Time

One challenge shared by a number of project participants was time. We assume that readers might often wonder how they can find the time to cover everything in their own classrooms which our authors set out to do. In many of the projects presented here teachers collaborated across nations in different time zones and with different academic schedules. Time and timing were clearly issues. In addition, natural events such as snow storms and school closures as well as holidays necessitated creative and often spontaneous adjustments to prior plans. In several projects, colleagues also reported that there were delays in responses by learners/groups of learners for various reasons which then also delayed the following interactions.

Another time-related question was how much development we could realistically expect during the time we had in the various projects when time was often dictated by variations in academic calendars. Different time zones also complicated the planning of meetings of different groups. Time is also a major factor for teachers, and we acknowledge that collaborating in projects such as the ones presented here is time consuming for teachers.

Addressing the last point first, we think that the time spent by teachers is an investment. Most teachers in the project reported they learned tremendously over the course of collaboration. Therefore, in addition to having carefully planned lessons for their learners through collaboration, teachers reflected on their own intercultural competence and learned from and with their immediate partners. They could also benefit from the whole group of teachers engaged in other projects and whose wisdom they could draw on when needed.

For other aspects of time and timing we found it most important to be flexible and to adjust plans when needed. We would even suggest going into a project under the assumption that alternative routes might have to be taken and possibly even with a few ideas in mind in case adjustments need to be made. As Peck and Wagner suggest in Chapter 7, one could envision multiple possible modules that could be combined according to the time allowed for the same project in order to ensure that learners are provided with the opportunity to develop certain skills even if certain parts of the project do not come to fruition.

Target language proficiency

As mentioned before, target language proficiency was an important factor in the design of the various projects. Yamada and Hsieh addressed this issue most directly by setting out to develop an approach for students with beginning or intermediate level proficiency of Japanese and English. Differences in proficiency between the undergraduate and graduate students in Korea and the USA, as well as between fifth, sixth and seventh graders in Argentina and Denmark represented certain challenges. If these differences in proficiency levels lead to students' frustration they can inhibit their collaboration. If, on the other hand, the students' need to communicate and their wish to complete a task together is strong, it is exactly the moments in which students need to negotiate meaning that lead to their language learning. While much can be achieved with thoughtful scaffolding of activities, at the lowest proficiency levels it might be impossible for students to express their understanding and opinions of complex concepts. Yamada and Hsieh in Chapter 4 therefore suggested code-mixing or code-switching as one of the possibilities to allow students to engage in a more nuanced conversation.

Mismatches between expectations

In some projects, especially in collaborations between different educational levels (high school and university students, undergraduate vs graduate students), there might be different expectations about what the learning objectives could be. Similarly learners might feel that there are differences in their level of intercultural competence at the beginning of the project. In Chapter 7, for example, undergraduate students in South Korea collaborated with graduate students in the USA. For the students in South Korea, the project offered a rare and novel opportunity in that it represented a transnational focus highly uncommon within national teacher education programmes, where educational theories and approaches are usually framed within and evaluated from a local context perspective. In the US context, some participants initially might have underestimated the opportunity to learn from the exchange as they felt that they were already 'interculturally competent' owing to their prior experience. However, many of them then came to the conclusion that one's own development of intercultural competence is an ongoing and presumably lifelong learning process.

One way to approach different expectations on the part of the students is to make them a topic of discussion in class. In the different projects, learners reflected on their own development of intercultural citizenship and criticality which urged them to address their own preconceptions. This also provided the opportunity for them to take ownership of their learning and discuss possible problems with other learners and their teachers. It might also be necessary to ask learners directly to have an open mind concerning their opportunity to learn in various situations.

Dealing with highly sensitive political issues

Another challenge can be that many of the topics in intercultural citizenship are rather sensitive and/or 'political'. In some contexts such topics might not be welcomed by learners, parents, other teachers or authorities. Even in contexts where it is more common to deal with sensitive topics, learners might still feel hesitant to express their opinions. Differences between groups and limited language proficiency can be additional factors in learners' discomfort with a sensitive topic. 'Action in the community' can then lead to challenges, such as resistance on the part of the learners, the school/university community or the community at large.

This does not of course mean that we recommend choosing only non-contentious topics. Topics that are sensitive in nature and that prompt learners to think deeply about issues related to human rights, the environment, conflicts, and identity and power, are at the heart of all citizenship education, including education for intercultural citizenship. In a number of projects we saw that often it is the struggles learners experience when engaging in intercultural interactions that offer opportunities for them to reflect more deeply on their preconceived notions and thereby develop intercultural citizenship competence. We believe that reflections related to (potential) conflicts in intercultural interactions are a crucial part of projects. Some of these reflections can be planned at critical junctures that can be anticipated, while others present themselves as (sometimes initially unwanted) surprises. We therefore urge teachers to choose such topics but to engage in careful planning in order to develop criticality and encourage civic action in the community.

Possible ways to scaffold such activities are to emphasize multiple perspectives, and ask learners to take a perspective different from their own, if the teacher fears that the conversation might otherwise become too emotional. It is also important to provide a safe environment in the classroom and one in which learners can express their concerns when they do not feel comfortable. When learners feel that they can be open about their discomfort, the teacher can then help them to understand these feelings better, and this in turn often provides opportunities for learners to learn about their attitudes concerning the sensitive topic. We might even go further and say that, without experiencing some discomfort in language learning, we cannot learn another language, and without some discomfort with some topics we cannot develop skills of criticality and intercultural citizenship. It is exactly when we need to negotiate meaning in learning a language and when we need to make sense of certain ambiguities in intercultural citizenship that we are required to learn new knowledge and skills as well as sometimes change our attitude.

Ways Forward

All experiments in innovation risk being interesting and inspiring single events which are not replicated in other times and places. What we have shown here is the desirability and feasibility of introducing intercultural citizenship into foreign language education. We are aware that we are a group who are enthusiastic and willing to make an effort to implement new ideas. We are also aware that we too need to maintain our efforts if the experiment is to become routine. It is only when intercultural citizenship is no longer thought of as innovative that we can be sure that it is accepted. One of the reasons for including two Chapters (9 and 10) by the same authors in the same universities is to show that it is possible to move towards a routine without losing the inspiration to look for new topics and new variations in methods.

Teacher education is crucial, and we have included chapters which deal with this, but how teacher education needs to change can only be determined locally. Equally important is the acceptance by authorities in particular schools and universities, and by those who determine regional or national curricula. The acts of persuasion needed can only be carried out locally but we hope that our book provides support for change.

Furthermore, we must not forget to communicate our purposes to learners. They come to our classrooms with preconceptions of what language learning involves, what its purposes are and how they will be taught. Quotations from learners in the chapters of this book reveal how they are initially surprised and may resist approaches in practice they have not met before. This needs to be anticipated and planned for; teachers should emphasize that learners can learn the skills of intercultural citizenship in the language classroom.

We do not pretend that we had no problems of this or other kinds but we do hope, in the final analysis, that the book will inspire other teachers like us to consider their educational aims and purposes, and at the very least try out the ideas and practices we have proposed.

References

Alred, G., Byram, M. and Fleming, M. (eds) (2006) *Education for Intercultural Citizenship: Concepts and Comparisons*. Clevedon: Multilingual Matters.

Barnett, R. (1997) *Higher Education: A Critical Business*. Buckingham: Society for Research into Higher Education and Open University Press.

Byram, M. (2008) *From Foreign Language Education to Education for Intercultural Citizenship: Essays and Reflections*. Clevedon: Multilingual Matters.

Index

ABCs model (Autobiography, Biography and Cross-Cultural Analysis) 47, 51–52, 54–55, 56–57, 72–77
accents 10, 13, 145
action elements
  environmental action project 105–127
  Football World Cup project 228, 233–234
  'future action' 232–233
  graffiti/mural art project 183–184, 185, 190–196
  Green Kidz project 144, 152–154
  Hungary/USA project 11, 12–13, 15
  importance for achieving international identification 253, 254
  and inclusion 83
  in the intercultural citizenship education framework xxii–xxiii, xxviii
  Japan/Taiwan lower-proficiency project 91–92, 95, 96, 98, 99
  Korea/USA intercultural citizenship project 162, 166, 171, 172
  Malvinas/Falklands project 205–206, 218–220
  naming the world 242–247
  not limited to travel experiences 16, 101
  and sensitive topics 257
  teacher education project 62–64
action research (method) 88, 95, 202, 234
Agar, M. xx
'all or some' dilemma (global citizens) 6, 11–15
Allport, G.W. 49, 54
Alred, G. xxiv, 56, 251
American Council on the Teaching of Foreign Language (ACTFL) proficiency scale 160
Arcuri, M.E. 131–158, 253
Argentina
  Football World Cup project 225–250

graffiti/mural art project 181–198
Green Kidz project 131–158
Malvinas/Falklands project 199–224
assumptions, challenging 52–53, 55, 89, 154, 167–168, 176–177, 190, 228–229
  see also common sense, challenging; 'taken-for-granted,' challenging
attitudinal change 27, 34–37, 92, 153, 173, 189
Autobiography, Biography and Cross-Cultural Analysis (ABCs model) 56–57, 72–77
autobiography as tool 51–52, 140–141, 142, 143
Autobiography of Intercultural Encounters (AIE)
  graffiti/mural art project 183, 184, 188, 189, 191–192
  Green Kidz project 140–141, 142, 143, 151
  Malvinas/Falklands project 204, 205, 207
  reflections on 254
Autobiography of Intercultural Encounters through Visual Media (AIEVM) 204, 207
autonomy, student 176–177

Baker, W. 98, 99
Barnett, R. xxiv, xxvi–xxvii, 46, 62, 64–66, 98, 100, 104, 119, 151, 184, 190, 192, 208, 209, 216, 232, 251
Barrett, M. 57, 222
beginners'-level language teaching 81–103
behavioural change 153–154, 173 see also action elements
biography 51–52 see also autobiography
Boler, M. 234
bonding xxvi, 51, 105, 146, 183, 186, 188, 253

British Council 27
Byram, M. xvii, xviii, xix, xxi, xxii, xvix,
    16, 28, 32, 34, 46, 81, 82, 85, 87, 93,
    95, 98, 104, 119, 120, 121, 132, 141,
    144, 148, 162, 163, 167, 183, 190,
    195, 205, 218, 235, 251–259

Candelier, M. 133
Cappelle, G. 60–61
case studies
    Football World Cup project 225–250
    Japan/Taiwan lower-proficiency
        project 87–102
    Malvinas/Falklands project 199–224
CEFR (Common European Framework
    of Reference for Languages (2001))
    xviii, xix, xxi
challenges 155–156, 173–177, 196–198,
    255–259
Chen, Z.L. 31
Chinese universities project 25–44
citizenship education
    assumptions about understanding of
        citizenship 177
    as basis for intercultural citizenship
        education 26, 82–83
    in China 29
    Citizenship Education in the Language
        Classroom project xvii, xviii–xxx,
        xxiii–xxv
    compared to foreign language
        education xxi–xxviii, 85
    consciousness-raising activities 222
    Football World Cup project 228
    and foreign language education 84–85
    graffiti/mural art project 193, 196
    Japan/Taiwan lower-proficiency
        project 82
    Malvinas/Falklands project 205–206
    sensitive issues 235
    sequential stages of critical cultural
        awareness 99–100
civic actions see action elements
civic and political engagement 218–220
    see also action elements
CLIL (Content and Language Integrated
    Learning) 87, 93
Cohen, L. 234
Cold War 82
collaborative working
    environmental action project 104–127
    graffiti/mural art project 181–198

Green Kidz project 137–139, 141–142
Japan/Taiwan lower-proficiency
    project 81–103
Korea/USA intercultural citizenship
    project 159–180
Malvinas/Falklands project 204–205,
    209–212, 218
teacher education project 45–77
collective memory 238
collective reconstruction of the world
    xxvii, 100, 105, 219, 220
common good 105, 142
common sense, challenging
    in Barnett's criticality theory xxvii
    Green Kidz project 144
    in the intercultural citizenship
        education framework xxviii
    Malvinas/Falklands project 211, 213–216
    teacher education project 53–55, 65–66
communicative competence see also
    intercultural communicative
    competence (ICC); proficiency
    and adaptive skills 36
    in definitions of intercultural
        citizenship 33
communities of practice 172
community involvement 61–62, 104–127,
    134, 183–184, 193 see also action
    elements
community of action, creating 171
comparative perspectives 188–190, 213
comparing and contrasting techniques
    environmental action project 120
    Football World Cup project 227, 240–242
    graffiti/mural art project 188–189
    Green Kidz project 137, 144–146
    in the intercultural citizenship
        education framework xxv
    Japan/Taiwan lower-proficiency
        project 87–89
    Korea/USA intercultural citizenship
        project 167–168, 169
    Malvinas/Falklands project 211–213
    teacher education project 51, 53, 55,
        58, 61, 72, 76
competence, definition xix
complex construct, global citizenship as
    15, 28
compulsory foreign language education
    14, 29, 92
consciousness-raising activities 99, 190,
    222, 242–247

content analysis methods 234
Content and Language Integrated
  Learning (CLIL) 87, 93
content-first language education 86–102
convenience sampling methods 29
co-prosperity/common development
  35, 37
Corbin, J. 89
cosmopolitan citizenship 4, 83
Council of Europe viii, xviii, xix, xxi, 14,
  53, 54, 82, 141, 204, 226, 234
Coyle, D. 133
Crawford, J. 5
creativity 33, 39, 191, 230, 232
critical cultural awareness/savoir s'engager
  Chinese universities project 27, 34, 57
  versus cultural awareness 98
  environmental action project 121
  graffiti/mural art project 195–196
  Green Kidz project 151–155
  Hungary/USA project 11
  in the intercultural citizenship
    education framework xxvi
  Japan/Taiwan lower-proficiency
    project 98, 99–100
  as key concept xxi, xxiv, 120
  Korea/USA intercultural citizenship
    project 169
  Malvinas/Falklands project 216–220
  most educationally significant 121
  sequential stages of critical cultural
    awareness 99–100
  teacher education project 55–56, 63,
    64–66
critical evaluation
  environmental action project 107,
    111–117, 119–120, 124
  Football World Cup project 235
  Green Kidz project 152–153
  Malvinas/Falklands project 209, 216
critical patriotism 222
Critical Pedagogy 98, 229–231, 232
critical skills
  in Barnett's criticality theory xxvii
  Chinese universities project 27, 33–34,
    35, 36
  in definitions of intercultural
    citizenship 33–34, 35, 36
  Football World Cup project 229
  graffiti/mural art project 192
  Green Kidz project 134, 152–153
  history of 33–34

Japan/Taiwan lower-proficiency
  project 91–92, 98, 99
Korea/USA intercultural citizenship
  project 159–160, 176
Malvinas/Falklands project 202, 216
primary school level 152–153
and the role of emotion 176
teacher education project 63, 64–66
critical thinking xxvi, xxvii, 27, 33, 39,
  63, 92, 93, 98–99, 144, 152–153, 192,
  216–218
criticality
  environmental action project 104
  graffiti/mural art project 184–185,
    190–196
  Green Kidz project 151–155
  Japan/Taiwan lower-proficiency
    project 98
  Korea/USA intercultural citizenship
    project 162
  Malvinas/Falklands project 209,
    210–212, 216–218
  overview of theory xxii–xxviii
  teacher education project 62
  transformative intellectuals, students
    as 232
critique-in-action xxvii, 100, 105, 122,
  124, 220
Crystal, D. 86
Cultnet research network ix, xvii,
  64, 66
cultural awareness 7, 33, 34, 98, 99, 170
  see also critical cultural awareness
cultural intermediary roles xix see also
  mediation
culture of peace 199–224
curiosity 11, 68, 119, 214–215, 229
curriculum development xvix–xxx

dancing, as cross-cultural
  communication 143
Danish 135, 137
Daryai-Hansen, P. 131–158, 253
data analysis techniques
  Chinese universities project 30
  environmental action project
    109–110
  Football World Cup project 234
  graffiti/mural art project 184–185
  Japan/Taiwan lower-proficiency
    project 89, 90–91, 95–96
  Malvinas/Falklands project 207–208

de-centring
    Football World Cup project 232, 234–238
    graffiti/mural art project 191
    Green Kidz project 145–148, 149–150
    Malvinas/Falklands project 209, 213–214
    teacher education project 53–55
definitions of intercultural citizenship
    7–11
democratic pedagogy 231–232
democratic values/attitudes vii, xxi, 83,
    85, 133, 225
Denmark 131–158
dialogic learning 47–49, 242
diaries (research method) 48–49, 106
Díaz-Greenberg, R. 232
discomfort, pedagogy of 234–238
discrimination viii, 12, 13, 15
documentary data 184, 207, 242
domain knowledge 64–66
Dower, N. 6, 11–12

education, value of viii–ix
EFL teachers 160
Elluminate live! 204–205, 207, 217, 254
emergent bilinguals 4
emotion 175–176, 188, 235, 237, 248, 258
empathy 105, 122, 124, 238–240, 247
English
    in China 26, 29, 39
    Football World Cup project 225–226, 234
    and global citizenship education 26,
        27–28
    graffiti/mural art project 182, 196–197
    Green Kidz project 133, 137, 143, 145,
        155, 157
    in Hungary 5
    in Japan 88
    in Korea 159–160
    Korea/USA intercultural citizenship
        project 163, 169–170, 175
    as language of international
        communication 4
    as lingua franca 4, 84, 85–86, 93, 101,
        133, 143, 169–170, 182
    Malvinas/Falklands project 202,
        204–205, 209–210, 216, 217
    'ownership' of 86
    as prerequisite for global citizenship
        10, 13–14, 33
    as 'prestigious' foreign language 92–93
    in Taiwan 92–93
    in USA 3–4, 161

English as a Foreign Language (EFL)
    181–198
'English as an Intercultural Language'
    (EIcL) 93–97, 101–102
English language teaching for non-native
    speakers (ELT) 85–86
environmental action project 104–127
environmental citizenship project (Green
    Kidz) 131–158
equality, in definitions of intercultural
    citizenship 8, 35, 37
Erasmus (mobility) 16, 45
essentialism 161, 163
ethics, in definitions of citizenship 8, 31
ethnographic methods 52
European Union viii, 82, 84
exchange schemes ix, 16, 45, 88, 131–158,
    159–180
expectations, managing 173, 196,
    256–257
experiential learning 49–50, 94
'external world' domain see also action
    elements
    in Barnett's criticality theory xxvii
    environmental action project 122, 124
    graffiti/mural art project 192
    Green Kidz project 151
    Malvinas/Falklands project 218, 220

Facebook 111, 112, 132, 139, 150, 188,
    204, 207, 254
Falklands/Malvinas project 199–224
Feng, A.W. 28
fieldwork trips 94, 101, 182
Finkbeiner, C. 51, 72, 77
Fleming, M. xix, 235
focus groups (research method) 141
Football World Cup project 225–250
foreign language education vii, ix, xviii
    Chinese universities project 27,
        33, 36
    compared to citizenship education
        xxi–xxviii
    content-based versus 'with content'
        86–87
    critical skills in 33, 36
    cultural awareness inherent part of 34,
        36, 170
    culture-centric versus native-speaker
        centric language teaching 93
    Green Kidz project 132–133
    Hungary/USA project 3, 16

incorporation of intercultural
  citizenship education ix, xviii–xvix,
  83, 84–85
Japan/Taiwan lower-proficiency
  project 81–103
Korea/USA intercultural citizenship
  project 160
mixed language approaches 101
and sensitive topics 222
foreign languages, importance for global
  citizenship 10, 13–14
Freire, P. 229–230, 231, 232, 233, 234,
  235, 242

Gimenez, T. 27
Giroux, H. 229
'global citizen,' use of term 4–5, 32, 59, 83
Global Citizenship in the English Language
  Classroom (Gimenez & Sheehan,
  2008) 27
global trade viii
globalization
  English as international language 4
  global versus local issues 27
  identity with supra-national entities 82
  and the media 32
  statistics on vii–viii
Glogster 204, 207
Golubeva, I. 3–24, 32, 251–259
Google Docs 162, 165–166, 170, 254
Google Translate 97, 137
graffiti/mural art project 181–198
grammar proficiency 86–87
grammatical differences 10, 13
'green crimes' 135
Green Kidz project 131–158
Greenpeace 140
group work 47, 48, 106, 173 see also
  collaborative working
Guilherme, M. xxiv, 218, 229, 230, 235

Hagen, L. 156
Hall, E.T. 51
Han, H. 26, 32, 34, 36, 38
Han, X.H. 26
Han Hui 4, 17, 25–44, 251–259
hate crime viii
Hermann, M.S. xx
high school 3, 14, 26, 38, 179, 252, 256
higher education 64, 89–90, 92, 98, 99,
  152, 154, 159, 181–198
Himmelmann, G. xxi

Holliday, A. 95, 235
Houghton, S. xxiv, 27, 99,
  104–105, 121
Houghton, S.A. 27, 104–127, 253
Hsieh, J. 81–103, 86, 92, 101, 253,
  254, 256
Huang, M.L. 104–127, 253
human rights issues 12, 15, 222,
  225–250, 252
humanity as common ground 105, 142,
  144, 187, 210
humanization 233
Hungary/USA project 3–24

iceberg theory 51, 52, 76
identity see also international
  identification; transnational
  communities
  adding new identities 56–61
  complex and multiple identities 148
  in constant dialogue 171
  individualism versus collectivism
    30–31, 37
  and the Intercultural Dialogue Model
    (IDM) 105
  Korea/USA intercultural citizenship
    project 163, 169, 171
  multiple identities 83
  national identities 30, 31, 35, 60, 83,
    97, 177, 220–221
  self-realization 120, 122
  with supra-national areas 82
  teachers' 220–221
  uncomfortable issues about 67
  'we' identities 97, 99, 142, 143,
    172–173, 185–188, 209–212, 219
inclusion, as part of global citizenship
  8–9, 83–84, 92, 101–102
interactional learning 47–49
'intercultural citizen,' use of term 32
intercultural communicative
  competence (ICC)
  in China 26–27
  citizenship and foreign language
    education xxi–xxviii
  coining of xviii–xix
  versus intercultural competence
    xix–xxi
  and the Intercultural Dialogue Model
    (IDM) 104, 119
  measuring movements towards 67
  process-oriented views 122–123, 124

intercultural competence xix–xxi
intercultural contact, levels of 37–38,
    49–50, 94
Intercultural Dialogue Model (IDM)
    104–127
intercultural environmental citizenship
    134, 157, 253
intercultural mediators 143, 148–149, 189
intercultural misunderstandings xix
intercultural speakers xviii–xix
internal world of individual xxvi,
    191–192, 227 see also self-reflection
international citizen, use of term 4, 32
international exchange students 16, 45,
    88, 131–158, 159–180 see also online
    intercultural citizenship projects
international identification see also
    transnational communities
    Football World Cup project 238
    graffiti/mural art project 183, 184–190
    Green Kidz project 138, 141–144,
        155, 156
    in the intercultural citizenship
        education framework xxv, xxvi, xxviii
    Japan/Taiwan lower-proficiency
        project 95
    Korea/USA intercultural citizenship
        project 169–170
    Malvinas/Falklands project 208–212, 220
    reflections on 251, 253
international school partnerships,
    criteria 156
internationalism xxiii, 3, 251
internationalization 16–17, 58, 83, 95
internet vii see also online intercultural
    citizenship projects
interpreting skills 11, 27, 144, 145, 149, 208
interviews (research method) 17, 27, 141
Italian 182
Italy 181–198, 240–241

Japan 38, 88–102, 105–127
Jia, X.R. 30
Jia, Y.X. 30, 32
Jing, H.T. 26–27, 38
Jing Hongtao 4, 25–44, 252
Johnston, B. xviii
journals, learning (reseach method) 95,
    97, 106
justice, attitude of 27
juxtaposition see also comparing and
    contrasting techniques

environmental action project 105
Green Kidz project 143
    in the intercultural citizenship
        education framework xxv
    Korea/USA intercultural citizenship
        project 167–168, 169
    Malvinas/Falklands project 211–212, 216
    teacher education project 53, 58, 61

knowledge
    graffiti/mural art project 189, 190–191
    knowledge transformation 123
    Malvinas/Falklands project 209, 216–217
    over-emphasis on 173
    as part of framework of global
        awareness 27
    teacher education project 62
Korea/USA intercultural citizenship
    project 159–180
Kramsch, C. 86, 96, 102, 235

La Plata-Padova project (graffiti/mural art)
    181–198
languaculture xx–xxi
language acquisition, and multilingualism
    research xxi
language competence xxi, xxxi, 6–7,
    86–87, 175, 207
laughter, as cross-cultural communication
    143, 148, 188
Lave, J. 49
laws and regulations 30, 31, 35, 36
leaflet creation tasks 193, 205–207,
    219, 225–226, 227–228, 240–242,
    243–247, 254
League of Nations xxxiv(n3)
learning journals (reseach method) 95,
    97, 106
Lee, W. 27
Leung, S. 27
lingua francas
    English 4, 84, 88, 93, 133, 143,
        169–170, 182
    Japanese 88
    Mandarin Chinese 93
    in mixed nationality classrooms 88, 93
    target language aided by a common
        language 101
    use of lingua franca develops
        communicative awareness 192
link projects ix
listening to others, as key skill 55–56

lower-level language classes in Japan/
    Taiwan project 81–103
Lundgren, U. 45–77, 253

Major, J. 235
'making the familiar strange' 53
Malvinas/Falklands project 199–224
May, S. xxi
McLaren, P. 233
media
    critical reading of 202
    Football World Cup project 225–250
    globalization 32
    Green Kidz project 136–137, 139–140
    Malvinas/Falklands project 202, 203,
        204, 212, 213, 216
    as source of intercultural contact
        37–38
    stereotypes 136, 202, 213
mediation
    in the concept of intercultural
        speakers xix
    between discourses xx
    intercultural mediators 143,
        148–149, 189
    mutual incomprehensibility xx
    in the 'same' language xx
meta-awareness 105, 191
migration vii–viii, 60
mini ethnography (learning tool) 52
minority groups viii
miscommunications xix, 175–176
mixed language approaches 101
mixed methods research design 140–141
mobile technologies vii
mobility and internationalization 16–17
mural art/graffiti project 181–198
Mural.ly 183, 204
mutual comprehensibility xxxiv(n2)
mutual incomprehensibility xx
mutual learning processes 231 see also
    collaborative working

Nakano, M. 38
naming the world 242–247
national culture, inheriting and
    developing 33, 34, 35, 36, 57–58
national identities 30, 31, 35, 60, 83, 97,
    177, 220–221
national perspectives, challenging
    129–130, 183, 213–216
national versus global citizenship 9

nationalism 8, 177, 199, 200
native speakers xix, 84, 85–86, 93, 102
Nevin, A. 232
noticing 48–49, 54, 55, 147

obligations of citizenship see
    responsibilities of citizenship
observing and discovering skills 144, 145,
    147, 149–150, 208, 212
O'Dowd, R. xvii, xviii, 196
online intercultural citizenship projects
    see also social media
    Chinese universities project 38
    graffiti/mural art project 181–198
    Green Kidz project 131–158
    Korea/USA intercultural citizenship
        project 159–180
    Malvinas/Falklands project 199–224
openness, attitude of 11, 27, 68, 119,
    146, 192
Osler, A. 83, 85, 222
Other
    Korea/USA intercultural citizenship
        project 161, 162, 163, 169
    and the media 202
    respect for xxv, 54, 61, 87, 98, 100, 111,
        133–134
'ownership' of language 88, 101–102
Oxfam 83

Padova-La Plata project (graffiti/mural art)
    181–198
Parmenter, L. 27, 37
participation in intercultural citizenship
    see also action elements
    'all or some' dilemma (global citizens)
        11–15
    Hungary/USA project 11–15
    Japan/Taiwan lower-proficiency
        project 96
    teacher education project 49–50
patriotism 30, 31, 35, 36, 222
Pavlenko, A. 231
pbworks xvii, xviii–xvix, 238
Peck, C. 38, 159–180, 253, 256
personal transformation 104, 113,
    118–123
perspective-taking skills
    environmental action project 105, 111,
        119, 121
    Football World Cup project 236–237
    graffiti/mural art project 191

perspective-taking skills (*Continued*)
   Green Kidz project 145–148,
      149–150, 153
   in the intercultural citizenship
      education framework xxii
   Korea/USA intercultural citizenship
      project 170
   Malvinas/Falklands project 209, 214
   teacher education project 52, 59, 64–65
Peterson, R. 231
Phipps, A. 230
pilot studies 28, 132, 133
plurilingual competences 133, 156
plurilingual curricula xxi
policy-making 16–17, 38–39
politeness strategies 159, 171, 172
political engagement
   in citizenship education xxii
   graffiti/mural art project 190, 195–196
   Green Kidz project 154–155
   in Hungary/USA project 14–15
   in the intercultural citizenship
      education framework xxii
   Malvinas/Falklands project 204, 206,
      212, 218–220
politische Bildung xxi, xxii, 82
Porto, M. 25, 131–158, 181–198, 199–224,
      225–250, 253, 255
posters, co-creation of 137–139, 142,
      204, 254
poverty 12, 15, 148–149
PowerPoint presentations 138–139,
      204, 254
praxis 233
prejudice
   environmental action project 121, 124
   graffiti/mural art project 191
   as key issue 12, 15, 31, 34
   Malvinas/Falklands project 210, 214
   prejudice and discrimination
      statistics viii
   and stereotypes 54–55, 148
pre-political engagement
   graffiti/mural art project 190, 193
   Green Kidz project 154
   in the intercultural citizenship
      education framework xxii
   Malvinas/Falklands project 204, 205, 212
presuppositions, challenging 152, 213
   see also assumptions, challenging
Prezi 182, 204, 254
primary school level

critical thinking skills 152–153
   Japan/Taiwan lower-proficiency
      project 81–103
   political engagement 154
problem-solving skills xxvii, 65, 95,
      100, 218
process-oriented views 122–123, 124
proficiency
   concluding remarks on 256
   graffiti/mural art project 196–197
   Green Kidz project 133, 137, 145, 156
   Japan/Taiwan lower-proficiency
      project 81–103
   Korea/USA intercultural citizenship
      project 160, 161, 169, 170, 175
   Malvinas/Falklands project 217
   and power 85–86
   reflections on 255
propositions, ideas and theories domain
      xxvi, 190–191, 216–217
Punch, K.F. 140, 141

questionnaires (research method)
   Chinese universities project 26, 28–29,
      41–44
   generally 6
   Hungary/USA project 21–24
   Japan/Taiwan lower-proficiency
      project 95–96

racism 13, 15
refashioning of traditions xxvii, 65, 100,
      218–219
reflexivity *see also* self-reflection
   and attitudinal/behavioural change 173
   in Barnett's criticality theory xxvii
   and divergent perspectives 172
   environmental action project 106,
      107, 111
   Football World Cup project 228–229, 235
   graffiti/mural art project 184, 189, 191
   incorporation in task design 122, 123
   and the Intercultural Dialogue Model
      (IDM) 119–120
   Japan/Taiwan lower-proficiency
      project 90–91, 94, 99, 100
   Korea/USA intercultural citizenship
      project 162, 172, 173
   language of 94
   Malvinas/Falklands project 204, 205,
      209, 210–212, 216–218, 219–220
   in pre-political engagement xxii

role of autobiography 141
and sensitive topics 257
teacher education project 48–49, 55, 65
Reid, S. xviii
relating skills 11, 27, 144, 145, 147, 149,
150, 208
relativism xxv, 98, 164
religion 57
respect, attitude of 27, 31, 33, 34, 35, 37,
54, 202
responsibilities of citizenship
attitude of 27, 86
Chinese universities project 30, 31, 34–37
environmental action project 113
Football World Cup project 235
Green Kidz project 144
Hungary/USA project 8–9
and inclusion 83
Japan/Taiwan lower-proficiency
project 86, 91–92
and language ownership 102
rights
balancing with responsibilities 31
in definitions of 'citizen' 30
human rights issues 12, 15, 222,
225–250, 252
right of abode 8
right to speak 102
Risager, K. xx–xxi
Ryan, C. 5

sample representativeness 29
Santoro, N. 235
savoir s'engager see critical cultural
awareness
savoirs xviii, xix, xxi, 95, 104, 121
Schifler, K. 131–158, 253
Schmidt, P.R. 51, 72, 77
school partnerships, criteria for
international 156
school visits (learning tool) 52–53
security 12–13
self-awareness 27, 105, 189–190
self-conceptualization as global citizen 27
self-reflection
in Barnett's criticality theory xxvi, xxvii
Green Kidz project 121–122, 123,
143–144, 152–153, 154
Malvinas/Falklands project 216, 217–218
teacher education project 65–66
self-transformation 104, 113, 118–123,
235, 237, 247

sensitive issues 222, 235, 257
sequential stages of critical cultural
awareness 99–100, 104
Sheehan, S. 27
Shor, I. 231, 234
Singapore 60
singing, as cross-cultural
communication 143
situated learning 49–50
Skype
Football World Cup project 226,
227–228
graffiti/mural art project 181, 182, 184
Green Kidz project 137, 138, 149,
155–156
Malvinas/Falklands project 204–205,
207, 217
social activity, learning as 47–49
social inclusion 82–84
social justice theories 162, 235
social media see also Facebook; YouTube
environmental action project 111, 112
Green Kidz project 132, 136, 139–140
Korea/USA intercultural citizenship
project 161–162, 168
social practice, language as 132
socio-cultural competence xviii
socio-cultural theory 47–49
socio-historical contexts 200–202
socio-political contexts 225, 227–228
solidarity 58, 230, 238–240, 244, 245, 247
Song, L. 26, 32
Song Li 4, 25–44, 252
South Korea/USA intercultural
citizenship project 159–180
Spanish
Football World Cup project 225–226,
234, 244
graffiti/mural art project 182
Green Kidz project 135, 137
Malvinas/Falklands project 199–224,
204–205, 209–210, 217
in the USA 6, 7
Spencer-Oatey, H. xviii
Stephan, C.W. 148
Stephan, W.G. 148
stereotypes 50, 54–55, 63, 136, 148–151,
187, 202, 204
Strauss, A. 89
study abroad 16
Sun, Y.Z. 33
Sweden 45–77

Taiwan
  environmental action project 105–127
  Japan/Taiwan lower-proficiency
      project 92–103
  'taken-for-granted,' challenging
      environmental action project 98
  Football World Cup project 235
  Green Kidz project 134, 157
  in the intercultural citizenship
      education framework xxvii
  Malvinas/Falklands project 202
  reflections on 253
  teacher education project 53–55, 58
Tang, P. 31
teachers
  as facilitators of learning 232
  foreign teachers as source of
      intercultural contact 37–38
  Korea/USA intercultural citizenship
      project 159–180
  teacher beliefs about intercultural
      education 26
  teacher education project 45–77
  teacher-researchers xvii
terminology
  for intercultural/global citizenship 4–5,
      25, 32
  translation issues 28
'This is me' exercise 51, 54, 73–74
time, as a challenge 255–256
time zones issues 174, 255
tolerance, attitude of 27, 33, 34, 35, 37, 178
topic-based approaches, and proficiency
      86–87, 88
transformative action 98
transformative intellectuals, students as
      232–234, 247
transformatory critique process xxvii, 65,
      99, 100, 153, 218–219, 232
translation issues 28
transnational communities see also
      international identification
  Football World Cup project 238
  in foreign language teaching xxii
  graffiti/mural art project 184, 185–187,
      195–196
  in the intercultural citizenship
      education framework xxii, xxv
  Korea/USA intercultural citizenship
      project 171–172
  Malvinas/Falklands project 207,
      208–212, 219

reflections on 253, 254
travelling to foreign countries
  in definitions of intercultural
      citizenship 7–8, 10, 15–16, 33, 34, 251
  as source of intercultural contact 38, 160
trips and visits 94, 101, 182

UK
  Football World Cup project 225–250
  Malvinas/Falklands project 119–224
UNI-collaboration platform 181–182
university-based projects
  Chinese universities project 25–44
  Football World Cup project 225–250
  graffiti/mural art project 181–198
  Hungary/USA project 3–24
  Japan/Taiwan lower-proficiency project
      81–103
  Korea/USA intercultural citizenship
      project 159–180
  Malvinas/Falklands project 199–224
USA
  definitions of intercultural citizenship
      7–11
  foreign language learning generally
      3–4, 6–7
  Hungary/USA project 3–24
  Korea/USA intercultural citizenship
      project 159–180
  lack of internationalization 58

values xxv, 27, 121, 124, 235
video recordings 135, 162, 166, 172
visits and trips 94, 101, 182
visual media 134, 136, 182, 204, 207–212
vocabulary differences 10, 13
vocabulary proficiency 86–87
VoiceThread 161–162, 163, 173, 174, 254
voluntary work 64, 105, 110–111
Vygotsky, L. 47, 48

Wagner, M. 3–24, 38, 159–180, 251–259
Waire, P. 196
war, as topic 199–224
'we' identities 97, 99, 142, 143, 172–173,
      185–188, 209–212, 219
Web 2.0 161, 168
Wenger, E. 49
wikis
  Football World Cup project 226,
      227–228
  graffiti/mural art project 182, 184

wikis (*Continued*)
  Green Kidz project 135–136, 137–138,
    142, 155
  Malvinas/Falklands project 200,
    204–205, 207, 221
Wink, J. 232–233
world citizen, use of term 4–5, 28, 32,
  59–60
World Cup project 225–250
world Englishes 93, 94

xenophobia 12, 15

Yakimowski, M.E. 3–24, 252
Yamada, E. xviii, 27, 81–103, 99, 196, 253,
  254, 256
YouTube 132, 135, 136, 139–140
Yulita, L. 199–224, 225–250, 253

Zarate, G. xviii, xix, xxi
Zembylas, M. 235
Zhao Yuqin 4, 25–44, 252